Out *of*

Egypt

An Odyssey of Enchantment

Vandean Harris-Philpott

Library of Congress Catalog Registration TXu-1-868-658

ISBN-978-1-951300-79-1

Liberation's Publishing LLC
West Point ~ Mississippi

Dedication

To my children, Denise, Janie, and Jonathan; My grandchildren
Derek, Naiela, Elijah, and all future grandchildren; My sister Melba,
my brother Clyde, their children, and grandchildren; My father and
stepmother, Madison and Arris Harris; and in memory of our late
mother Jane Anna Ware, and to our ancestors.
This is for you!

"It is the Responsibility of every adult to know their history and
culture, to preserve it and then pass it on to the next generation. The
youth have the responsibility of using that knowledge, assuming their
rightful place in history and then passing this information on to the
next generation. This is not an obligation; it is a luxury."

-Anthony Browder

Table of Contents

Vandean Harris-Philpott

Introduction

The initial intent of this book was to document the bits of my mother's side of my family's history, as told to me by my elders, along with what I was able to ascertain from the research I managed to conduct, for my children, grandchildren, and future generations of our family. Having so little information about my mother (since she died when I was only three years old), I felt that to couple what I've been told about her and her family history with my life's experiences, combine it with the historical events that would happen during my lifetime, and how I dealt with them, would at least be a start from where my children could know and understand our family's legacy.

As my written story began to unfold, I could see a greater purpose for this book; one that may be of benefits to others, especially young people. While writing I had the opportunity to look back on my life's journey, and in doing so began to see that events I initially thought were stupid and unforgivable mistakes turned out to be opportunities that would inspire greater growth. Unaware, at the time these events or challenges occurred, that our lives are divinely orchestrated, and that they often happen to arm us with greater wisdom, I realized that setbacks and disappointments are meant to teach and/or push us toward future growth. Could it be that too many of us give up efforts to pursue our goals because of these challenges? It is my hope that those, who may be reluctant to pursue their goals because of circumstances in their lives (the kind that show up and present themselves as misfortunes or mistakes that can never be overcome) find this work as inspiration to keep going.

Considering the expanded goal for this book then, I will offer some shortened versions of my experiences. In their shortened form, these stories may give the impression that my journey was easy, or to some degree, even fictitious. Be assured that this was not necessarily the case. I experienced many difficulties, setbacks, and disappointments, as well as some bizarre spiritual moments, and many achievements. I labeled the not-so-pleasant experiences, such as discrimination, bigotry, sexism, racism, tribalism, and elitism as necessary, universal human challenges. For as my life unfolded, I could clearly see that what initially appeared to be mistakes, obstacles and/or setbacks, would eventually be neutralized by some form of gift or opportunity that resulted in greater understanding, and/or accomplishments.

For example, when my husband left us in California, I was indeed, hurt, disappointed, frightened, and confused. In retrospect however, I could see that it was during those times I would achieve the higher education necessary for the imminent future endeavors I was to undertake. Likewise, what appeared to show up as discrimination in my life only made me more determined to achieve; such experiences also taught me how to treat others when I found myself in positions of authority.

Events that began to occur after I left the Foreign Service, a job that turned out to be both exciting and challenging, confirmed that it was time for me to leave that rare position. Three beautiful grandchildren showed up a short time after that, and having returned home, I was able to be close by, and got to participate early on in each of their lives. Leaving that prestigious, but dangerous, job also cleared the way for me to begin a career that I could only dream about in the past. It also paved the way for returning to my beloved Tupelo, the place of my birth, where my mother made her transition, and where I would experience some remarkable achievements there as well.

As my life continued to unfold, I somehow began to see through the external events and whatever temporary discomforts that accompanied them. From an early age I had been aware of a presence that was always with me. It was this presence that often allowed me to see beyond the physical manifestations I initially saw or experienced. Knowing that it was there to guide, support, and protect me, I understood that all I needed to do was accept that no external fate could ever deliberately be harmful to me, for I knew that whatever the situation, it was I who had the choice to dwell in place or move forward. As I matured, both physically and spiritually, I began to understand that as a young child desperately missing her deceased mother, I had interpreted this presence as my mother. I would eventually discover that the presence was God showing up as my mother.

This book does not claim to prove or disprove any written religious or historical dogma of any kind. Its only objective rather, is to record what I was told, by my elders, the history of our family and to record my own life's journey. My only reason for conducting the small amounts of historical research was due to my desire to verify dates and the timelines of events that I was told occurred; those that might have coincided with my great-grandfather's arrival in America and how they might have affected the decisions he made during his lifetime--decisions that would eventually impact those of us who came later. Once I was satisfied that these timelines and dates did indeed match, I had no doubt that the stories passed on to me happened just as they were told.

As you read, you will find that much of my life's story is inter-twined with my family's history and their current experiences. I have also included events, both historical and contemporary, that impacted my life. The reason I chose this style is to show how history does, indeed, affect us currently. Keep in mind however, that like the words of my elders, I am using my life's journey to document our history for my children to pass down to theirs, my descendants. My experiences and my perspectives about them are just that--mine, and how I processed and/or reacted to them. This book is not an attempt to convince anyone of anything.

With that being said however, it is my desire that everyone who decides to read this book, enjoys my adventures. I hope also that young people really understand that while traveling their own journey, what happens along the way is not as important as how we react to what happens. Additionally, I wish my words convey that our life journey is somewhat like a script and as the writer of this script, one can stop at any point, and re-write it if, or when he/she does not like where it is heading; we have that choice! While writing about many of the events in my life, I often found myself laughing out loud at some of the script changes I made, just in time.

Writing this book has been therapeutic in many ways. Not only did it give me the opportunity to forgive myself for things I initially thought were mistakes in my life, after realizing that these so-called mistakes were a part of a growing process designed specifically for me, I began to appreciate them more, as well as the people sent to travel each part this journey with me—even the challenging ones.

As stated earlier, the original intent for this project was to document my family's history and some of the relevant events that affected my life for future generations of my family. While describing certain of these events, I realized that some of the books and/or articles I'd read, many of which supported my ideas and/or had an impact on my life's experiences, may not be readily available to the reader. I, therefore, decided to include some of the information contained in these works into my book. These included articles and books written by African writers, who explained their lives from their own perspectives, much of which I found only in Africa, and African historians from other parts of the world.

Finally, I appeal to the reader's understanding if some of my adventures, experiences, and yes, life's lessons, appear over-simplified. To discuss and/or elaborate on each and every aspect of what has been shared, surely, would have taken this book in a direction other than its main purpose. Perhaps another book or two (on a particular topic) is warranted. So, while my overall goal is that my family glean enough from these words to continue our ancestral journey with pride, I also hope that anyone who takes the time to read this book find some value in my experiences and be inspired to pursue their own quest, no matter how farfetched it may seem. There are many light/funny moments described herein and I hope everyone enjoys reading about them as much as I have enjoyed describing them.

Because I associate the different stages of life with the four seasons in a year, I have identified the stages of my life as such. Therefore, each section of this book is set up according to seasons. For example, my early childhood years are associated with early spring; my adolescent and young adult years with spring and late spring respectively; my adult years with summer and so on. This was done because, in my view, as we grow and mature, we receive enlightenment, develop better understanding, and then blossom, after which activity wanes; and then we rest. And, not unlike all other of God's creations, we eventually depart. But do we actually leave?

As I researched my family's history, I realized that like the perennial plants in my garden that fade away in the winter only to spring up again next year, perhaps I am a continuation of my mother(father) as she(he) was her mother(father), therefore, I am my grandmother(father), as she was her mother(father)...and life goes on eternal as does the next upcoming seasons.

More importantly, after I reviewed my life, (by writing this book) I've learned to let go of any ideas of mistakes or so-called failures I've made. I can now see my past (and present) as necessary experiences for future growth; I now see a connecting pattern of events and ultimately the divine plan meant for me alone. By reviewing my life with me, I hope that you can see that this just might be the plan for all of us.

Part One

Early Spring

Vandean Harris-Philpott

You Can't Go Back, or Can You?

It has been said, "You can't go back." Yet here I am, after nearly fifty-years, back home in Mississippi. Depending on the reason one wants to go back, I guess the above quote can hold some truths. Since my earlier departure from Egypt, Mississippi, at age twelve, I have studied extensively about, traveled to, worked and/or lived in 19 different countries around the world. Yet my life-long desire to return to the place of my birth in Mississippi, had not changed.

My mother, on whose family history much of this book is based, was born in Egypt, Mississippi, in the early 1900's on a large parcel of land promised to her grandfather, Ephraim Ware, by his employer, but never given. This land, on which her father Frank was born, was actually purchased after emancipation, by Frank and his wife Ada. The land, which is still occupied by my mother's family today, holds the key to my longing to return to Mississippi.

My grandfather, Frank Ware, had married his childhood sweetheart, Ada Morrow, and from that union bore three children-- a boy and two girls. Uncle Angelo, the oldest, was followed by my Aunt Evelyn (Auntie)--"the knee baby," as the middle child was called in those days, and my mother, Jane Anna, "the baby." They all lived on their grandparents' farm, that was situated on the nearly one hundred and twenty acres of land, which they willed to be distributed evenly between their three children upon their transition.

My mother, "the adventurous one," was the first of the three to leave the family farm. After ending a "turbulent" relationship with her son's father, and returning home, she decided to move out on her own. So, with her little son in tow, she set out for the "Big City" (of Tupelo), to find work. "Such a move was a huge endeavor for (still) a young woman in those days." After all,

Tupelo was some 35 miles from the back roads of Egypt -- a large expansion of wooded countryside with miles and miles of rich, fertile farmland, and "it was almost unheard of for a young woman to go out on her own like that." Nevertheless, my young mother proved she was ready for the challenge when she and her best friend Georgia, who was also her first cousin, hitched a ride on the back of her big brother's delivery wagon one weekend.

Cousin Georgia was in her mid-nineties when she confirmed this story, which had already been told to me by my Grand-Aunt Mariah. According to Cousin Georgia, whom I had the honor of getting first-hand information (though many years later), my mother, "around twenty-five at the time" informed her brother, who made weekly deliveries to the milk cannery in Tupelo, that she and Cousin Georgia wanted to do some shopping in Tupelo and wanted to ride along on his next trip there. On the day their trip took place, my mother instructed Uncle Angelo to collect them at their cousin's (Hanna) house, whom they'd planned to visit after completing their shopping, when he was done with his deliveries. Since their real plan was to explore ways to remain in Tupelo, the two young women knew that Hanna, would be their best source for the information they needed to best carry out their plan. Having grown up in Egypt before marrying and relocating to Tupelo with her husband, Hanna was happy to have relatives visiting from Egypt, and, after learning of their plans, "delighted to give advice on how to best implement them." She recommended the two young women stay in her home until they could secure a place of their own. So, Uncle Angelo returned to Egypt that day without them.

As she reminisced, Cousin Georgia gave her version of when and how my mother and father met. "After about a year of living and working in Tupelo, the dashing young Madison Harris caught sight of your mother. He joked (with them) 'that one day while taking a break from his duties at his auto mechanic shop, "I caught sight of Jane Anna and observed her for several weeks as she rushed up the hill from the bottom of North Spring St. at the same time each day. She often trotted as if the worst thing in life was to be late to wherever she was going. At some point I began feeling for this lady, who'd never look my way because she was always in a hurry to get up that hill. Although I wanted to approach her, I wasn't sure how since it was improper to just call out at her from the shop, which was situated on a corner, across from the hill. So, I decided to just wait, hoping that the opportune time would eventually present itself.

Then one day, as she rushed the hill, your mother tripped and fell. Watching as she struggled to get up, Madison said he rushed out to assist her to her feet, but 'was taken aback as she pulled away when he tried to start a conversation. Thanking him, she quickly explained that she must go, or she'd be late getting to her job.' Your mother worked as a maid for a white family that lived at the top of Spring and was apparently worried about losing her job. Seeing this as his only chance to get to know her, Madison said he quickly replied that 'a pretty woman like you should not have to rush anywhere, and quickly offered to drive her up the hill in his car. Thinking that maybe her reluctance was because she didn't know him, Madison was beside himself when your mother accepted." Cousin Georgia joked, that my father was obviously unaware that nearly everyone in Tupelo, including my mother, knew who he was, although she had not planned on meeting him that way. "Dubbed as the dashing young entrepreneur from Brooksville, Mississippi, your father was one of the few Black business owners in Tupelo at the time," she boasted.

Cousin Georgia also told of the dilemma in which my mother found herself (while living in Tupelo) when she was presented with a marriage proposal from my father, which she could not accept without the customary family scrutiny and consent-- "especially since she'd made one bad choice." Explaining that, "In those days, when a young man was seriously interested in a young woman, it was mandatory that he seek permission from her parents before asking for her hand in marriage, especially if he wanted to be accepted into her family." This ritual, of which I was already aware, involved the young man first visiting the family, and trying to hold an intelligent conversation as possible, with anyone that would talk with him, often while the parents discretely observed the interchange from a distance. Given the intense scrutiny he would face, this first step was not an easy task for most. It helped if the young man already knew some of the young lady's family members, preferably a brother, who could put in a good word or two for him.

After this initial observation and scrutiny, the young man is then faced with a series of questions about his folks and his religious faith. Once her parents were satisfied that he was fit to pursue or 'go with' their daughter (although still within viewing distance), the parents would leave the couple to themselves--in the sitting room. It was only after a young man was known by the family, could he announce his intentions to marry their daughter and thus, perhaps, receive their blessing. This would usually be after months of excruciating observations and examination, after which the couple was allowed some time alone, but still be under careful observation.

Although my mother had been married before, she was still considered a young woman, and apparently had to abide by the established courting rules, which were strictly enforced at that time. Besides making sure he was a man with honorable intentions, another purpose for this courting process was to ensure relatives did not inner marry, which was very possible, given that, in those days (shortly after emancipation) families often lived in small clusters, not unlike those of African villages. These clusters, which started off small, developed into large territories, and eventually into small separate townships. So, it was not unusual for one to "hook up" with a distant relative, thus, the inevitable questions, "Boy, what's yo daddy's name?" or "Who yo folks?" It was also important to make sure that the woman wasn't bringing a hell-raising sinner into the family, thus the question, "what church y' all attend?"

I had been taken aback, after returning to Mississippi, when upon introducing himself to me, a gentleman immediately began giving details on his church along with the name of his pastor. I was later told that still, when a man is seriously interested in a woman it is customary for him to do this. Having long forgotten about this ritual, I was caught off-guard when it actually happened to me and was left wondering if the gentleman was promoting himself or his church.

At any rate, once father made his intentions clear (that he wished to marry my mother) Cousin Georgia recounted that, "in my parents' case, with the absence of her parents in Tupelo, my mother's eldest cousin Hanna performed the initial screening of my dad. However, he still had to travel to Egypt to stand before my grandparents, Frank and Ada Ware." Before doing this my father made sure he made friends with my mother's elder brother, Uncle Angelo, who would perform the second level of scrutiny, after which off they went to Egypt--on Uncle's milk delivery wagon.

Constituting a perfect match, especially since they each had a little son (from previous relationships), my parents were married in 1940. Cousin Georgia joked that it didn't hurt my father chances, that he promised to take my mother to live "up north" someday. That dream, however, never came into fruition for my mother. After giving my father three children (two girls and a boy) she made an early transition from this life. My new little brother, Madison Jr., died a short time thereafter. I was three years old at the time.

Among the few things I still remember about my mother and our relationship was the joy I felt when she would take my sister and me on walks in our neighborhood. I recall being pushed in a baby carriage while my sister strolled along beside us. Eventually, my father would purchase a house (at the top of North Spring Street) for my mother, doors away from where she'd worked years earlier. These walks seemed miles away to me at the time, and I'd get so excited about going outside for such a long adventure I could barely contain myself. Years later, during a visit to my hometown as an adult, I was surprised to discover that the walks were just a stone's throw, up the hill in front of our house—to our church, in fact, Springhill Baptist. Memories of our church included sitting on my mother's lap during Sunday school as she listened to the lesson for the day, and the many sweets we enjoyed afterwards.

One of the more haunting memories of my mother, however, was trying to wake her during, what I learned later was her "Wake" where relatives came to say their last good-byes. This memorial was held at our farm in Egypt. My father had taken me and my siblings to Egypt "to visit our relatives for a few days" earlier. We had not seen our mother since, when suddenly, there she was. I recall being so happy to see her I could hardly wait for her to pick me up, and just hold me. Upon seeing her, I practically jumped out of the arms of the person holding me but was being held so tightly that I could not manage to do so. Additionally, my infant mind could not figure out why she was lying there, in that strange looking bed, all dressed up, with her eyes closed. Nor did I understand why everyone was just standing there, sadly staring at her. Moreover, why was she not responding to my cry?

While I was confused about not being allowed to touch my mother, I was even more so when my two siblings and I had to remain in Egypt that day. To me, it appeared that she and my daddy (who, for some reason, couldn't stop crying) were going back home to Tupelo without us. And, when she did not return, I wondered why they had disappeared and left us again. I never saw my mother again after that. Nor did we see our father much either. When he did return, although he brought many goodies, he always looked sad, and never mentioned our mother.

During one of his visits my father announced that he was going "up north". Although I had no idea where up north was, based on the excitement exhibited among the adults, I got the sense that it was far away, and my heart jumped at the idea that I was going somewhere--with my parents no less. When my father explained to my sister and me why we could not go, but that he would return for us later, even though I tried to understand, I could not help feeling an overwhelming sense of abandonment. So, armed with his mechanical skills, my father set off for Chicago, and for the next several years, poured himself into building a successful auto repair business there. "Working all day and late into the night," when he explained death to me much later in life, "helped to keep [his] grieving at bay."

As promised, my father eventually returned to Egypt, but only to get my sister and me. The next thing I knew we were in Indianola, Mississippi, where we would spend the next couple of years or so with his sisters, Vandine and Coreen, each at different times. Although we were surrounded by scores of relatives there also, I recall feeling very stressed and helpless during this period of my life. It seemed that as soon as we had gotten adapted to one place, we were off to another. Where was my mother and father, and my big brother? I would often question my aunts about this situation, but never received a satisfactory answer. Apparently, in those days, it was not customary to tell children about death, so I never understood where my mother had gone, nor why we had to always live at our cousins' homes--with their mothers and fathers.

At some point, my mother's sister, Aunt Evelyn, apparently requested that my father bring my sister and me back to the family's farm, "so that we could be with our brother," my mother's first child, Clyde, who had remained with her. So, with another promise that he would come back for us once he established himself in Chicago, my father took his two little girls back to Egypt, Mississippi, where we would reside for the next five or so years in a household of fourteen children (including my mother's three), and three adults, Auntie Evelyn, her husband, and our great Aunt Mariah, surrounded by scores of mosquitoes. As a three-year-old child, at that time, I missed my mother terribly; It would take years before I understood that she had died.

***

While living with my mother's side of the family, I constantly heard stories about how she left Egypt to live in Tupelo. It was also during this time I believed that my mother started visiting me. Though most of her visits were at night, she'd sometime come during the day, like the time I got left behind in a cotton field. Thinking that I was on one of the two wagons that carried the entire lot of us children down to the bottom part of our farm to work in the fields (about three miles away from the house), it wasn't until later that evening, after discovering that I was not in the house, that my brother and two cousins were sent to look for me. Despite the mosquitoes singing around my head, I had fallen asleep under a row of tall cotton and did not know that everyone had left. Needless-to-say, I was eaten alive by the mosquitoes, which I hated with a passion, especially after having been told that "having sweet blood", and them loving it, I attracted them.

Upon their approach, my brother and cousins found me "sitting by the lake scratching and talking to [my] herself." I was actually talking with my mother, who had already informed me that they would be coming for me and promised to remain with me until they arrived. When the search party found me and asked if I was frightened, I tried to explain that I was not because my mother was there with me. I felt it strange that everyone (except my brother) began teasing me about my response. In fact, of late, my mother seemed to always be there when I was afraid and/or could not sleep. What I could not understand initially was why she never stayed, if for no other reason but to confirm to those who never believed me when I told them about her visits. Still having the mind of a young child at that time, I consoled myself by reasoning that for whatever reason, she had to rush back to Tupelo, where, I had also convinced myself she still lived. As I grew older, however, and my mother's visits grew less often, I gradually began to understand and accept that she had passed away.

In the meantime. the stories told about my mother's adventures became my own dreams. I promised myself that someday, I too would live and work in Tupelo, which for me. at that point in my life, was the largest place in the entire world. But first, as did my mother. I must get out of Egypt.

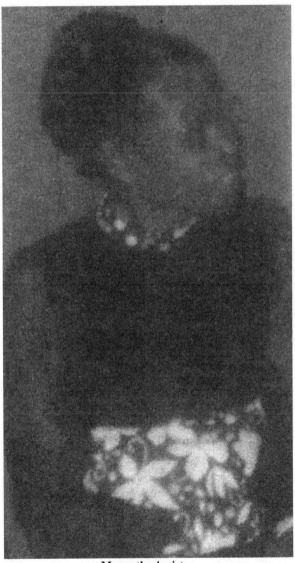

**My mother's sister,
Evelyn Ware-Sims
(Year Unknown)**

Vandean Harris-Philpott

The Parting of The Red Sea

My first trip out of Mississippi took place when I was about eight years old. My father had visited often since he left us there with our aunt, uncle, their eleven children (they initially had twelve--one was deceased) and our Grand-Aunt Mariah. This time however, his visit was different. Shortly after his arrival, he announced that he had found a wife and would be taking us to live with them in Chicago. After hearing this, I could barely contain myself. But with my small body, which by now resembled a spotted calf due to the many sores (the result of mosquito bites), I found it necessary to ask if Chicago had mosquitoes. I felt satisfied once the puzzled look on my father's face released into a comforting, "I don't think so."

I can still recall my first reaction upon arriving in Chicago and driving up to a large gray stone building with three levels of windows, seemingly stacked on top of each other. After parking, my father proudly announced that we had arrived and pointed up to the last level of windows indicating that that was where our home was located. His announcement nearly put me in a state of shock. The idea of living three floors off the ground was very unsettling-- maybe more so than the mosquitoes. Even now, remembering that reaction, I sometimes smile when I walk by a tall building inhabited by human beings. Compared to the wide-open space I was accustomed to on the farm in Mississippi, upon discovering that this was where we would be living, perhaps I wasn't so excited about leaving Egypt after all. I remember consoling myself by reasoning that at least my daddy would be there to catch me if I fell from one of those windows my eyes stayed fixed on, as we climbed the stairs to the porch. I also assured myself that finally having someone that I too could call mommy was an extra bonus, so on I cautiously climbed.

Maybe now, I thought, I would receive that little something I'd observed Auntie give her children, that somehow my siblings and I rarely, if ever, got. What that little something was I could neither identify nor describe at the time. Perhaps it was the tender way Auntie combed the hair of her own children, or the fuss she made when straightening their clothing before sending them out of the door to school or church. It could even have been the undivided attention she gave while listening to their concerns, or the pride she showed for their accomplishments.

Although I knew my aunt loved us as well, I somehow never felt that little, yet necessary something. As a result, I soon began to think that maybe I didn't deserve that kind of love and began wondering if maybe this was why my mother left us. My aunt was never mean to us, nor did she discriminate when it came to disciplining the entire lot of us. And, by age five, I had already learned the signs and could act quickly to avoid any kind of extreme punishment.

***

Even though Auntie clearly had her entire household of children, (which at times numbered more than sixteen or more when some of her brother's [Uncle Angelo] ten were visiting from St. Louis) under control, the house could sometimes mimic a zoo-like atmosphere. In spite of her well-established control system, complete with its well-respected pecking order in place, the younger ones would occasionally grow restless while sitting around the fireplace listening to the older ones compete at storytelling. During these times, mostly on weekends, Saturdays in particular, Auntie would often be seated at her foot-peddled Singer sewing machine, making clothes for her many children when the hitting and whining started. At the beginning, she would just ignore us. But as we got bolder and the noise became louder, she would start humming a particular tune, attempting, perhaps, to drown us out; yet she would never utter a word, warning us to behave. Each one of us already knew not to approach her and tell on or whine about another. Without failure, the one that did so would be the first to receive a whack.

By the time our ruckus reached the point that could annoy the gentlest of saints, Auntie's mono-tuned humming would begin to include a louder "bum-a-lum, bum-a-lum". Trying her best to block us out, each bum-a-lum, bum-a-lum was soon followed by an urgent "hu-hu-hu¬hum," which by now had increased in both octave and intensity. I learned early on that when she reached a certain octave level, she was about to blow. And it was at that point I would find a secure place out of her reach, usually under a bed or dresser. For some reason the others, most of whom were older than me, never seemed to have noticed this I've had enough point.

As the ruckus among us children intensified, still humming her "I'm almost fed-up tune," (still unnoticed by everyone except me), my aunt would slowly lift her weary body from her chair, and disappear into another room, often the kitchen, where she would find herself a stick of stove wood or anything that could inflict the most pain without actually killing us. Then, suddenly, Auntie would burst through the door swinging her weapon of choice. From left to right she'd plow through the sea of children, seemingly without any concern about what or whom she'd hit. A scene replicating Moses' parting of the Red Sea, with bodies diving from left to right, Auntie too, created a great divide as she passed through the middle of us still not saying a word, just bum-a-lum, bum-a-lum, only now she hummed it with force and conviction. When it seemed, she was satisfied that everyone was dead, she'd make her exit, re-enter the room from which her weapon came, gently place it back in the spot from which she found it, and return to her sewing machine as if nothing ever happened. I remember thinking how remarkably she could hold such a dignified, almost graceful posture, while slinging her weapon of mass destruction.

It was only after she had re-positioned herself at the machine and sewing again that those who survived her swift and blunt blows would re-emerge. It was nothing less than a miracle that everyone survived. Then, without a sound, the able bodied would collect and care for the wounded. And, even if half of one's brain was left hanging out, absolutely no one, not even the youngest, dared approach my aunt in an effort to receive sympathy. The best one could expect the remainder of that night was an older sibling's pity, or one who cared enough to provide bandages that could hold one's brain in his/her skull until the next morning, at which time for some reason Auntie, seeming to not have any clue how the wound was inflected, would nurse the person back to health with her homemade potions and remedies. When I think back on those

events today, I am still baffled by the fact that none of the other children ever prepared themselves for Auntie's rage. And, with a smile, I also wonder what would have

Me on left at around 8 years of age and My sister during our first stay in Chicago, 1952.

happened if, like me, everyone had hidden so that when Auntie came through, there was no one on whom she could release her fury.

***

As time went by in Chicago, I became aware that my sister and I were not getting that something from our stepmother Murene either. Perhaps, I reasoned, it's because like Auntie she was often too busy. After all, she had three children of her own, who also lived with us. Although I'd observed Murene displaying the same gentleness with her children, that my aunt showed hers, somehow, I did not mind. At least, I felt, I am with someone to whom I belong--my daddy. And, if having Murene and her bunch around was the only way I could remain with him, that was okay with me.

Then one day I overheard my father discussing with one of his relatives, who lived nearby, the possibility of having to take my sister and me back to Egypt. It appeared that his cousin's wife had confirmed my father's suspicion, that his new wife was neglecting his children in some way. It is hard to express the distress I felt at that moment, so I won't. What I will say is having lived for so long with such large families in Mississippi, I wasn't used to getting much attention anyway, and did not see it as a problem. After all, there was only three of them compared to the twelve or more I had grown use to in Mississippi. Nevertheless, the arguments between my dad and Murene, often about her treatment of us, intensified, and the next thing I knew Murene was packing her belongings. And, after hugging us good-bye one day, she gathered her children and left. Not long after that, my sister and I found ourselves back in Egypt.

Saved

After returning to Egypt, we were re-enrolled in the little one-room schoolhouse situated in the pasture across from our home, where we'd begun our primary schooling a few years earlier. While I was still grieving over the fact that my daddy had left us there again, for some reason I felt a bit of comfort being back. Here at least, I noted, is a place where more attention is paid to a child's ability to comprehend his/her lessons than on what they wore to school each day. Although our feet had to be cleaned (free of mud) before entering our classroom, we didn't even have to wear shoes to school if we didn't want to in Egypt. An additional bonus was that we got to chase the cows during recess. And even though the entire school consisted of one large room (divided up by grades), upon attending school in Chicago, I soon discovered that I was leaps and bounds ahead of my classmates in terms of my educational level and capabilities.

Having traveled out of Mississippi, I now knew that there were places in this world beyond Tupelo. Upon this discovery, I decided that perhaps before finally settling in Tupelo, as I'd planned when I grew up, I would first explore other places. And soon I began longing to do just that. I now found myself lying awake long into the nights, paying attention to the trains whistling through the small town (located across the highway at the top of Egypt road), wondering where they might be going.

I still smile when I think about this small town (also called Egypt) which consisted of one general store carrying everything from food and clothing to farming equipment. The Post Office was situated in the rear of the store. The town also had a church, in which Blacks were not allowed, which I could not understand after being taught in Sunday school, that God loved and was the father of us all. Why, I wondered, would he allow such separation? Although no Blacks resided within the little town either, while

25

shopping and/or collecting their mail many would gather on the side of the general store's veranda (not on it, which was for Whites only) to learn about the latest happenings around Egypt's territory.

The town also had two nightspots, one for the Blacks and one for the Whites, each at a safe distance from the other. These social outlets or juke joints were frequented mostly by the young folk, who lived throughout the surrounding farmlands of Egypt. After a long work week Egypt's young adults would relieve their boredom by dancing themselves to near exhaustion each Saturday night. Knowing that someday our day would come, those in our household too young to go to this weekend retreat, would longingly watch those of clubbing age readying themselves for the good times they planned to have each weekend.

Since we had the largest wagon in the community, ours was the vehicle of choice. And, long before they'd depart, our house would be all a-buzz with excitement, since many in the community (mostly girls) would gather there waiting to be the first to climb aboard considering that the seating was on a first come basis. My cousins would collect others along the way up Egypt road needing a ride to town. At any rate, although I was not really interested in the weekend jute joint retreat, I did promise myself that someday I would get on one of those trains, which rushed through the town of Egypt, but never stopped, that I would find out where it did stop, and go to wherever it wanted to take me.

One afternoon, during one of the rare occasions on which I got to have my Auntie all to myself, I decided to share my future plan with her. Because she knew I liked gardening, Auntie would sometimes allow me to help attend, and/or collect the produce she'd grown. On this particular day, I got the privilege of helping to pick and clean the vegetables she selected for that day's dinner. My usual behavior when alone with her was to "talk and talk and talk" and, on this occasion I began talking about my plans to travel the world when I grew up. During one of my rare pauses, at which time I expected some feedback from her, I became aware of a long silence. After sneaking a closer look at my aunt's face, I could see the mist forcing its way into her eyes. As it became clear she was fighting hard to hold back her tears, and unsure of what to do or say next, I spent the remainder of our time in the garden in silence. Apparently, something I'd said had hurt her deeply.

Then one day, while sitting on the bottom step of our porch, pretending to be occupied with my shuck doll[1] as opposed to listening to the "grown folks talk," I heard my aunt discuss our garden conversation with the women who'd often gather there on Fridays after their work week ended. Exclaiming that not only was I my mother's spittin image, one woman declared that I had also inherited her restless spirit. Disregarding my presence, she went on to reference my mother's marriage to my father "an outsider." "Candy (my mother's nick name) couldn't wait to get out of Egypt," she continued, and in near panic, yelled "Oh lawd chil, has she been to the monen banch[2] yet?" When my aunt responded that I had not, all the women agreed that she should make sure that I did so as soon as possible, "so that if, like my mother, I was determined to be so adventurous, I needed to be saved." "Um hum, no telling what might happen to that chil out there in that mean ole world," another reminded everyone.

Although I had heard about the mourning bench, I wasn't entirely sure what was supposed to happen since no one had taken the time to explain it. So, when the revival took place that year, I sat on one of the front rows in our church, as instructed, along with my sister and the other candidates. Most of us were children between ages 6-12, and a few older back sliders, most of whom I

---

[1] A toy doll made from a dried corn cob on which the dried husks (leaves) remain (or nailed on) the top. The husks are then separated into strands and used as the doll's hair, while the cob represents its body.

[2] Mourning Bench - Where one turns his/her life over to God, after which they are baptized, and "washed whiter than snow."

had witnessed boarding our wagon heading for the Saturday night juke joint.

As the revival week drew to an end, I and two others of the unsaved around my age, and my sister, were still sitting. Exhibiting great concern, on the eve of the last night of the revival, my aunt asked us why we had not yet felt the Spirit? As puzzled as ever, I was the first to respond that I didn't know why and wondered out-loud how it was supposed to feel. She then explained that when a person feels the Spirit, they would be so happy, he/she would jump up and shout. Apparently like some of the others I'd witnessed during that week I concluded, most of whom were from the Saturday night jute joint group, whom I thought had gone crazy at the time.

Auntie continued by explaining that the declared spirit-felt person would then proceed, or be escorted, to the chairs facing the congregation, and after being questioned by the pastor, testify that the Holy Spirit had indeed touched and saved them. This way she boasted, "everyone would know that the person had been saved." Although I was left wondering about the ones that had just quietly taken a seat facing the congregation, I chose not to ask that question.

When I attempted to explain that I would be too embarrassed "to jump up and shout in front of all those people," my aunt assured me that when the Spirit touched me, I'd be so happy, I wouldn't even realize I was shouting; nor would I care who was watching. Now that I knew what to expect, and, convinced that I wouldn't be embarrassed by shouting in front of an audience, I went back to the mourning bench that following evening and waited along with the other remaining sinners and my sister, who eventually took the quiet approach. However, nothing seemed to be happening for the rest of us.

Then, suddenly, just as I began questioning myself again, I felt two strong arms wrapping themselves around me. In a daze, I thought to myself that surely this must be the Holy Spirit. Being rocked back and forth by a force I knew was not my own, I remember thinking, my goodness, it's happening. But when I looked over to see my aunt clinging to me in what seemed like a state of desperation, I realized that she was the one rocking me--I was almost disappointed. Crying now, Auntie began begging God to please save her poor dead sister's child. Soon, several of my aunt's sister friends joined her. As they circled us fanning and begging the Lord, I felt myself being lifted from my seat and floating to one of the chairs facing the audience. I heard someone cry, "Lawd, Candy's baby has been saved." The church went wild. When the Pastor approached and asked if I love the Lord, not quite sure what had just happened, I quickly responded in the affirmative. And, within seconds it was over—so I thought.

The following Sunday, the entire household buzzed with excitement. I, along with several other of Auntie's brew, including my sister, and three of our other cousins (Uncle Angelo's children) who had been sent down from St. Louis, to be saved also, had all been saved and were getting baptized. After church services that day, all of us new Christians were dressed in the white gowns, Auntie had spent the night sewing, and ushered down to the lake. Standing there on the banks and after making a few observations, I quietly asked my sister if she was afraid to go into the water. After her response, she asked if I was. I said no, but went on to assert that I wasn't going in. When, in near panic, she asked why not, I pointed to the cow on our far left, with his tail held high, pissing in the water. Although everyone else witnessed this show, they ignored it, and proceeded with the baptizing.

At any rate, apparently more afraid of my auntie's wrath than that of God's, when it was my turn to go into the small body of water, although I was petrified, I did not have the nerves to resist. So, I held my breath and proceeded to go in and be "washed as white as snow"--cow piss and all. When it was over, I could not help wondering if my aunt and her friends had forced me to the saved chair for my salvation, or to save face among their fellow

Christians. I also wondered why God would want us to be dipped in this dirty water; what does all this have to do with loving God, I questioned. Oh well, I thought, at least I was saved. To this day, however, I still experience great anxiety when entering a pool of water--whether it be filled with animals or with people.

The Process

To the younger children in our area, picking cotton was the "rite of passage" to becoming a grown-up--a stage we were all eager to begin. So, still too young to take on the responsibility of picking my own row of cotton, when I did get to go to the fields, I, along with the other three children in my age group, was assigned jobs such as "water totter and errand runner." To teach us the art of cotton picking, we were sometimes allowed to practice on the rows of our older siblings, who would often compete among themselves at being the fastest and most productive. With the assistance of one of us, the slower ones could sometimes achieve this goal. More often than not however, we'd cause them more work than more cotton.

Our apprenticeship entailed going ahead on a row with a bucket or whatever we could find to fill with cotton and bring it to be emptied into the sack of the person working that row. The more seasoned pickers did not want us to help them because of the "snag factor". Since our little hands were not large enough to encompass an entire cotton bulb, we'd often leave half of the cotton in its hard and prickly shell, and thus the snag factor. This caused double work for the more seasoned pickers, and inevitably slowed him/her down. For reasons I never understood, to be left behind while picking cotton was almost an abomination.

Apart from our regular "gofer" duties, we younger ones would usually play among ourselves between the rows of tall cotton until we'd either get tired or get on the nerves of our elders (due to too much horsing around), after which we'd be ordered to "go take a nap under the wagons"-- our transportation source during those times.

After completing a cotton-picking cycle on our farm, to either earn extra money or to help a neighbor, my aunt would allow the older children to work on other farms (usually the white ones) in the area. During one of these money-making out-sourcing occasions, I felt lucky to be chosen by my brother, who was now in his adolescent years and rarely paid me any attention, to help fill his sack. Having grown up in the city (Tupelo) and not too keen about this task, he was one of the slower cotton pickers. With the promise of earning a whole nickel, I jumped at the opportunity considering we'd be working for the infamous Mr. Elmer King, the gas station and store owner, whose place of business sat on the highway at the top of Egypt Road.

Although it may not have amounted too much to a seasoned picker, I picked my little fingers off that day, making sure I did not leave one snag of cotton in those bulbs. Besides trying my hardest to impress my big brother, I also knew we would be going to Mr. King's store when the day ended. While my brother could not boast of having picked the most cotton that day, he did make some earnings, and when we all filed up to the store to collect our pay, I was excited about having earned the nickel he gave me.

Having earned my own money for the first time in my life, however, I wasn't quite sure what to do with it. Should I spend it or just keep it? Upon seeking his advice, my brother solved my dilemma with a recommendation that I spend three cents and keep the rest for later. Armed with what I decided was a sensible financial plan, I strutted up and announced to the little golden-haired girl behind the candy counter that I was there to buy something. The girl was about my age and seemed as eager to talk with me as I was with her. Since I was not sure what else I wanted along with the two Bazooka bubble gum pieces I had chosen for my sister and me, the little girl, who had already introduced herself as Nancy before asking my name, began making suggestions. After we both agreed on a package of Kits candy, that contained four small portions of individually wrapped pieces, which I felt could also be shared with my sister, we began chatting about whatever little girls talk about.

Then, suddenly, I found myself being snatched away from the

counter. I looked up to see anger in the eyes of my eldest cousin. Puzzled but not daring to resist him since he was near the top of our family's pecking order and was respected by all of us below him, I allowed myself to be handled. Nevertheless, I was totally confused, as well as annoyed by his actions, never mind the embarrassment I felt when I became aware that all the people in the store had started laughing, as I was being lifted up by my collar and forcefully escorted out of the store.

We had gone quite a distance when I sensed that everyone was afraid to speak after the brief tongue lashing, I received upon mounting onto our two-mule team wagon. As I watched the store disappear in the distance however, I managed enough courage to ask what I had done wrong. Surprised that I would have the audacity to ask, my cousin warned that I was just too bold for my own good, and that if I did not mind myself, I would get us all killed someday.

Just before I was about to go into shock over what he had said, he went on to point out that I was talking and laughing with the little white girl as if I were her equal. When I tried to defend myself by explaining that I was more than her equal because she had told me that she was nine years old and that I was almost eleven, he snapped back that I had lived "up North" too long and said no more. Since it was understood that he was highest in the chain of command in the absence of his parents, no one else dared say anything either. Although I could not understand his behavior, I too kept silent since my cousin was clearly very upset with me. Besides, I did not want to be the one responsible for getting us all killed.

As the entire household was a-buzzed about that day's events, especially the sin I had committed, I went to my grand aunt as I'd always done when I wanted answers. Aunt Mariah, my grandfather's sister, having lost her second husband "to the grave" had come to live with her surviving niece, Auntie Evelyn. Well into her eighties at that time, Aunt Mariah seemed to know everything about everything, and after hearing my version of what happened that day, explained the reason my cousin reacted the way he had.

Aunt Mariah explained that "although slavery had long ended, some the descendants had maintained some of the wretched ways of their slave owning ancestors, including personalities and behavior. And, for this reason, she explained, many Negroes[3], in the South were still afraid to be friendly with white people, especially after what had happened in Money, Mississippi that summer."

In August of 1955, while visiting his grandparents in Money, Mississippi, a fourteen-year--old boy from Chicago had been abducted in the middle of the night by two white men who claimed that he had whistled at one of their wives. Emmett Till's body was later found in the Tallahatchie River' weighted down with a cotton-gin fan. He had been beaten and tortured to death. Although I was shaken by young Till's story, I was more interested in knowing why Emmett's relatives allowed the two men to take him away that night? After I asked this question, Aunt Mariah explained that "His relatives were not aware of the accusations at the time, and considering the times, they had not expected that two grown men would kill the child."

"Anyhow," Aunt Mariah continued, "like in Emmett Till's case, a person never knows how white people would react to such boldness from Negroes, (as I had displayed) which was often interpreted as 'those who are too sure of themselves." She went on to explain that while the little girl at Mr. King's store may have enjoyed talking with me, "since they (the grown-ups) expected Negroes to be more docile, they could have reacted differently."

---

[3] A Latin word meaning black, Africans were first called Negro by the Portuguese, who are said to be the first of the Europeans to arrive in Africa. The Portuguese called Africans Negroes because of their dark skin tones, and the name Negro remained after Africans were brought to America.

When I asked if she thought Mr. King would come after me that night, she assured me that he would not, and pointed out that the reason my cousin behaved the way he did that day was to avoid trouble. "But don't you worry, she added jokingly, they know not to come down Egypt road looking for nobody." Still puzzled and unable to let the subject go, recalling another story about slavery she'd explained earlier, I probed further by asking why the slaves were taught to be so docile. Aunt Mariah began explaining what she called "The Process."

"In order to ensure that the Africans transformed into good slaves," she began, "upon their initial arrival in America, the first group was put through an intense breeding process, after which they were either sold or killed off. This process involved turning the children of this first group into a completely different people than what their African parents were. The slave makers accomplished this by establishing techniques designed to strip a child of any connection to, and knowledge of his or her ancestry, by erasing all memory of such concepts of a family and, especially of their African traditions, religions, and culture. This strategy was to instill a new way of being -- that of a slave -- with no memory of one's past."

"The process actually began at the time the African was captured in the homeland," Aunt Mariah continued, "at which point a breaking down technique first began. After being captured, individuals were separated from those they knew and/or those with whom they could communicate. Upon arriving at their final destination, captured Africans were further separated --from those to whom they had been chained and stored on slave ships during the long agonizing months they spent crossing the Atlantic Ocean. This was done in case a person developed any kind of bond with their fellow prisoners. Once the captured were sold to a final master, the process became even more inhuman.

After a well-planned demeaning process, the African would be bred and branded like animals. African males were ordered and forced to impregnate as many African women as possible, but not allowed to reside, marry, or form any kind of family relationship with them. In fact, in order to avoid bonding with the females, once a male had sired enough children for one master, he would be sold or traded off to another plantation to continue breeding with his new master's female slaves.

Females had been purchased based on their physiques, which if strong looking, were thought to be good breeders. A 'good breeding' female was forced to have one child after another until she was worn out, like an old horse, and unable to bear more children. The whites justified their behavior by convincing themselves that Africans were only one quarter human and therefore had few, if any, human feelings and/or emotions.

If the male slave dared show any emotions and/or refused to leave his plantation when commanded or tried to return and form a connection with the woman and family he helped to create, he'd be killed, as would any female who tried to keep her child beyond the suckling period (a period her master determined the child could survive without its mother's breast milk). At this point the babies would be taken to a training house to be raised without his/her natural parents and taught how to be an obedient servant to its master--that is, how to be a slave."

"For example," she continued, "from the time he/she could understand directions, an African child was constantly told that he/she was inferior to their white counterpart, and that their kind was put on earth by God to serve their white masters. They were also taught that they initially came from a place where people were wild and uncivilized, and that they were lucky to have been chosen to be in America among civilized people." When I questioned if everyone complied, she explained that "those slaves who found the courage not to accept these teachings or refused to comply were severely punished or sometimes beaten to death in front of the others, thus putting fear in those remaining." Aunt Mariah went on to explain that, "With few other choices, many slaves submitted to their plight and became obedient and docile. After a few decades of this breeding process the slave makers did not have too many problems controlling their slaves since the 'slave mentality' had been so deeply embedded. These newly-created beings, who now knew little or nothing about their African origin or heritage, were now called American Negroes."

Just as I was about to start crying (for my people) my aunt quickly pointed out that, "Fortunately some still didn't submit completely, especially since newly-arriving Africans like her father were always arriving and would inevitably contaminate the new breed with knowledge of who they really were. Thus, Negroes

Photo by Phyllis Harper; A local newspaper article about my Aunt Mariah's excellent memory and storytelling abilities at 105 years old. GREAT, GREAT AUDIENCE — Mrs. Mariah Lou Cozart, 105, relies on a long stick for support for walking, but she can still tell a good story — as illustrated by the rapt attention from some of her great, great nieces and nephews. (Year 1972)

were constantly coming up with strategies to outsmart their owners, and/or persevere until opportunities presented themselves to overcome slavery, which is the reason we are free today!" she exclaimed. After hearing this, I promised my aunt and myself, that I would never submit to being docile or inferior to anyone. Moreover, I would respect only those who respect me--as apparently the little golden-hair girl did. I felt sorry for my eldest cousin, who obviously feared these people. I promised Aunt Mariah also that someday I would go back to Africa and that I would send for her. She smiled and said, "I know you will."

Out of Egypt

Lying in bed that day, I felt so ill, I found it difficult to even raise my endlessly pounding head. My Aunt Evelyn had tried every home remedy she knew to get my temperature down. I felt so bad that I could not tolerate the taste nor the smell of the food she offered me. Even water tasted bad. In an effort to keep me strong, Auntie insisted that I at least take some milk. But upon entering my mouth, the milk immediately came back up--"fully cooked."

In those days, African people in the South rarely went to hospitals since they were in cities miles away. However, when I hadn't gotten any better, I was finally taken to be examined by a doctor in town nearby. Although I was barely conscious by then, I heard the doctor explain that I was in an advanced stage of meningitis, and that it was too late for him to help me, so we went back home.

As my body laid still later that night, I remember feeling a bit annoyed that my head had been covered with a white sheet which, for some reason, I could not manage to remove. A while later, for some unexplainable reason, I was looking down at my sister, who was kneeling by the small cot on which I was still lying, crying her heart out. At that same moment however, I recall feeling an overwhelming sense of happiness--after all, I was with our mother, who was holding my hand and looking down at my sister also.

Since she had appeared to me many times during my early childhood, especially when I was sad, afraid of something, or needed consoling, I had become used to my mother's visits. In fact, I thought it was normal. Nevertheless, lately, when I'd tell my auntie about my mother's visits, I begun noticing that she would go off to herself and cry. At that time, I could not understand why she was not happy to know about her sister's presence, and even more puzzled when the older of her children firmly instructed me to stop telling Auntie about "these so-called visits." They explained that I only imagined having seen my mother. Equally puzzled as to why I could not get my mother to show up when I wanted, to prove that she did visit me, I eventually began believing them when they explained that she was not real.

Then one night, my sister, who was afraid of the dark, was told to go into the kitchen to get something for Auntie. When she refused, pleading that she was afraid to go into the dark room alone, she was threatened with a spanking if she did not do as told; I took my sister's hand and told her not to worry; that our mother would be there to protect us. So off we went in the dark kitchen together.

Upon entering the kitchen my sister was surprised to see that our mother was indeed standing there greeting us with her usual smile. While I do not recall any verbal exchange that night, I know that she remained there until we had found what we were looking for, after which she somehow conveyed that we "go and take it to Auntie." We both waved good-bye and obeyed. After that, my sister tried to convince everyone that while in the kitchen that night, she too had seen our mother, and although no one could gather enough courage to check, they chose to not believe her either. It was at that point that I stopped doubting our mother's visits.

On this occasion however, my mother's visit was different. This time she was holding my hand, and since she was, I thought perhaps she was taking me with her--to wherever she'd always disappear after her visits. Although I knew better by now, I became excited at the thought that she might be taking me back to our house in Tupelo to live with her again. Eventually however, my mother finally looked down at me and began to explain that I could not go with her. She went on to say that I must go back to be with my sister, who really needed me more. She also explained since her appearance upset her sister, while she would always be with me, I would no longer be able to see her. In alarm, I began clinging to her.

To comfort my distress, my mother explained that I had a lot to accomplish in life, and that I should not worry about anything. She also told me that she knew about my dreams to travel, and after stressing that I should go wherever in the world I wanted without fear, she reminded me again that while I may not see her, she would be always there with me. Before leaving, and without actually explaining it, my mother conveyed that, like her and her mother, I was going to have three children, two girls and a boy--in that order. Not sure why she added this, nor understanding how, I could have children, I nodded okay.

Suddenly, I heard a knock on the door and was abruptly awakened. When the person entered, I could hear Auntie expressing her sorrow, and explaining that she had done all she could, but that I had passed away anyway. Recognizing my father's voice as he sobbed and spoke, I jumped up. Pushing the white covers off, I called out to him--Daddy! It was a sight to see my father come rushing toward my bed, while everyone else in the room (except my sister—I don't recall where my brother was), ran in the opposite direction. After all, I was supposed to be dead. But I felt great, no fever, and no pain.

Looking at her for some kind of explanation, Auntie began to tearfully describe to my father how I had been burning up with fever the preceding evening. Before going to bed herself, she continued to explain that she'd checked me one last time, found that I had turned completely cold, and had stopped breathing. It was at this point she sent two of the older children to town to send the telegram to him. Unable to respond to Auntie's explanation, my father then turned to me and asked how I felt? I exclaimed excitedly, that I felt good and that I had been with my mother. While the grown-ups just stood there staring at me, I noticed that my siblings and cousins were beginning to return to the room. Assembling around my little cot I could hear the questions about my coming back to life, and my auntie shushing everyone as she instructed them to bow their heads while she prayed.

As they prayed, I noticed that my father had a very pretty lady with him. When I asked about her the next morning, he explained that she was his new wife. I recall thinking, oh no, not again. But, I thought, this could mean spending a little more time with him. So, to make sure they would take us with them, I tried hard to appear sick again. I think my father knew what I was up to because when we were alone, he cautioned that unless I got better in the next day or so, he would have to leave and come back for me later. When I assured him I was okay, he smiled.

I do not recall the remainder of their visit, except that Arris, whom I'd learned was my father's new wife, fussed over my brother, sister, and me like we were her precious little kittens throughout their entire stay. When it was time to leave, she began packing my sister's and my belongings while appealing to Auntie to allow her and my father take my brother as well. After much resistance from Auntie, to which I did not understand, and after promising my brother that she would send for him one day, we left without him. I will never forget the sad look on my brother's face when we left him, for the second time.

Several months of living with my father and his new wife had passed when I finally began to understand what that something missing was that my Auntie and Murene unwittingly transferred to their own children, that somehow escaped me. It was that unwitting tender, patient, understanding, attention, and unconditional love (no matter what the child does) that only a non-distracted mother can give a child. Somehow Arris was able to transmit these feelings to my sister and me. She would eventually confess to us that she had always longed for children. She also shared that although she tried, she was never able to have any, and that my sister and I were the answer to her prayers. I need to be clear, here, that I had no doubt that my Auntie loved us, but the woman had eleven children of her own! Because she always treated us so special, I believed that our mother knew that Arris would be the answer to our prayers as well. Strangely enough, my mother never appeared again after Arris came into our lives. Finally, out of Egypt, I grew up convinced it was my mother who sent her to us.

Vandean Harris-Philpott

Spring

Mixed Emotions

Old enough now to understand the differences (between city and country living), it had become clear to me that life in Chicago was not going to be as easy as it had been in Egypt. While it was wonderful experiencing the undivided attention of one's own father and a mother, who provided nothing short of unconditional love, had it become necessary for me to have to choose to remain with them or return to Egypt at this juncture (nearing my confusing adolescent years), I may have chosen Egypt. Having spent most of my life with my Auntie and her family, I was finding it harder to forget them, and Egypt, this time. After all, they had been the only constant family in my life for so long, I had begun thinking of my first cousins as my sisters and brothers. Consequently, after settling into our new environment, I would often find myself longing for my larger family, especially those in my age group.

I found myself reminiscing often about the fun times we had playing with the children along Egypt road, most of whom were our second to fourth degree cousins. I missed the freedom to travel up and down this road without fear, something we could never do on the streets of Chicago, where we were constantly told to be cautious of strangers. One major challenge for me to overcome was having to wear shoes year-round in Chicago, even after school!

I longed also for many other aspects of the Mississippi way of life, which I soon learned did not exist in Chicago. These included family events such as the boxed dinners at church every fifth Sunday. Although it was no longer our current experience, I'd often smile when reminiscing how us younger ones would leave these feasts feeling sick from overstuffed bellies. This picnic-like occasion was designed for summertime fellowship purposes, but for a family with fourteen children, they were almost like famine to feast. Each church family would bring cardboard boxes filled with

47

their best dishes to share with fellow worshipers. This event was held outside, under the shade trees, after the church services ended.

Once the tables were set, everyone could go from table to table selecting his/her favorite foods. Most of us children already knew who made the best desserts, so after stuffing ourselves on the regular foods, often from tables of those other than our own, since no one was paying attention, we would race to be first in line for the dessert table, where every family's dessert was placed in order of type. This table featured everything from homemade ice cream to pies and red velvet cakes. As long as we behaved ourselves, and asked politely, we could eat all we wanted. While fruits were displayed on its own table, seldom, if ever, would one see a child there. I also found myself reminiscing about fishing at the lake in the back of our farm. Accompanied by scores of other nearby cousins, we would make so much noise playing we rarely caught any fish. I smiled as I'd recall how I once nearly beat the life out of one of our more mischievous cousins, and thus earned the title "tomboy." This cousin (Little Willie) and I were both about eight years old. One day the older kids spotted, caught, and killed a snake that had lingered too close to us younger ones. Knowing my fear of snakes, since the snake was already dead, Little Willie decided to scare me with it.

Having established a reputation of being the most fearless of my sister and me, my cousins rarely teased or harassed me as they would her. On this occasion, Little Willie decided he would teach me a lesson and with a precise aim, threw the snake at me. After I removed and recovered from the trauma of the cold dead creature that landed around my neck, I went into a trance and nearly beat Little Willie to death. When he arrived home that day, apparently upset about the bruises I had inflicted on her child, his mother stormed our house but left furious at Auntie for not spanking me. Auntie had already heard the story and advised her that instead, she should correct Little Willie's behavior.

Christmas was also a time of great joy in Egypt. In Chicago I soon learned that Christmas was mostly about buying gifts. The only store-bought gifts we received in Egypt at Christmas were sparklers, firecrackers, and a few pieces of candy, which was "all Santa had left by the time he got down to the end of Egypt Road," where we lived. Each of us was encouraged to make a gift for our favorite brother or sister. Additionally, the older siblings would collectively make toys for the younger ones. To prove that these toys (though homemade) were left by Santa, they would show us the sleigh marks imprinted in the dirt road in front of our house--I was amazed that this same claim was made year after year, even after I had long learned that this was not true.

One night before Christmas morning, when they thought all of us younger children were asleep, I watched from a window as our older siblings made prints with a wagon wheel on the dirt road in front of our house. The following morning after proclaiming Santa's visit, evidenced by the sleigh tracks, I decided it was best to continue going along with the tale, either because I did not have the heart to let' them know that I knew better or because I did not want to miss out on my share of "Santa's" treats. Christmas also meant a host of visiting relatives and friends from around our area (all with the same sleigh story), as well as cousins from up North. With all these happenings, our humble gifts were not that important.

What I missed most however, was sitting around the fireplace on cold winter nights listening to stories told by our older siblings who would try to out-do each other by creating impromptu stories, most of which were spooky. We did not have television during those days and we younger ones loved how the older ones competed to tell the best story. Additionally, Aunt Mariah, my grandfather's sister, told wonderful stories about our ancestors, dating all the way back to Africa, and how her father (whom she'd always point out that he was not a slave) ended up in Egypt after immigrating to America from Africa.

Having lived with them for most of my life then, I now found it difficult living without them and all that I had grown to know and love; I missed my larger family terribly. I also missed what I'd begun to understand and appreciate was a simpler way of life. Although the ultimate decision would be to remain with my dad and new mom, I'd often console myself with the promise to someday return to Egypt -- after going back to Tupelo, of course.

Life in The Big City

As we grew older, life in Chicago did not get much easier for two "little country bumpkins" like my sister and me. Even though I had been saved before assimilating into this new and different world, and having had at least a nodding acquaintance with religion, I was to find that being a saved Christian was not enough to save me from the trials and tribulations yet to come.

Before reaching my teen years, for example, I would have several occasions in which I found it necessary to defend myself and my sister, who was of a gentler nature, from both neighborhood and school bullies. While I recognized that someone of my four feet, eighty-five pounds stature should simply walk (or run) away from some of the confrontations that always seemed to gravitate my way, I somehow found it hard to do so.

Christianity aside, by now I had come to believe what my mother had assured me during her spiritual visits when I was a small child in Egypt. Although life was challenging in Chicago, her words not only made me feel that I could accomplish anything I wanted to, but they also instilled traits that left me with extreme, and sometimes, daring courage. So, although I would never start a fight, I would never back down from one either. I would do battle at the drop of a hat, especially if I felt justified in doing so. One of my most memorable encounters was with two girls nearly twice my size.

Two young bullies, who were aware of my sister's reluctance to fight back, kept promising her a beating at the end of the school day, "at 3:15," a phrase that meant one was going to get his/her butt whipped after school. Confident she would not fight back, these girls had been harassing my sister for months, basically to make themselves feel important. Their constant threats terrorized her, and while my sister was really not that timid, having never encountered such harassment, she "was not sure how to handle it,"

51

nor would she talk to me (her little sister) about it. I'd heard about the bullying but could not do anything since the girls had never followed through with their treats. Besides, they were much bigger than me.

Then, on the last day of school, nearly out of breath, a friend came running towards me. Attempting to explain that my sister was in trouble with what little breath she had left, I had difficulty deciphering what she was trying to tell me. She then grabbed one of my hands and literally pulled me to the other side of the school yard. I could see the excited crowd long before arriving at the scene. Urged on by the crowd, the two girls (who had harassed her all semester) were taking turns pushing my sister in an attempt to make her respond to their assaults. Thinking how unfair that they were two against one, I became so furious that upon my approach I could actually feel my body lift from the ground.

The girls were so much bigger than me however, while running toward them, the only strategy I could think of was to jump on the back of the larger one and pin her arms to her body (by wrapping my legs around her waist) in an attempt to contain her, while hopefully my sister would handle the smaller one. It turned out that this girl was much stronger than I had anticipated. Refusing to be defeated however, I decided to keep my legs clamped around her waist and just hold on for dear life. The girl tried hard to sling me off, and just as she was about to succeed, my jaws clamped down on her neck.

As the crowd gasped in unison, I could feel the blood oozing down the side of my mouth. In a daze, it was only after I became aware of my sister and the other girl begging me, that my teeth released their grip. When they finished assisting with nursing the girl's wound, a few of her friends (followed by a small crowd), escorted her home. As the larger crowd dispersed, based on my actions, someone called me a vampire and from that point on I was known, both at that school and the neighborhood in which we lived, as "Van, the little vampire." My sister and I had no more bullying problems after that. Aware that the girls had long been terrorizing my sister, I received only a reprimand from the school officials with a warning not to fight again. My parents ended up having to foot the hospital bill for the wound I inflicted to the girl's neck, however.

I had learned to play baseball in Mississippi and, as a result of accompanying my father to scores of baseball games at Chicago's Wrigley Fields, and playing with him and our cousin (on my mother's side), whom, for some reason we called, "Uncle Nick" (who was my dad's age) during their down time, I had mastered the game. As a result, I could out play most of the boys my age, in our neighborhood. However, I was not sure if it was because they feared me, or if I really was a better player. I would learn years after his death that Uncle Nick was Cousin Georgia's baby brother, whom daddy had helped get settled in Chicago. At any rate, by the time I realized that I had to behave more like a young lady, we had moved to another neighborhood, and it was there I began high school. Our big brother had finally come to live with us, and by now my sister and I had gained both status and prestige from having a handsome brother on whom nearly all the girls had a crush.

With several years of city living behind me, I began excelling in most of the extracurricular activities I'd undertake. In high school I sang in the choir, played violin in the orchestra, and participated in the drama club. Recalling my deceased mother's assurances during our talks, I really believed I could achieve anything I set my heart on, and I was on a roll. Although I was equipped with unshakeable self-assurance however, I would still have to endure challenges that would put a serious strain on this confidence before maturing into the woman I would become. And, while some of these challenges were predictable, I was nowhere near prepared for others.

I am the third person on the front row. at Beidler Elementary, Class of 1959. Note the sixth young lady, on the front row, wearing two different shoes. Another young lady, perhaps in another classroom, is wearing her other shoe. This was to signify that they were best friends in those days.

Growing up in Chi-town

Life was very busy for me during my teen years. Having evolved from a mere auto body shop business, my father had now acquired two stores and a restaurant in which I spent most of my time after school, as well as my weekends working as a cashier and/or bookkeeper. By age fourteen I was already performing managerial functions for our businesses. It was also during this time that I would observe some very bizarre behaviors practiced by my people.

My new neighborhood was called K-Town, an acronym for the streets in the community, most of which began with the letter K. K-Town was the home of a notorious street gang called The Kobras. I had heard many stories about the violent behavior of this group, consisting mostly of young Black[4] male school dropouts. Most of The Kobras' mischief were fights with a rival gang called The Vice Lords (also Black), whose members lived in a community nearby. Although I had been well versed in African American history (thanks to Aunt Mariah), I still could not comprehend the rationale behind Blacks fighting each other.

It was now the early sixties and the fight for civil rights was in full swing, as well as the Black Power movement along with its message of decolonization of the Black community. The feeling was that the community would rather manage itself than be integrated into the larger society. Black Power advocates wanted

---

[4] By the early 1960's African Americans had rejected the title negro, the name given during slavery, and in light of the Black Power movement began preferring to call themselves as Black. Later in our history, someone questioned if there was a place on earth called Black, after which it was decided that like others who came to this country from elsewhere, Black people should identify with the place from which they came-; and while most didn't know where on the Continent, they knew we all came from Africa.

African Americans to control their own economical, educational, and political destinies, as well as the institutions within their communities. This movement also triggered a change of attitude among gang members.

In addition, African Americans in the North were keenly aware of Martin Luther King's non-violent efforts against oppression and segregation in the South. Many of us had watched helplessly as the evening news broadcast the abuse imposed on hundreds of marchers as they tried to peacefully protest against this oppression in the South. The southern police force used attack dogs and water hoses to discourage the marchers while crowds of bystanders threw rocks and eggs at them. Seeing such hatred and disrespect so vividly displayed each night in our living rooms not only infuriated young African Americans, but it also left many doubting if non-violence was the right approach. Besides, most had figured out by then that discrimination and segregation existed in the northern states as well--by custom if not by law. It was during this time that Chicago's Black gangs really began to ponder who their real enemies were. I think they were happy when Malcolm X declared that King's non-violence approach wasn't working, because when Malcolm suggested the "by any means necessary" tactic, he quickly gained the full attention of all of the gangs on the West side of Chicago. They now had a cause.

The transition from the non-violence movement to the Black power activism began in earnest when Malcolm X resigned his leadership from the Black Muslims and foamed the Organization for Afro-American Unity. This decision ignited the Harlem riots, and it wasn't long before the rioting soon spread to other northern cities, including, Chicago, where they were initiated mostly by the youth gangs.

It was also during this time that three young civil rights workers (James Chaney, the African American, along with Michael Schwerner and Andrew Goodman, two Caucasians) were murdered in Philadelphia, Mississippi. Though the Neshoba

County sheriff and two of his deputies were among the nineteen suspects, there would be no convictions and the charges were eventually dismissed. It would be over forty-two years (on June 20, 2007) before the U.S. House of Representatives passed a bill to establish a new division of federal prosecutors at which time FBI agents focused strictly on these and other unsolved murders from the civil rights era.

Not sure how close Neshoba was to Chickasaw County, where Egypt was situated, I recall begging my father to send me back to help protect our family. He assured me that he was keeping his eyes on the events in Mississippi and "would let me know if I needed to go save everyone." Although I figured he was being sarcastic, I consoled myself with Aunt Mariah's assertion, that "no one would ever come down Egypt Road looking for no body."

It was against this backdrop that the riots in Chicago began. The word was already circulating around our school that the gangs were going to band together and do their share to stop exploitation in the Black Community. I was not quite sure what this meant until it happened. Late one mid-week afternoon, a group of young men (gang members) came into our store and warned my father that he should close early that coming Friday, and that he should tie a black ribbon on our store's security bars, indicating that his was a black business. Since my father didn't close early for anyone, when he followed their orders, I knew something serious was about to happen.

After closing our store that Friday evening, my father informed me that he would remain there, but instructed me to go home and not go out of the house for any reason. We lived about one and a half blocks off of Roosevelt Road, where this (our main) store was located. Roosevelt was a main street that stretched from downtown Chicago through the Black community up to Cicero, a small suburb populated mostly by Italians.

My father had already telephoned and apparently instructed my mother what to do about me. He knew somehow that I was ready to go out and join the fight. When I arrived, my mother was glued to the television, watching the news. I was shocked to see many of the buildings up Roosevelt on fire. Some people were yelling "burn baby burn" (a term that had been coined by activist Stokely Carmichael of the Student Nonviolent Coordinating Committee, SNCC), while others were running in and out of stores with televisions, radios, and even washing machines, among other things. It then became clear to me that my father had stayed behind to save our store's inventory.

When my mother explained that they were looting, I jumped up and headed for the door. Surprising me with a strong hold I couldn't escape, she grabbed me just before I made it out. Knowing that my father was at our store alone, I begged her to let me go to help him. Refusing my pleas, she held on tighter. I am compelled to pause here and offer my own reason why the riots were so violent in Chicago.

Not unlike other large Cities where the anger was ignited because of unemployment, the lack of recreational facilities, and degraded living conditions, Chicago's main gripe was with the predatory business practices and high interest rates for inferior products sold in our communities by the mostly white owners, who had firmly established their businesses therein, but who did not live there. With an easy "no money down" policy, one could get any household item they wanted from these stores as long as they agreed to use the strict credit terms set by the store owners. Before one finished paying for these cheaply made products however, they would inevitably break down. Considering the high interest rates attached, which took years to pay off, a debtor would have paid two to three times the cost of an item if and when he/she completed the payment plan. It was well known that these absentee business owners became rich from their earnings in African American communities.

As the rioters progressed down Roosevelt Road that week, they were preceded by the same band of young men who'd previously passed out the black "Passover ribbons" to the African American businesses in our community, and warnings to everyone to remain inside their homes that evening. It puzzled me that during the rioting the police were nowhere to be seen. Rumor had it that the authorities did not bother because the Blacks were destroying their own neighborhoods and, that since the Jews owned most of the businesses, the authorities did not care.

I also wondered if the destructive behavior in our community had anything to do with the fact that it had become well known by now that after purchasing what one thought would be a permanent home for his/her family, the purchaser would soon learn that they had been deceived. It was during this time (1960's) when Chicago's West Side had become the pilot community for interracial living in which a handful of middle-class African Americans were encouraged to buy homes on "contract". Although sold at unscrupulously inflated prices, the contract process offered an easier purchasing process while promoting the pride of home ownership over the disadvantage of renting. The purchaser would soon learn however that a contract sale did not allow the buyer to accrue any equity in the home, nor the fact that if a single monthly payment was missed, he/she would immediately lose the property as well as any down payment initially made on it. The family would quickly be evicted after which another naïve family would be encouraged to purchase the property on contract; and the cycle went on, fueled by quenchless greed on behalf of the seller.

At any rate, my father remained at the store throughout the night, and apparently did as he was told. As a result, our business was spared, as were the other Black businesses on Roosevelt Road. However, by the time President Lyndon B. Johnson sent the National Guard to suppress the unrest, our community had been almost totally destroyed. The destruction would remain ignored for years. I thought it interesting that the Guard did not arrive until just before the rioters were about to enter into Cicero.

The Gems aka Lovettes

My entire family were devout churchgoers, and just as I had done in Mississippi, I sang in our church youth choir in Chicago. Having to work in my father's store most days after arriving in Chicago, singing became one of the few social outlets I had during my teen years. Therefore, I looked forward to choir practice every Saturday evening. Our youth choir had become one of the best on Chicago's West side, and as a result, the church we attended was selected to host the community's gospel musical every fourth Sunday. This event was frequented by many people from the surrounding neighborhoods including Bertha, who would become my best friend and confidant during my teenage years, and her older brother Willie, on whom I had a serious crush despite his being older, and who never seemed to notice me except to compliment me on the songs I'd lead.

I also sang in my high school choir. Eventually, my singing talent was recognized by one of our school music instructors, who encouraged me to participate in what turned out to be the school's first annual Jamboree. The school's music director, Ms. Bane, had created and launched this program to provide students (who displayed a talent for entertainment) the opportunity to practice and develop their individual talents in a contest-styled setting. Accompanied by school mate and student pianist, Raynard Minor, I won the female solo contest that first year. The Jamboree got rave reviews which caused it to become a yearly event.

By the second year Raynard, had become the pianist of choice for most of the solo and groups participants in the Jamboree. That year, a friend with whom I had completed grammar school, Jessica Collins, had also entered the contest as a soloist. After encouraging Jessica and me to do a duet, Raynard convinced us further, to find two other students and form a group. We selected our fellow school choir members, Teresa (Casey) Washum and Dorothy

Hucklebee. And, during the era of the Supremes and Marvelettes of Detroit, out of John Marshall High School, the Lovettes were formed.

With Raynard, who by now had become our pianist exclusively, the Lovettes began participating in other local talent shows around the Chicago area. Although we were well chaperoned, knowing how religious our parents were, it surprised everyone that they not only allowed us to participate in the entertainment world, but also to travel throughout Illinois performing R&B music. Our group was eventually discovered by a talent scout representing Chess Recording Studio, and the Lovettes soon became part of the Chicago music industry.

The group eventually included my friend Bertha. Although she did not attend Marshall High School with the rest of us (she attended Crane High), I wanted to share this wonderful new experience with her and insisted that she be included. So, with a group of five young teenage girls, Chess records renamed us *The Gems*.

The Lovettes (Gems), 1962 Raynard Minor (Center), and from left to right: Vandean Harris, Teresa Washum, Dorothy Huckleby, Jessica Collins and Bertha Watts

The Gems recorded several records, but to our surprise, the local radio stations never played them for more than a few weeks after each were released. Additionally, the distribution of our records seemed never able to get beyond the northern mid-western markets, something we as young and popular musicians, did not understand. Needless-to-say, we never had a hit record. On the other hand, because our harmony was so well formed (thanks to Raynard), we became the musicians of choice for the more seasoned recording artists at Chess, needing background singers. Ironically, while our musical talents always produced hits for others, it did not do the same for us. Some of the R&B legends for which we provided background voices included Billy Steward, Etta James, Fontella Bass, and Mittie Kyia. We also accompanied on the recordings of groups such as the Dells, and the Radiants.

Years later, after leaving the group, I would learn that (during our teen years) the reason the Gems never progressed beyond our local status was by design; that our recordings were intentionally never promoted beyond two to three months of airtime and on record outlets. This decision was said to have been made by others, on our behalf, and was beyond our youthful and naive control, at the time. "Because [we] had such fine-tuned harmony (partly due to Raynard's relentless coaching during his efforts to get us prepared for the local contests we entered) however, from the very beginning, management at Chess decided to maintain our group as background singers for as long as possible, or at least until we completed high school." This way "not only would the Company have a cheap source for a badly needed product (background singers), but it also lessened their risk of something happening to us under-aged artists while we were in their care."

Later, as an adult, while I could understand their reasoning, I still couldn't help feeling that we had been taken advantage of, especially after learning that allowing us to record periodically had been strategically planned. But to assure we never reached wider notoriety, our recordings were never to be promoted beyond two to three months. Whatever the reasons were for our lack of extended fame during that time, I have to admit that I enjoyed my short singing career. My routine would eventually become such that I'd go to the Studio three or four days out of the week to do background singing, if our group got lucky, and be allowed to perform one of our records when accompanying other artists on their performances at nearby concerts. Although it never got beyond an after-school job with occasional stage appearances thrown in, singing provided a social outlet for me. It was during this time that another major change took place in my life.

Ignorance: Is It Really Bliss or a Curse?

As a young and desirable entrepreneur, my father was constantly approached by women who could not understand why he was so dedicated to his church-going wife when he "could enjoy the company of more glamorous females and live a more exciting life." It was against this backdrop that my father temporarily gave in to the temptation. And while I do not recall the details, I do remember arguments that resulted in my father, periodically, not coming home for several days at a time. The strain finally became too much for my mother, and she eventually decided to spend some time at the home of one of her sisters.

Now eighteen, my sister, had gotten married the year before and moved to Texas with her husband, who had just completed his initial training in the Army. My brother had long moved out into his own place. And, while everyone in my family was apparently occupied with their own lives, at nearly seventeen years of age, I'd often find myself all alone in our second floor flat. No one, except my best friend Bertha, who'd often provide a shoulder for all my teen problems, as I did hers, knew about my situation.

Having sensed my infatuation with her brother Willie, Bertha had long ago cautioned me to stay away from him, whom she warned was too mature for me. Though he never encouraged me, Willie was aware of my crush on him, and would often tease that one day, when I grew up, he would take me out. As fate would have it, one evening during an entire week of unsolicited independence, that is, before my mother and father discovered that they had both left me at home alone, Willie spotted me sitting on my front steps. He came over, and after observing the residual tears in my eyes, inquired if I was okay. When I confided that I could not spend another night in our home alone, he insisted that I come to his family's home, which was directly across the street from ours, and stay until his mom could contact my mom. Interestingly, none of my friends knew that my mom was really my stepmother. It turned out that his mother and Bertha were not at home when we arrived that evening, so Willie invited me down to his room (in the basement) to listen to some music until they returned.

In an effort to cheer me up, Willie joked about the rumors he'd heard about me and Jimmy (my high school sweetheart), being the best dancers in the neighborhood. He then challenged me to show him some dance moves, which I felt confident in doing. Knowing how to dance in Chicago was a serious matter in those days; if one had the nerve to venture out on the floor not knowing what to do, or without knowing the latest steps even, he or she risked being laughed off. So, in preparation for our neighborhood "Saturday night socials," which were often held in someone's basement, Jimmy and I, along with our closest friends, would spend most of our free time practicing the latest dance steps.

Having fun trying to out-dance each other, Willie and I were both relieved when a slow record finally started to play. As he pulled me close to him my heart almost jumped out of my chest. After much seductive maneuverings, Willie planted a kiss that engulfed me with a flame so powerful I could hardly breathe. Sure, Jimmy and I had done some occasional petty necking, but our innocent explorations never went very far, nor had they produced this kind of feeling. I began shaking like a leaf on a tree, blowing in the wind. By the time I gained some control of these new and powerful feelings (with Willie's soothing stokes), I became so caught up in my usual, analyzing the situation, Willie had already carried me to his bed and was well on his way to forcing himself inside me. In an attempt to stop what I knew was about to happen, his calming voice completely mesmerized me into submission, and I suddenly found myself in a position of no return.

When it was over, I wasn't sure what to feel. While one part of me was savoring the warm feeling that still encompassed my entire body, another part was feeling anger at being forced into something for which I was neither ready nor prepared. Sensing my confusion, Willie began apologizing, claiming that he did not realize I was a virgin. "After all," he defended, "when you sang in that group of yours, you sound like you know what you are singing about."

Although we had accomplished a bit of composure by the time Bertha and their mother arrived, I was still in a daze. Trying hard to focus on what had just happened and, at the same time, process Mrs. Watts' anger--I wasn't sure if she was upset to learn that my parents had left me alone, or if she knew what Willie and I had done. In any event, with a promise that she would contact my parents the next morning, she instructed to me to sleep in Bertha's room. When I told Bertha what happened that night, she cried--I cried too.

Both my parents had returned home by the next afternoon. Profusely apologizing to me, they promised to never leave me alone, like that, again. Their reunion, however, was bittersweet. After I nearly passed out while working at my dad's grocery store one evening, he sent me home to rest. My mother noted, and wondered out loud, why I had lost so much weight. Indicating that I did not know, I explained that I couldn't keep any food down lately. Thinking that I might be coming down with meningitis again, my dad insisted she take me to see our family doctor.

The diagnosis shocked us all and changed my life forever. According to the doctor, in about seven short months I would become a mother. How could I be expecting when I was a virgin, I wondered--something which the girls in my group and I (still) proudly proclaimed when we'd talk about the other, more loose girls at our school, who by the way never appeared to end up pregnant. As a matter of fact, Willie had confirmed I was a virgin! In my naivety, it never occurred to me that our encounter had ended my virginity.

Upon learning my condition, and noting that even though I was approaching seventeen, that I really didn't understand what was happening, a nurse explained the facts of life to me, after which I wasn't sure how to feel. I knew that I was angry but did not know where to or toward whom it should be directed. Why hadn't anyone explained these things to me, I wondered. Recalling that all my stepmother ever said was "keep your dress down," I also wondered if I would be pregnant had I'd known a bit more. Perhaps I should have been interested enough to learn things on my own. Be that as it may, all my friends and I were concerned with at that stage in our lives was making it in the music industry.

My only consolation was that at least I would get to marry Willie. After all, this is what happens (I naively thought) when a girl gets pregnant. When I confided in Bertha however, I learned that at twenty-one years old, Willie had already fathered two children (by two different women!), and was not interested in marriage, which is why she had warned me about him in the first place. And, although she would soon learn about my condition (thanks to my parents), I was too ashamed to face Willie's mother. When I did, I learned that Willie had moved away.

Needless-to-say, my Group was devastated by the revelation of my pregnancy, as was my boyfriend, Jimmy. Unable to continue with performances during that time, I was advised to take a maternity leave. However, I was still allowed to do background singing at the studio. Ashamed that her brother was responsible for both my condition and the position in which it left our group, Bertha quit the group and would no longer talk to me. Things had indeed fallen apart.

Jimmy was in the twelfth grade at the time, and since everyone knew us as a couple, he insisted on marrying me in spite of my condition. Even though we had never been intimate, he "did not want me to carry the label of an unmarried teenager." However, both our parents were totally against our very naive solution, all reasoning that Jimmy was still in high school and would not be able to get a job that could pay enough to provide for a family. My father also reasoned, that if Jimmy dropped out of school, he doubted if he had the maturity to take care of a family at this juncture in his life. Thus, the marriage solution stood a greater chance of turning what appeared to be a bad situation into a disaster. He then assured me that he would take care of my child and me until I was ready to go out on my own. That made sense to me and while it was necessary for me to drop out of school during that spring semester, I continued singing at the studio, recording on background sessions, and working part-time at my dad's stores.

Still, Jimmy stuck by me throughout my pregnancy even telling those who didn't know, that he was the father of my child. He was also constantly present after my little girl was born, and I allowed him to give her her first name. Determined that "one day he would indeed marry me," Jimmy insisted on giving my little girl his last name as well. After graduating that following year, he joined the Navy, and since we both were of age by then, we got married shortly after his initial training. It was not long after his first leave, in the Navy, I learned that I was pregnant again.

I believe I was more upset about this pregnancy than my first. After all, to make sure that we did not have any more children until we were ready, or at least until he completed his tour in the Navy, Jimmy and I had used every precaution we knew of. It's hard not to smile when I recall how we assured ourselves that I could not get pregnant so soon after the first one, when we could not locate the protection, we'd used one night and how we both laughed when we discovered, the next morning, that it had slipped off inside me. I now began wondering why women had so little, if any, control over their bodies?

When everyone learned I was pregnant again, they jokingly dubbed me "the baby-making machine." Although I knew my family and friends didn't mean any harm, I felt devastated. I began thinking that having children so early in life was my destiny, of which I had little or no control. And, while I had the support of a good man, considering I was the lead singer in our group and despite their effort to convince me to continue, I decided to at least take some time off. Beside my preoccupation with one toddler, and another one on the way was too much for my young mind to handle. Then I recalled a young lady that had been showing up at the studio of late, for whom the producers seemed to have not found a place. Minnie Riperton had been discovered earlier that year, but had a voice so unique, the studio writers were having difficulty finding a suitable song for her. Knowing that it had been rumored that Chess did not want to lose her, I recommended that she take my place while I take a much-needed maternity leave.

***

During my time off, my friend Bertha, who had started talking to me again, was the only person I could talk to about my feelings. Although I was expecting my second child, she was surprised to learn how little I still knew about the whole process of procreation and tried to explain it as best she could. Armed with some information now, I made a vow to never get pregnant again--or at least not until I was good and ready. After all, I still had to give birth to a boy. Nevertheless, I recall still being very upset with the women in my life during that time, who never said more to me about the facts of life other than "keep your dress down and your legs closed," a technique that obviously did not always work. I vowed that before, during and after puberty, I'd teach my daughters all they needed to know about womanhood and life, including the very sensational but natural feelings that can sneak up on one, in moments of venerability, regardless of how "good" one tries to be. I would explain that these feelings are naturally embedded in both male and female, for the purpose of procreation. And, that once they reached puberty, at which time they are most fertile, when they participate in unprotected sex, the probability of getting pregnant was greater than not.

Now that I had no illusions about how life happens, I would also let my children know that when they find themselves in an uncompromising position, and those strange, new, and exciting feelings arise ("and they will" I'd assure them), the only defense one has sometimes is knowledge and/or some form of protection. I would be up front with them about how and where to find information on how to access protection for themselves if they were not comfortable asking me or their father about it. Problem was, at this juncture, I was still not sure what all this knowledge and information was myself. Indeed, ignorance may be bliss, but it could also be a curse.

This grouping of the Gems from left to right includes D. Hucklebee, J. Collins, T. Washum, Me, and Minnie Rippeton. 1967

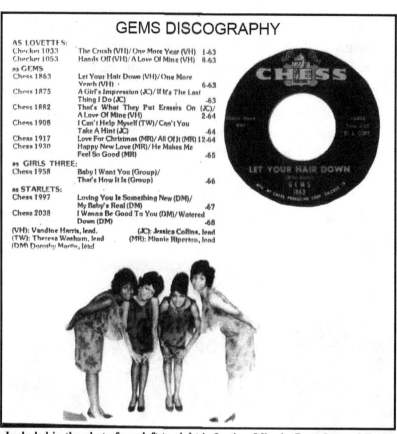

GEMS DISCOGRAPHY

AS LOVETTES:
Checker 1033	The Crush (VH)/ One More Year (VH)	1-63
Checker 1053	Hands Off (VH)/ A Love Of Mine (VH)	8-63

as GEMS
Chess 1863	Let Your Hair Down (VH)/ One More Yearh (VH)	6-63
Chess 1875	A Girl's Impression (JC)/ If It's The Last Thing I Do (JC)	-63
Chess 1882	That's What They Put Erasers On (JC)/ A Love Of Mine (VH)	2-64
Chess 1908	I Can't Help Myself (TW)/ Can't You Take A Hint (JC)	-64
Chess 1917	Love For Christmas (MR)/ All Of It (MR)	12-64
Chess 1930	Happy New Love (MR)/ He Makes Me Feel So Good (MR)	-65

as GIRLS THREE:
Chess 1958	Baby I Want You (Group)/ That's How It Is (Group)	-66

as STARLETS:
Chess 1997	Loving You Is Something New (DM)/ My Baby's Real (DM)	-67
Chess 2038	I Wanna Be Good To You (DM)/ Watered Down (DM)	-68

(VH): Vandine Harris, lead.   (JC): Jessica Collins, lead
(TW): Theresa Washum, lead   (MR): Minnie Riperton, lead
(DM) Dorothy Martin, lead

Included in the photo from left to right is Jessica, Minnie, Dorothy, and Teresa 1968

Late Spring

Vandean Harris-Philpott

California Here I Come

Upon joining the Navy, Jimmy had been sent to the Great Lakes Naval Academy for training. He was later assigned to Long Beach, California, and from there sent to Vietnam. After his tour of duty there, he was re-stationed in Northern California, and although we had gotten married and had a second daughter by then, we had not spent much time living together as man, wife, and family. So, when my husband asked me to give up my singing career and join him in California, considering what he had done for me in the past, I had no problem complying. In addition, I could sense that something was brewing from the subtle indications in his most recent letters. It was not until well after I arrived in California however, that I learned that indeed, something was brewing. The eventual revelations were so painfully blatant I wasn't sure how to handle the drama that followed.

Our Two Daughters, Janie and Denise, 1966

In Northern California, Jimmy had been assigned to the naval base in Alameda. Scottie's, a local club where the sailors hung out after returning from sea, was where it had all begun. According to my husband, who later confessed during an attempt to get me to forgive him, during one of his nights out, before I arrived, he met a young lady, who also lived in Alameda, and Scottie's was a local hang out for her and her friends as well. Convincing himself that he could never get serious about anyone who'd obviously entertained many other sailors, since he was missing home, Jimmy explained that he began talking with her. "But what started out as a friendship developed into a full-fledged affair [he] thought would end after [I] joined [him]."

I'd begun working for the U.S. Postal Service while still in Chicago and was able to transfer to California. After his Naval service, Jimmy secured employment with the Postal Service also, though in a different location and different shift. Once the children and I arrived in California, we soon settled into the lifestyle of a two-parent working family. Our plan was to purchase a home as soon after his military service as possible.

Our children were still very young at that point, and the childcare arrangement we'd established involved the two of us taking turns keeping them. During the evening swing shift, during which time I worked, Jimmy would take care of our girls while I cared for them during the day, when he worked. This way, we reasoned, one of us would always be available for our children, and at the same time, be able to put the money we would have sent on childcare toward a home. It was during this (1968) time, Martin Luther King, Jr. was killed.

I shall never forget the sadness that swept across the Post Office Annex that April afternoon. I, along with more than a hundred others, was sorting mail when the announcement came across the loudspeaker. Dr. King, who'd vehemently promoted the non-violent approach to equal rights, had been targeted many times before but few believed that anyone would actually murder him-- not this spiritually conscious, Christ-like, human being, I wondered out loud.

However, I could not help but recall that just days before, during one of our breaks, someone had mentioned that threats on his life had become more numerous of late, and that perhaps Dr. King should lay low for a while. Dismissing this situation, Dr. King proceeded to Memphis, TN, where he was to give a speech in support of the garbage collectors' strike. During that occasion, he was shot down while standing on the balcony at the Lorraine Hotel with a few of his colleagues discussing the collector's situation.

Before the announcement (of the assassination) that day, the gigantic room in which I worked was full of lively chatter, and it took a few minutes before us workers could process this awful news. The information left most of us standing in a daze, while others began falling to their knees in prayer. Still others cried out loud as if their own father had just died. I found myself wondering who on earth would want to murder a man that promoted nothing but peace and love. My mind rushed back to how Jesus was killed doing the same thing. Is this what happens when one steps up to show us the way, I wondered.

The sense of loss was so overwhelming that literally no one, including our strict supervisors, could continue working that day. We all just stood there in shock. Some, in an attempt to comfort themselves, tried to comfort others. A bit of relief came only after the Postmaster, a Caucasian man, got on the loudspeaker and asked us all to bow our heads as he prayed. He prayed for us all that day--Blacks, Whites, Hispanics, Asians, and everyone else.

Those customers waiting for the timely delivery of their mail were out of luck during that time because for the next week or so, although the majority showed up for work, having been inundated with the same televised footage regarding that awful event via the news, and finding it hard to accept that Dr. King had been murdered, most of us moved around our workstation like zombies. It was only after he was buried that thing eventually began to resemble some sense of normality. I recall wondering if and when all hell was going to break loose, now that the one who appeared to be the only one to maintain the peace was dead during those troubling times. Unlike many other places around the United States however, California's Bay Area remained somewhat calm.

***

Despite all that was going on at the time, I was apparently so happy to finally have our family together, I hadn't noticed any improprieties in our marriage, especially during the first year of our reunion. However, the outside relationship, which eventually

77

revealed itself, would change our lives forever, and the long intense battles that followed put a serious strain on our marriage.

I would eventually figure out that unlike my husband's routine, which included hanging out with his old Navy buddies (often at Scotty's) during his downtime, in addition to my working full-time, my routine consisted of taking care of our children, our home, and had no downtime. Actually, it never occurred to me that I had taken on the role of the proverbial stressed-out, over-worked superwoman; all that I was doing seemed normal to me at the time. After all, I had come from a family of hard-working women, including my stepmother. A reality check revealed that the many responsibilities that I'd taken on, often left me too exhausted to be the friend I had been to my husband during our earlier years.

Jimmy and me on a night out during happier days, sometime during the late 60's

Believing that all I did was the sole responsibility of women, it never occurred to me ask my husband for more help, and, apparently, he didn't know to offer. I now began wondering if maybe his infidelity was partly my fault.

After being forced to confront our current situation, Jimmy promised to end what he declared was only a friendship. We agreed to eliminate this hiccup in our marriage and work harder to not allow any outsider to destroy what we had built together so far. However, after his "friend" began calling our house with bold requests to speak to him, and his attempts "to let her down easy, more and more fights ensued, at which point I was not sure if I was the wife or friend. Finally fed up with the situation where my husband tried to end an affair "without hurting the feelings of the other woman," which I honestly believed he did try, I informed him that until he decided which of our feelings he preferred to protect, I was going back home to Chicago. And, in spite of his pleas, my husband and I experienced our first separation.

Vandean Harris-Philpott

What's Love Got to Do with It?

Having learned that I had returned to Chicago, Bertha contacted me at my parents' home. During our conversation, she informed me that she had gotten married and that her husband worked in the music industry as a promoter. After telling him about my singing ability, she was convinced that if I chose to remain in Chicago, they could restart my singing career. Not quite sure where my future was heading, considering the recent separation from my husband, I agreed to accept a singing engagement arranged by her husband to see where it would lead. It turned out that the "gig" Bertha's husband secured, at one of Chicago's popular night clubs, was also a contest. It wasn't hard to figure out that he wanted to see if I really could sing. Having not performed for months, and with no rehearsal time, I won third place. Impressed, he offered to manage my career as a solo artist.

In the process of deciding whether or not I wanted to proceed with what appeared to be another chance in the music industry, Willie showed up. He informed me that he had heard about the probability of my working with his brother-in-law and wanted to encourage me by giving all the support he could. He also took this opening to apologize about our past. Making a plea that, given the chance, he would gratefully spend the rest of his life making up for it. He reasoned that we (my children and I) did not need to be in California, miles away from our families, and that perhaps it was fate that caused Jimmy and me to separate.

I could see the sincerity in his eyes and thinking that he had gotten through to me Willie made the mistake of pulling me near and kissing me. Shocked that his kiss was still as electrifying as it was the night of our first encounter, I panicked, and with a promise that I would let him know what my plans were, I quickly excused myself and left. Although I was saddened by our current situation, I still felt totally committed to the man that stood by me after

Figure 1Me with Bertha and her husband during the night at a singing competition they arranged for me, 1969.

having been abandoned by Willie. While recognizing that I still had a weakness for and maybe, even still loved him, given our past, I was not about to trust my heart to him again. After all, I reasoned, what's love got to do with it? Love had not kept him there before.

When, years later Willie and I met again, having matured a bit more, and having gained a better understanding of how historical events (which will be discussed in a later chapter) could have affected our young lives and the decisions we made, realizing that he was just as much a victim of our times as I, I found it easier to be around him now. I had contacted him after visiting his sister Bertha, during another trip to Chicago, and decided to I take my first born to meet him. Although she knew that Willie was her biological father, she had grown up knowing only Jimmy as her "daddy." By introducing them at this juncture, I felt, would give her the option to decide whether or not she wished to remain in contact with them.

At any rate, Jimmy had already begun calling with apologies, and begging me to come back home, during this first breakup. Ironically enough, he called again that very night I had the encounter with Willie. I told him I was ready

to come home and, after saying good-bye to Bertha the next day, my girls and I were on a train back to California.

Vandean Harris-Philpott

Here We go Again and Again

Before our second separation, Jimmy had encouraged me to return to school to acquire a few clerical skills and to finish my high school diploma. We were both still working for the U.S. Post Service and had re-instituted our previous routine. As time passed, I began to experience extreme tiredness along with a constant ill-feeling throughout my abdominal area. When we could not figure out why, we went to see a doctor who revealed that I had been pregnant and had suffered a miscarriage. Apparently again, I'd been so busy working and taking care of my family I had not recognized the symptoms.

Later that year, during the Christmas mail rush, Jimmy's shift was called in to assist at my work location. I looked up just in time to see him approaching my workstation with a strange look on his face. Before his final arrival, he'd begun profusely apologizing about something. As he came nearer, I could see the mist in his eyes. Snatching the mailbag full of heavy boxes from my hands, he asked, "Is this what you do all day?" When I nodded yes, he continued, "No wonder you're so exhausted when you get home!" In spite of what had happened to us of late, I still recognized that my husband was a very kind and sensitive human being. It was during this time that we decided I should return to school.

Taking advantage of the light-duty work schedule I had been given, that resulted from the health issues I was experiencing, our plan was revised accordingly. I was to return to school and obtain the clerical skills necessary to qualify for the office assistant position on which I'd been temporally assigned. I'd been working light-duty on a part-time basis, and Jimmy had changed his shift to accommodate our new plan. Our perfect schedule was such that I could be at home in time to have dinner ready when my family members were all at home during the same time. My husband and I had time for each other as well as for our children.

Everything was going fine, and I recall being so happy, I felt like I was living a fairytale life again. However, it turned out that I did not get the office position we were counting on, and I had to return to my regular job assignment. To accommodate a new schedule, it was necessary that I return to my 3:00 pm to 12:00 am shift. The children were now in the Head Start program for a few hours each day. This old arrangement provided my husband the opportunity for a well-deserved break from his evening-long babysitting regimen and the re-occurring sleepless nights he'd been experiencing more frequently lately, to relax before going to work the next day. Unfortunately, he decided also to use some of this free time to rekindle the relationship with his lady-friend as well.

Then, one afternoon, during which I had taken an unexpected day off, the telephone rang, and I picked it up simultaneously to Jimmy picking up the extension. The incoming call instantly announced the voice of an angry woman shouting at him because he had not shown up that day. Although I made sure they knew I was on the line, by the time Jimmy became aware, it was already too late. The woman was so irate she did not seem to care. Apparently, so much in love with my husband, the woman insisted that it was time I knew who she was, "because I'm not giving up so easy this time" she screamed. It turned out that this was the same woman that caused our first separation. And, needless-to-say, that telephone call started another war between us, especially after her assertion that I did not know him as well as she did. Whatever the case, it was becoming more difficult for me to blame "the other woman" when, clearly it was my husband who had frequented her house. I could only pray that he had not brought her to ours.

This drama did not end until Jimmy announced one day that he needed a break, "to clear his head." Consequently, "Fed up with her continued boldness," he explained that he'd decided to go back to Chicago to stay with his family for a while. Agreeing that indeed, maybe this was what he needed--a break from this California madness, I conquered. So, along with the promise that he would also see a doctor at the Great Lakes Veterans Administration (VA) while there, to address the flashbacks and nightmare problems he'd been experiencing, Jimmy took off in our newly purchased, brand new car. I would learn later that his girlfriend had gone with him.

Feeling beyond betrayed, I also decided to let it go. I continued working and doing what it took to keep my mind off my shattered life. I also decided to go back to school and complete the requirements for my high school diploma. Just as I was about to enroll in a community college however, Jimmy and I found our way back to each other--again. Unfortunately, the process of us breaking up and getting back together would continue several more years. The final split involved my taking our girls and leaving my husband, with all the associated drama, in Chicago, where he had brought us, after our third (or was it the fourth?) reconciliation attempt.

Apparently, the excitement of living with his California girlfriend in Chicago, without the burden of having a wife and children present had worn off and having decided that she wasn't what he wanted after all, Jimmy made another attempt to salvage his family. And although I was afraid to confirm it, I assumed he'd gotten the help he needed from the VA. After many telephone calls, Jimmy eventually convinced me (or maybe I just wanted to believe) that he had grown up now but felt that our relationship might stand a better chance back in Chicago where both our families lived. So, after much begging, I submitted again, and my husband came to California to personally collect his family. He took us to a beautiful townhouse apartment situated at an equal distance between our parents, who lived on the West, and South sides of Chicago.

With the exception of an occasional nightmare Jimmy still experienced, we were finally living peacefully again, and everything was going fine until the California woman showed up with the police! While asserting that the girls could stay, she demanded that I leave, because the premises in which we lived belonged to her and my husband. Although the problem was settled, when the police learned that I was in fact the wife (and the mother of our children) and because Jimmy had not included her name on the lease, this situation created still another rift in our relationship. Refusing to let go, and after many failed attempts to rekindle their relationship, the girl decided to cause trouble in other ways--not worth mentioning here.

Me after completing my High School Diploma, 1960

Totally unable to take anymore, I announced I would be going back to California, and to the dismay of both our families, with my two little girls in tow, I eventually took off, but not before learning that although Jimmy had finally gotten rid of the clinging woman, from California, apparently while she and I were constantly competing he had found comfort in still another outside woman!

Reasoning that perhaps, as my father had suggested, in spite of my husband's good intentions, and/or love for me, we had gotten married much too early in life, and with my having a "ready-made" family, he did not have much time to grow up. Since I felt he deserved it, especially after considering the adjustment problems he experienced after his tour in Vietnam, I decided again, to give him more time. In the meantime, I had my own growing to do, something I felt I could not do in Chicago. So, with my two little girls in tow, I set out to

California again.

After our departure, I learned later that Jimmy had followed his newest friend back to Mississippi, where she lived before trying to make it in Chicago. Feeling satisfied that, at least I tried to do what was right, I remained in California, and continued going to school. I eventually enrolled in Contra Costa Junior College, where I graduated with an AA degree in business administration.

Vandean Harris-Philpott

In Search of God

Looking back on my life and how it had unfolded so far, I began doubting myself and my religion. Although I attended church, as I was trained, I began thinking that I must be doing something wrong, since it appeared that no matter how hard I tried to be "a good girl/wife/person," and/or do the right thing, everything I had done so far ended up producing negative or (at best) questionable results.

For instance, I was not promiscuous, so why did I get pregnant so young and, on the first encounter no less! During my teens, I had heard of many girls in my age group bragging about the many intimate encounters they'd had yet, to my knowledge, none of them had gotten pregnant. Why had I, who wanted to reserve my first time for that special someone with whom I would share my vows, and my life? The fact that both of my early intimate encounters had produced two wonderful children presented an even greater irony.

Although I loved my children dearly, and at this juncture could not imagine living without them, I could not understand how fate could allow a young girl's innocent infatuation for and trust in a person to result in an unexpected pregnancy. And, with someone in whose life that person was not interested in participating at the time. Not unlike my teenage friends, who dreamed of marriage someday, I too preferred having my children "the right way", or as society dictated; that is planned for after being married for a while. Additionally, why had both my singing career and marriage failed, in spite of all the efforts I'd put in both of them?

Perhaps God was punishing me for not taking my religion seriously. After all, my auntie had to literally drag me from the mourning bench to the acceptance chair when I was a child in Egypt. And, what about the comment I made at the baptizing pond? I wasn't concerned that my soul was about to be "washed whiter than snow." My only concern that day was that I was about to be dipped in water that cows had pissed in. By the way, this is why until today, I will never step into a public pool. At least, not until somebody convinces me that people do not urinate in them while swimming. Perhaps, I hadn't been saved after all, and this was my punishment. These thoughts ignited my need to understand how God and his religions worked. Thinking that this knowledge could assist me with making amends with him, I became consumed with the need to find and understand more about God.

My only point of reference, at that time, was the Bible. However, the more I read it (about three times), the more confused I became. The favoritism God appeared to show some at the expense of others was incomprehensible to me. As a young mother, I could not imagine favoring one of my children over the other. How then, I wondered, could God, who had created all of us, be so cruel to some? Another disturbing story for me was that of Hagar. Since this conflict mimicked my own life's experiences so far, here is where my search began, and became an obsession.

Focusing on the lower status of women, I noted that this practice seemed to be condoned in the Bible. The double standard presented there seemed to give men the right to use and abuse women as if they were not human beings or had no human feelings. I wasn't at all happy about this revelation but became totally upset after reading about poor Hagar's plight in the story of Abraham and Sarah. In alarm I thought, my goodness, if God condoned this, we (females) do not stand a chance in this world!

As the story unfolds, once Sarah learned that she was barren and could not conceive a child for her husband Abraham, she recommended he sleep with her Egyptian handmaiden, (Hagar) in order to satisfy his need to sire a child. Apparently, Hagar was a young maiden who, although never been touched, had no control over her life. I was shocked at how easy it was for this "man of God" to accept the gift of another human being to fulfill his own desires, without any regards about how she, the handmaiden, felt about it.

Much later in the story, Sarah was finally able (or blessed by God) to bear her own child, which she did, but eventually became concerned that Hagar's son might share an inheritance with her son. Sarah therefore ordered Abraham to "get rid of that slave woman and her son," after which Abraham sent Hagar and their child into the desert! It was amazing to me at how easy it was for Abraham to do this now that he no longer needed the handmaiden's womb. When comparing this story to how women are treated in today's world, I wondered if God's seemingly condoning of Abraham's behavior is how the behavior of most modern men, i.e., the double standards and attitudes toward females, are currently justified. Was this also "God's will?" Having been told that while Hagar's son Ishmael would be the father of the Arab nation, and Isaac father of the Jewish nation, I wondered also if this is where the problems between the two began, that is, Abraham's treatment of Ishmael's mother, and his favor for Sarah's son, Isaac, over him. Equally upsetting to me was the violence described in the Old Testament, such as that in the book of Deuteronomy. How, I questioned, could a God who had power over heaven and earth justify allowing one group in his creation to slaughter another, "...every man, woman, and child!" Other history books I had read on the evolution of nations all over the world appeared to follow the examples described in Deuteronomy--to conquer and kill all. Wasn't this earth large enough for all of us, I questioned. Even more disturbing was that religion appears to be the motive behind this violence, as many wars were fought to intimidate people into following a particular theological philosophy or religion. Needing explanations, I went to my pastor to seek assistance.

The head pastor at my church, explained that I needed to pray for understanding before reading the various chapters of the Bible. After much prayer however, I was still at a lost to understand, so I decided to visit other Christian denominations, i.e., Catholic (my husband's faith); and later, Methodist, Lutheran, Pentecostal, and Jehovah Witnesses, in an attempt to understand their positions on this and certain other subjects. I even took a peek at the Mormons. I concluded that no matter how explicit the Bible was on a particular subject, each denomination interpreted the texts to suit its own purpose, or theological position. Having grown up in the Baptist church, I had already witnessed many indiscretions among the faithful, and questioned some behaviors early on. I was beginning to believe then, that these various religions were the creations of man, not God. I was already on the verge of losing faith in my own denomination, especially after considering a situation that took place earlier in my adult life during which I discovered that my pastor's wife, with whom I shared rides to work, was cheating on him with a deacon of our church.

***

While still working at the Post Office, I had begun carpooling with the wife of the minister of my church in Oakland. After nearly one year, the minister's wife, whom I honestly looked up to, apparently felt safe enough to share her transgressions with me. One night, after our shift ended, she asked if I minded that she makes a detour (from the normal route to my house), to pick up a package from a friend. Puzzled why she would even ask since she had already made the detour before I answered, I nodded in the affirmative. We turned on to a dark street and pulled up alongside of another car, and although her actions mimicked those of an actress in a mystery movie, I was still unaware of what was happening.

After parking, the pastor's wife left our vehicle, opened the door on the passenger side of a vehicle in which a male figure sat on the driver's side, and slid inside beside him. They talked for about five minutes, after which she gave him a peck on the cheek and returned to our car. I still had no idea about what was going on. After all, she was the pastor's wife, and since she was old enough to be my mother, it didn't even occur to me that she would be doing anything wicked. Nonetheless, when we proceeded on our way, she felt it necessary to confess that the man in the car was her boyfriend. Having already recognized him as one of the devout deacons at our church, I was so taken aback after this revelation I couldn't speak all the way home. She, on the other hand, chatted proudly about "her boyfriend " all the way there. I did not sleep at all that night. I wasn't sure if it was her hypocrisy that upset me so, or the fact that she was doing the same thing, to a member of our church, that another woman had done to me. What's with these California women I wondered. I laid awake stuck in this quagmire through most of the night.

What was most unsettling about this situation was this woman's ability to smile and be friendly with that deacon's wife with seemingly no guilt. I believe however, that it was her willingness to share her sin with me was what made me decide to leave the church altogether. It had become very difficult for me to sit in the choir stand each Sunday, singing God's praises, while facing the deacon's wife, who sat loving with her cheating husband, knowing what I knew. More disconcerting was the reverence the pastor's wife accepted from the other parishioners and deacon's wife, who respected her as a devoted first lady. Although I could not claim myself any holier, it became very uncomfortable for me to watch this fiasco every Sunday--I left the church.

Why then (I continued wondering), had I, who tried so hard to do the right thing, experienced so much adversity, while someone who didn't seem to be concerned about who she'd hurt, appeared to have everything go in her favor? It was at this point I became obsessed about finding the truth, and thus began a quest to explore religions other than Christianity. In the meantime, I kept praying for understanding, as instructed.

***

During my independent studying, I became aware of the "Lost in Translation" argument, and at times wondered if perhaps misinterpreting the Bible, on the part of some, was intentional. Whatever the case, some of the assertions and conclusions therein surely must have added to the confusion among the various religions' understanding of certain events. For example, I discovered that in the ancient world of the Near East, i.e., Assyria, Syria, Iraq, and Iran, where many of the Biblical events took place and later written about, phrases such as "burning by fire" was a capital punishment widely practiced during that time in Babylon (today's Iraq). Bible translators imply that such punishments were only inflicted on one particular group of people.

Additionally, considering that words like "hell," which in Aramaic (Jesus' native language) means "mental suffering, anguish, inner torment and regret," and terms such as "burn in hell," still used today--commonly as a metaphor, could have been used by writers of the Bible, as metaphors, or to emphasize the importance of an event, as opposed to the literal meanings given such terms by later translators. I also read many accounts on where heaven is supposed to be. For example, while many Western religions argue that it is up above the clouds, where only the righteous will go after death; others use assertions in the 17th chapter of Luke as proof that the Kingdom of Heaven is within— us all! In this chapter Luke goes on to tell how we can achieve this heavenly "state of being." Was it possible then (I wondered), if Western religions have taken other biblical metaphors literally, and as a result interpreted scripture to mean that God, for example, would burn human bodies or souls as a punishment if they did not follow his orders? Would this make sense from a God who is all about love? Ultimately, I preferred to believe that God is indeed love and would not treat his/her own children so cruelly. In spite of these discoveries however, I was still unsatisfied, and continued searching.

Eventually, I ran across Osoko K.K. Ameve, an African writer, who defined religion as merely a belief system and the cultural practices of the various people in the world. Ameve explains that there are as many religions as there are people, and that every part of the world has its own religious philosophies, including the many countries in Africa. He points out, for example, that the Arabs have their Islam, the Chinese their Taoism and Confucianism, the Persians their Zoroastrianism, the Japanese their Shintoism, and the Europeans many kinds of Christianity, and so on. After reading The History of the First Council of Nice, which capped my understanding of modern religion, I was convinced that Ameve's theory, just might be true.

The purpose of the Council at Nice, held in Nicaea, in A.D. 325, by Emperor Constantine, supposedly the first Christian Emperor, was to establish the basis on which the Christian doctrine was to be worshiped in the future--even though Peter and other key components of the faith had already established the doctrine, including when the Passover was to be celebrated. Additionally, it appears there were several conflicting schools of thoughts in the Christian faith regarding who Jesus was in relations to God. While one argued that the Trinity (God the Father, Jesus, the Son and Holy Ghost, which I would learn later, was the mother), were all one, the other dominate school of thought, namely the Aryans (established by Arius, an Egyptian Presbyter or elder), maintained that God had an existence separate from the Son (Jesus).

Having already learned that basis for the Christian faith could be traced back to Africa, and that Alexander, an Egyptian Bishop and key player in the Council of Nice, favored and convinced Constantine on the former doctrine, I thought it interesting that this Greek Emperor Constantine felt it okay, or even had the power to change religious doctrine to fit his likings--especially since these words were supposed to be God's (unchangeable) own. I would eventually discover that it all had to do with the power he (Constantine) had acquired through wars.

I was even more surprised to discover that by the 16th century, Christian doctrine had been changed several times to fit the needs of those in power, the most prominent of which was the King James Version of the Bible, whose creation was necessitated, in 1534, after King Henry VIII and the Church of England separated from the Vatican. In 1604, after authorizing a committee of fifty scholars, including philosopher Shakespeare, the King James Version set the rules for what books the new Bible would contain and declared that no other version could be used or read. Interestingly enough, during King Henry VIII's reign, laws were enacted prohibiting women from owning or reading a Bible unless they were of the "noble class."

By the time I completed books like Christianity Before Christ, by G. Jackson, The Hidden Years of Jesus, by George M. Lamsa, The Origin of The Bible... by Osofo K.K. Ameve, The Browder Files, by Anthony Browder, the History of the First Council of Nice, by Dean Dudley, and several others regarding the history of religion, I was forced to conclude that indeed, every religion has its own agenda, and these agendas had little to do with God.

What continues to be an enigma (to me) is why those who worship in the many Christian sects persist in taking Jesus (an Armenian Jew, who sought to free his people from the grip of the Roman Empire, during his time), from his people and declaring him their God. While I had come to understand that, like prophets in other parts of the world, who tried to convey this same sense of hope to their own people during their times of social upheavals, foreign occupation, and colonization etc as Jesus had done for his people, why had Jesus been elevated to be the "only son of God' among Christians, especially when Jesus himself tells us, via the Bible (the book of his Jewish ancestors), that what he had done, we can do also.

Considering all that my research had revealed, raised a Christian, the only religion with which I was most familiar at the time, I decided to comfort myself with Luke's assertion (17:20) that "the kingdom of God is within us [all]." And, while I began to understand intellectually, that religion deals with the mind of their adherents and encapsulates the traditions and cultural heritage of a particular people, this verse, along with other readings that supported this idea, helped me to find the peace I so desperately needed at that time in my life. If little else, my search somehow, confirmed what I already knew: that each of us must go within and seek God for ourselves--in our own way.

I decided, then, that while others (the more spiritually developed ones) can assist with guiding us in this process, I still wanted to seek a better understanding of how the various religions around the world interpreted it, and at this juncture, I needed to learn how to manage my life in relation to God. More importantly, I needed to understand how procreation and gender roles play in this—that is, if God loves us all (both male and female, not to mention all races) equally and unconditionally. I also had a burning need to know why adherents of various religions fought wars throughout history over this, our one God? But my search had to be put aside for now since I had more pressing issues that needed my attention.

Angels Beneath My Wings

Since having lived a life focused on trying to live up to what others expected of me had not worked thus far, I decided that perhaps I should take another approach, and do what I thought was best for me and my girls. My parents had been very happy that we had returned to Chicago, and although they were concerned when my marriage began to show signs of trouble again, they had not hesitated to assist with the children when I requested. We lived with them while I worked two jobs during that winter and saved up enough money to implement my unshared plans.

When I announced that I was going back to California, and finally accepting that he could not convince me otherwise, my father literally broke down and cried. Although I loved being near my parents, and greatly appreciated their support, I had long decided that Chicago, which represented a lot of pain and sadness for me, was not where I wanted to live. So, determined to follow an unexplainable desire within me, I pushed on.

Upon arrival in California, my daughters and I were picked up from the airport by my friend Sarah who, like myself, was a single parent at the time. When I phoned her earlier about my plans to return, she was very happy and offered us accommodations in the small apartment she shared with her two small children until I could secure one of my own. I was lucky to find a job at a large department store right away, and after saving several paychecks, I naively accepted a small kitchenette apartment in an old, renovated motel not far from Sarah's place. Although I had noted some of the characters hanging around the complex during my tour with the building manager, after he assured me it was very safe, I accepted it. Besides the low rent, which was very manageable for me at that juncture, I was also cognizant of the fact that four small children in my friend's small apartment too long would eventually wear negatively on our friendship.

Unfortunately, it would soon become a challenge to reside in our little abode. Shortly after moving in, I began hearing the doorknob rattle during the night. Convincing myself that no one would dare try to break in, I reasoned that someone must have mistaken our door for theirs. These incidents kept happening more frequently however, and, at times, so forcefully they began to awaken the children during the night. Knowing that had the person succeeded in entering my home, he/she was putting their very life at risk, I became more annoyed than afraid. I was confident I could murder anyone (with my bare hands), should they try to harm me and, more importantly, my children.

Soon, I became worried my girls were not getting enough sleep, so I began putting a chair under the doorknob for extra security. I also reported the matter to the manager, who promised to keep an eye and ear out for the culprit. In the meantime, I would remain awake most of the night, waiting for any intruder that dared to open my door. Then one day, after picking the girls up from childcare and upon returning to our little kitchenette, we found it in disarray. Someone had broken in. Although we had nothing valuable enough to steal, our clothing was scattered all over the

place. After calming the girls, I reported the incident to the manager after which he changed our locks. He also suggested that perhaps I move downstairs, in the apartment next to him and his wife, so that he could keep a closer eye on us. The problem was it wouldn't be available for another two weeks.

Me and my girls (on our own) after returning to California 1970.

Needless-to-say, the girls were afraid to go home after this, but since I had no other options at that point, I agreed to his proposal. In the meantime, our routine became staying out as long as possible, doing various activities (i.e., shopping, movies, eating out, visiting, or just walking around), until the girls were exhausted before returning home each day. This way, I reasoned, they would fall asleep quickly after going to bed, while I remained alert during the nights protecting them.

The following weekend, the girls and I were invited to a picnic by my friend Janice, with whom I had worked with previously at the Post Office. After we adults had nearly eaten ourselves to death that day, and all the children were playing among themselves, the adults decided to play a game of baseball. Confident that this was my game, when it came my turn at bat, I hit a pop-up ball in the direction in which I was to run to first base. So excited that I finally made a hit, and determined to make it to at least, first base, I took off without noticing Tyree, Janice's boyfriend (Wayne's) friend, running towards me with his eyes fixed on the ball. The next thing I recall was lying on the ground surrounded by my children, who were crying, along with my worried looking teammates. When I had completely regained consciousness, and after learning that we had come to the park by bus, Tyree insisted on giving us a ride home. Too embarrassed to let him know where I lived, I quickly rejected the offer.

Tyree, as all the people I met at the picnic, consisted of a group young adult who had just finished college and/or the military, and was now working and living their well-planned future. During some of the conversations in which I had participated that day, I recalled admiring both the choices they all had made in life, as well the lifestyle they were now living. While I felt I had done okay on my own so far, and that I would eventually get to where I wanted to be, weighted down with the responsibilities of a single parent, I was finding it a bit harder than I'd expected. And, right now, I also knew that I did not want Tyree to see where I was at this point. Trying hard not to hide his embarrassment for literally knocking me out, Tyree insisted I "take the lift for the kids' sake." After noting that my girls were indeed tired, while I remained reluctant, I was a bit happy he insisted. Besides, I was still woozy and did not feel up to a long bus ride home.

Upon arriving at our residence, Tyree was unable to conceal his shock, and blurted out, "This is where you live?" I answered timidly in the affirmative, and quickly began to explain that it was only temporary. Noting the characters hanging around outside, Tyree parked his car and insisted on walking us inside. Once I unlocked the door, we all were surprised to see that the apartment had been broken into. "Not again!" I groaned. At that point, Tyree demanded I pack some clothes and come with him, "Right now!" he shouted before I could protest. He went on to suggest that we would return for the remaining things later. I meekly obeyed. We drove along in silence until I managed enough nerve to ask where he was taking us. As if in deep thought, he softly responded that we would stay at his place that night. As we traveled on, I attempted to explain my current situation and what my future plans were. When I finished talking, he asserted boldly, "Well, you won't be staying there any longer."

Without pausing I asked how Janice was going to feel about him taking us to his place, (which he shared with her boyfriend) without her knowledge. After explaining that he understood what I was trying to achieve, he then asserted that he could do what he pleased in his place. After a short pause however, he went on to acknowledge that their bachelor apartment was not appropriate for us, and he had something else in mind. After arriving at his apartment that evening, Tyree made a brief phone call, after which he informed me that he was taking us to visit "some friends". After loading us in the car, off we went to the home of Lawrence and Mary Lee.

The Lee's had two little girls about the same ages as my two.

After properly introducing us, Lawrence and Tyree disappeared into another room, leaving me, his wife (Mary), and the children to ourselves. All the children seemed delighted to have playmates their own age, and, although it was a bit late in the evening, I began to appreciate Tyree for being so insightful. They eventually called Mary in to join them. Graciously excusing herself, Mary requested I serve all the children the food she had prepared. The visit was turning out well.

When they all returned, Mary started the conversation about our staying with them by asserting that she and Lawrence were not prepared to take "no" as an answer from me. After dinner, the four of us adults sat and planned my life for the next few months. Mary, who was a stay-at-home mom, kept my children the next day while I went to work. Tyree and Wayne picked me up from my job after work that evening and took me to my little kitchenette. After summoning the manager to let him know I was moving, they helped pack what remained of our household effects, then took me back to Mary and Lawrence's, where we resided for the next five months.

The time spent with the Lee family turned out to be very pleasant. I would learn later that although Tyree and Wayne were best friends, Mary and Wayne had grown up together in Georgia. In fact, Mary's family were lifetime members at the church in which Wayne's father was pastor. After Wayne and Tyree befriended each other at their workplace, learning that he too was from the South, Wayne introduced him to the Lees after which they all became like family, away from home. Since they all were a few years older than me, I would also learn (from them) a lot about how to survive on my own in California. Observing how these young adults lived and worked hard to achieve the lifestyles they wanted, with both dignity and respect, while still having lots of fun, I concluded that these were the people whose lives I wanted to emulate. This included going back to school to further my education. Lawrence and Mary refused to take any money from me during our stay with them, so I was able to save a comfortable amount before I eventually found a very nice apartment and was able to move sooner than expected. Needless-to-say, Tyree, Mary, Lawrence, and Wayne, became life-long friends, whom I felt where angels beneath my wings, as well as role models. I would eventually meet still another angel.

Shortly after we moved, while shopping at a retail outlet, I met Spencer. As manager of the store in which he worked, Spencer assisted me with picking affordable furniture for my new place. Without going into details on what turned out to be another life-long friendship, suffice it to say Spencer encouraged and supported all my plans when he learned of my aspirations. He would also empower me in other ways, including encouraging my pursuit of my first college degree. After assisting with a move to get my girls and me settled into a more permanent residence, Spencer actually took me to the nearby local college to explore how to proceed in my getting admitted. As a result, I enrolled at Contra Costa Junior college that Spring semester of 1972--less than two years after returning to California.

The Lee Family. Left to right are Lauren, Lawrence, Mary, and Stacy, 1970

Part Two

Early Summer

Vandean Harris-Philpott

Aiming Higher

It was the end of the spring semester at Contra Costa College (CCC) and the last day of my African history class. As I sat relishing my final grade (an A), I couldn't help but appreciate Professor James Lacy's teaching style. Little did I realize, at the time, that this encounter with Professor Lacy would set the course of my life for the next thirty-five years, or so. Having spent several years living and working on the continent of Africa, Professor Lacy would augment his lectures with actual personal examples, slide shows, and/or guest speakers such as Alex Haley, the author of Roots, and Africans from the Continent. So fascinated with the information he provided, I'd often sat in class daydreaming and actually seeing myself living the same experiences he'd had.

While sharing his experiences enhanced my understanding of Africa, the professor's reminiscences also brought back memories of my childhood in Egypt, Mississippi, and the stories my grand Aunt Mariah would tell (all fourteen or so of her grand nieces and nephews) as we sat around the fireplace on cold winter evenings. These stories consisted mainly of those told to her by her father (my great-grandfather), about the great ancient Empires in Western Africa and how powerful they were, as well as his travels and adventures to and from Africa. It was remarkable how Aunt Mariah's tales of West Africa's great empires agreed with what I was to learn throughout my African studies courses.

Although she had not provided the actual dates that these African empires existed, my grand aunt's time reference, which she speculated was "sometime after the life of Jesus," proved to me she knew what she was talking about. My research estimated that Ghana, the first of the Ancients (written about), was around 400 A.D. and thrived as one of the most powerful empires in the world until around 1070 A.D. Al-Bakri, an Arab scholar, is thought to have given the most complete account of ancient Ghana in 1067.

His writings describe Ghana's commercial, legal, and political systems as the best in the world at that time. He also tells of Ghana's great wealth, claiming that the king had "a nugget of pure gold weighing thirty pounds, of absolutely natural formation, to which his horses were tied."

The Ghana Empire was followed by Mali, which began evolving about the year 1000 A.D. Said to have used the same methods for controlling trade and administering its territory as did Ghana, Mali went on to become even more wealthy and powerful. Mali was also the home in which the world first centers for learning (Timbuktu) was located. This empire lasted until around the mid 1400's A.D.

The last of the three (recorded) empires was that of Songhai. Songhai began its rise around 1332 A.D. when Mansa Musa, the powerful king of Mali, died. Although Mansa Musa's empire began losing control not long after it began, it is said that the fall of Songhai took One hundred and fifty years to complete. The empire lasted until around 1528. I recommend Irani Abubakari Obadele's, A Beginner's Outline of the History of African People, for those who wish a brief but very good account of these early West African empires. The book includes ancient empires of the Congo, Nigeria, Great Zimbabwe, and those in other parts of Africa as well.

To me, Aunt Mariah stories were so fascinating I had become notorious, among all the children in our family, for being "the last one sitting," absorbing every repetitive detail long after the others would tire and discretely wonder away. Among my favorite stories were those of how and when my great-grandfather, whom she speculated was who my mother had gotten her adventurous nature, came to America. After proudly proclaiming that he was not a slave, and that Ware (his surname) was, in fact, African, Aunt Mariah recollected that my great-grandfather's journeys to America began sometime in the late 1800's. Considering that Papa Ephraim (she called him) was born in 1844 (which by the way, is exactly

100 years before I was born), he would have been somewhere in his twenties at the time.

I would later learn that the name Ware was indeed African. My research found that there were at least two kings in Ghana with this surname: King Katakyi Opoku Ware I (1700-1750), who ruled from 1720 until his death in 1750. He was credited with being the "empire builder." The other, King Otomjuo Opoku Ware II, was born in 1917, and ruled from 1970 until his death in 1999. Both kings were from the Ashanti tribe. (More about these kings later).

According to Aunt Mariah, her father, Ephraim Ware, began working around ships at a very young age. Although I do not recall her ever saying where, Aunt Mariah explained that he began working in this industry by helping the older men in his family load export products on ships at the docks along the coast of West Africa. These ships transported goods all around the world. As he grew older, Papa Ephraim was eventually hired aboard one of the ships and began traveling with it. The ship on which he worked frequently brought goods such as cocoa, coffee, and rubber, to the West Indies, South, and Central America,[5] and to the southeastern coast of North America. During one of these trips to the Florida coast, Papa Ephraim met one Colonel Eli Abbott, a planter and slave owner from the Chickasaw territory of Mississippi. After observing Papa Ephraim's performance, during a project on which he appeared to be in charge, namely, supervising the unloading of goods from the ship and directing the logistics of the various commodities by their designated states of destination, the Colonel offered him a job in Mississippi. By this time, the shipping of slaves from the continent had been abolished by the British, and because of this opportunity presented to him, my great grandfather "decided to stay in America for a while."

---

[5] They Carne Before Columbus. by Ivan Van Sertima, who documents proof that Africans traveled to and in the America's, both as traders, and settlers, long before the Europeans.

Colonel Abbott, who'd earned this title during the Seminole War in Florida, had returned there sometime during the 1860s on business. My research on the Seminole wars and the timeline during which both the Colonel and Papa Ephraim could have met in Florida seemed to back up my aunt's stories.

***

There had been three distinct Seminole wars. It appears that the first started in 1817 after a Native American tribe (the Seminoles) migrated from the North (Georgia). Under General Andrew Jackson, U.S. military forces invaded the areas inhabited by the Seminoles at Pensacola and St. Marks, scattering their villagers, and burning their towns. This war began over attempts by the U.S. authorities to recapture runaway African slaves living among bands of Native Americans. It ended in 1818. Since Eli Abbott was born in 1799, he would have been about eighteen or nineteen years old at this time. And while he could have participated in this first Seminole war, considering that it was local to Florida, that it lasted less than a year, and that he lived in Georgia at the time, one can deduce that he did not participate in this one. Even if he had, he had not yet earned his colonel title.

The second and third Seminole wars took place and ended in 1835-42 and 1855-58 respectively. The 1835-42 war followed the refusal of most Seminoles to abandon the reservation that had been specifically established for them north of Lake Okeechobee located west of the Mississippi river. This war affected the white settlers in Mississippi who had coveted this land and sought to oust the Seminoles under the Indian Removal Act. Since the census records, I found, do not place Mr. Abbott in Chickasaw County until the 1850s and, considering it was only after 1859 that plans to establish Pikeville, Mississippi as a business interest in the County, it is reasonable to believe that Mr. Abbott did not participate in the 1835-1842 war: or if he did, it was not because he had interest in the Chickasaw area at that time.

Additionally, Colonel Abbott is credited for naming Egypt, an area situated about eight miles east of Buena, originally known as Pikeville. Pikeville was merely a post-village at that time, with a few almost impassable roads on which a pike was built. This pike was to cross a large creek called Chookatonckee and did not become a settlement until 1842. Further research implied that Mr. Abbott earned the title of Colonel during the war in Florida, after a confrontation resulting from renewed efforts to track down the Seminole remnant remaining in Florida; it is likely then, that he did participate in this Seminole war which took place between 1855-1858. It is also likely that this is when the title Colonel was earned. While this war did not cause much bloodshed, it ended with the "most troublesome band of Seminole refugees" coming west, toward Mississippi, where by now, according to the census records of 1860, Mr. Abbott was living in Chickasaw county with his family.

Sometime between 1858 and 1864 the now Colonel Eli Abbott was commissioned with constructing the portion of the newly designed Mobile & Ohio railroad that was to stretch from Corinth through Northeast Mississippi to the State line in Alabama. And, considering that my great-grandfather had traveled to America's east coast several times during that time period, I believe my Aunt Mariah's account of how the colonel met him in Florida is correct. It is conceivable also that the Colonel would have earned his title and participated in the construction of the M&O railroad project.

In any case, the Colonel was using former slaves on the railroad project, and, according to Aunt Mariah, having observed the ease at which Papa Ephraim got his crew to work with the locals without using any kind of harshness or brutality, was very impressed. Deciding that he could "use a man like this African," after promising him eventual ownership in a portion of land in the newly established Pikeville development in Mississippi, the Colonel convinced Papa Ephraim to join his workforce as supervisor on the railroad construction project that was to cross the Chookatonckee Creek bottom area in Chickasaw County.

"Papa Ephraim accepted the offer, and during the years he spent working for him, earned the Colonel's respect even more as he shared with him his vast knowledge of world geography, including that of the African continent. Having often heard Papa Ephraim refer to the soil in Pikeville "as rich as that of the Nile Valley in Egypt," the Colonel renamed Pikeville, Egypt."

One may have observed that as an institution, slavery had been abolished by the time Papa Ephraim accepted the job offer to live and work in America. Apparently, my great-grandfather was aware of the political climate in America during the time and believed that he could in fact comply with the Colonel's request. However, although the slaves were freed in 1862, not everyone acknowledged and obeyed the law, especially those in the Southern States. As a result, Lincoln found it necessary to issue another proclamation later in 1862 on September 22nd declaring that as of January 1, 1863, all people who did not comply with the proclamation "shall then be in rebellion against the U.S." I ask that the reader permit me to digress here to point out a few facts my research found relevant to the slave situation in Mississippi at the time. I will get back to my, or Aunt Mariah's story shortly.

***

While those enslaved in the South were freed, one could argue that they were really not free since they were still not allowed to participate in decisions affecting their own welfare; especially since that they were released into a system that had not prepared them for survival. This fact is clearly demonstrated in a book written by Ronald L.F. Davis entitled _The Black Experience in Natchez, [Mississippi)._ In the chapter discussing _"Good and Faithful Labor,"_ Mr. Davis describes the life of the freedman in Mississippi during the mid-1860s:

> The low wage experiment, initially tried by the Federal government on leased and abandoned plantations during the war, had been un-popular with most district freedmen because it

retained many of the features of slavery...most unsettling of all was the fact that a system of yearly wages involved a work routine similar to slavery, one in which workers were compensated with such low pay that few or freedmen were able to save enough from their salaries to buy land or to pay a fixed rent.

Situations such as this inspired Frederick Douglas's speech during that period addressing this same issue. Mr. Douglas argued that "the colored must be admitted into this society as a full member in good and regular standing into the American politics. "While Mr. Douglas referred specially to the right of suffrage, the larger fight of Reconstruction included the civil rights of the African American to take care of himself and/or provide for his family. Providing for one's family involved owning the property on which one made his living. Although freed African Americans had the right to purchase land then, they were not able to do so.

Apparently, the issue of Americans of African descent owning land in the South ran deeper than just not being able to afford it. From all indications this situation also affected my great-grandfather (a free African) who, although having earned his land, was still unable to officially attain it. And the portion promised was never legally transferred to him, supposedly because he was not a citizen of the United States; nor was he a former slave belonging to the Colonel. Not unlike other Blacks during that time, however, he and his family were allowed to continue living on the land while they worked.

In any event, out of Mr. Douglas's efforts and those of other freedmen and organizations, such as the National Equal Rights League, in January of 1865, an order was signed by General William Sherman, granting freed black families forty acres of tillable ground. It was said that while Sherman saw this as a temporary solution to his temporary refugee problem, the freed slaves saw it as a permanent repayment for their services to the old plantation owners. The issue of land redistribution would ultimately join that of the African American voting rights issue during the reconstruction period. The order signed by General Sherman referred to property abandoned by or confiscated from slave owners in South Carolina but would eventually apply in other Southern States including Mississippi.

Judging from Aunt Mariah's stories, having made several trips to the East coast of America by the mid-1860s, my great-grandfather was aware that blacks could now purchase land which was why he accepted the Colonel's offer. Apparently, he had not anticipated all the obstacles mentioned above, which applied to him as well, especially since he was a foreigner--of African descent. However, his efforts did eventually pay off. According to Aunt Mariah, the land promised to Papa Ephraim is the same land that, with the help of my grandmother Ada was later purchased by her brother (my grandfather), Frank Ware, who was born thereon, and indeed was a U.S. citizen. My mother was also born on this land, and it is still owned and inhabited by my family (Papa Ephraim's descendants) today.

Aunt Mariah's story goes on to account how, during one of his trips to America, my great-grandfather brought with him a "very beautiful velvety black-skinned" lady whom he had met in Jamaica, where he'd often stop during his trips around the world. He brought her to American to settle down with him in Egypt. This lady, "whose beauty was the talk of the community," became my great grandmother. Her name was Evelene and from their union my grandfather Frank, his brother, and three sisters, including Aunt Mariah were born.

After locating our great-grandparents marriage license, which showed they were married in 1872, other records indicated that Grandpa Frank and Aunt Mariah were born before that date, 1868 and 1867, respectively. While births before marriage can definitely be explained during those times, this information, right or wrong, throw a twist in my confirmations. Since I had other priorities at this juncture, I chose not to pursue this matter. Perhaps later generations of our family can research further.

MARRIAGE BOND.

THE STATE OF MISSISSIPPI, } 2^d District
CHICKASAW COUNTY.

KNOW ALL MEN BY THESE PRESENTS,

That we, Ephraim Ware and Ed Cunningham held and firmly bound unto the State of Mississippi in the sum of One Hundred Dollars, for the payment of well and truly to be made, we bind ourselves, our heirs and assigns, jointly and severally, firmly by these Signed by us and sealed with our seals, this 12 day of 187 But this Bond is to stand void, on condition that there exists no legal cause why the RITES OF MARRIAGE not be celebrated between the above named Mr. Ephraim Ware and Miss Euline Cunningham, for which a License has this day issued.

Ephraim his Ware

Ed his Cunningham mark

696

STATE OF MISSISSIPPI, }
COUNTY OF CHICKASAW.

any Minister of the Gospel, Judge of any Court within the State of Mississippi, Justice of the Peace, or other Officer authorized to Celebrate Marriage—Greeting :
You are hereby authorized to Solemnize the RITES OF MATRIMONY between Ephraim Ware and Miss Euline Cunningham
A certificate whereof you will return hereon within six months of this date.
Witness, H. Y. Casey Clerk of the Circuit Court
of said County and the seal thereof, affixed at office in Okolona this 13th day of December 187
H. Y. Casey Clerk.

By Virtue of the above License, The Rites of Marriage were duly Celebrated by me, between Ephraim Ware and Miss Eu. Cunningham 7th day of Janeway 187
Washington Drake

Throughout the time my siblings and I lived in Egypt, there were no television, so our lives, along with those of our eleven cousins, were filled with the wonderful stories Aunt Mariah would tell, which in effect, were remnants of our family's history. I still smile when I reminisce very mention of Papa Ephraim's name, which indicated Aunt Mariah was about to start a story or history lesson we children had heard so many times before, one by one each child would discretely find a reason to disappear. I, on the other hand, stayed and soaked up every detail the stories offered. For some reason, unlike Tupelo, Africa didn't seem so out of reach during that period of my childhood. And, while I somehow knew that indeed it was far away, I recall promising my Aunt Mariah that I would someday go to Africa and find our family.

***

Today marked the end of my second semester at Contra Costa College, and by now I had participated in several activities involving Africa, including a fundraiser to assist victims of the drought in Central Africa. Knowing that Professor Lacy's last lecture would leave me feeling like I had just traveled to Africa, as they always had, I hurried to his class in anticipation. In addition to his final lecture, the professor had promised still another treat for this end of semester class, and I could hardly wait. Although I had no idea how it was going to happen, by now I was so ready to go to Africa; I had already begun charting a five-year plan, something I had become accustomed to doing over time.

Me, in a planning session for a fundraiser to assist Africa's drought victims while attending CCC, 1971

Drive ends today

By Calvin Walker

Today African Relief Week ends with a program beginning with a noon rally on the patio. Colton Westbrook will speak on his recent trip to Africa. Contributions to the drive will be recognized by Stanford Robinson.

The Family will offer a program of dancing followed by a fashion show at 1:15, a poetry reading at 1:30 and other entertainment until the program concludes at 4 p.m.

Noon rallies daily on the patio sparked the drive jointly sponsored by the Black Student Union and the Student Council.

William Freeman spoke on Monday with The Family providing entertainment.

On Tuesday, a CCC student from Ghana, Kumi Amankwah and Stanford Robinson of The A.F.R.I.C.A. organization spoke. The Universal Blacks, a congo group, entertained.

Native fashions were demonstrated on Wednesday. Instructor James Lacey spoke on African history as it relates to Black Americans.

Student Body President O.T. Anderson also spoke and the Universal Blacks again entertained.

Counselor Charles Allums was the principal speaker at the rally yesterday.

Throughout the week of fund-raising, emphasis was on cultural aesthetics and information about the effects of the drought and famine on the 17 countries of Africa.

More than three million square miles of the African continent are affected by the seven years of dry weather.

Since 1968 more than one-and one-half million people have died and millions of acres of crops have been destroyed.

The United Nations and the Organization for African Unity estimate six to ten million people may die, millions more acres of crops will be destroyed and as a result more livestock will die too.

Goal for the fund-raising on this campus was set at $8000.

Van Philpott was co-ordinator of the drive.

Drive Ends Today Article

A Real Life African

Just as Professor Lacy completed revealing his reasons for inviting our guest speakers and explaining what he hoped we would gain from the information they were to share, the door opened and in walked Basuye. Although he was accompanied by two other African gentlemen, my eyes affixed on him only. I remember thinking, My goodness; a real live African! Surprised by the attraction that kept imposing on my thoughts throughout Basuye's talk, I decided that I must leave the room before anyone else noticed--after all, I was still a married woman. As soon as the group had completed their presentations, I made a quick dash for the door. Professor Lacy noticed my leaving, however, and quickly beckoned me to come back and meet his guests.

It was astonishing how much Basuye's persona matched that of my husband's. Although they could not pass as identical twins, everything about him seemed to be the same, including his height, size, coloring, and disposition. My husband and I had been separated for nearly two years now, and I missed him very much-- when I wasn't busy working, taking care of the children, and/or studying.

After a personal introduction to the trio, Basuye looked at me and asked which ethnic group was I from in Nigeria. At first, I thought the comment was meant to flatter me. However, when he went on to explain that the markings on my face were strange to him, I realized he was serious. Stunned, I could only stand there while my mind raced back to the incident that caused the small, nearly invisible, twin marks down the right side of my face, which was a result of one of the fights I had during my adolescent years in Chicago, yet I could not figure out how to even begin explaining. After seconds passed, though it felt like about fifteen minutes, I heard the smiling professor explain that I was an American, and after examining the marks, to which Basuye referred, he explained that they were probably scares left from a childhood accident. I quickly shook my head in agreement.

While I was relieved that someone had broken the silence, in addition to feeling flattered that Basuye thought I was an African, I was a bit annoyed that the professor found it necessary to explain that I was not. As I stood there, seeing no one else except Basuye, I tried to think of something intelligent to say. It was at that moment I noticed he had two similar marks on his face, although his twin marks were on both sides, and going in opposite directions. Basuye would later inform me that such marks, imprinted during infancy, in some tribes, symbolized the ethnic group to which a child belonged in his area of Nigeria.

Still in somewhat of a trance, I remembered little else of what was being said, for the next thing I knew the conversation had ended, and Basuye was escorting me to the door. Before departing, he invited me to a small gathering at his place that evening. He also offered to pick me up when I informed him, I did not have a car.

Needing to let him know that I had children, which had been my way of informing those interested about my marital status, I explained to Basuye how I would love to go, if I could find a babysitter for the evening. I already knew that this statement would ultimately lead to a conversation on the subject of my availability. Although I could see both the surprise and disappointment on his face, Basuye took the phone number I offered anyway. While I did not expect him to, I instructed him to call me later to see if I had secured a babysitter. Even though I was not interested in a love affair with him, I clearly recognized the attraction emitting from both of us. At that juncture however, I was still waiting for my Jimmy to return home.

To my surprise, Basuye called, and later that evening I found myself in the company of about ten other African graduate students, both male and female, discussing everything from local current events to international politics. Eventually, the conversation got around to colonization in Africa, the effects it had throughout the continent, and Nigeria's struggle for independence during the 1960s.

I was only a sophomore at a junior college at that time, and while I really enjoyed the discourse (especially from the Africans point of view), I felt a bit uneasy about keeping up. I was very pleased however, when during the drive home, Basuye complimented me on my knowledge of world affairs, Africa's various liberation movements, and how I was able to hold my own throughout the discussions.

I decided against telling him that in one of Professor Lacy's classes I had researched the subject thoroughly, in preparation for a paper I wrote comparing Africa's liberation struggles with that of the African Americans struggle here in the U.S. During my research, I became totally immersed in the tactics Kwame Nkrumah used, some of which were being used concurrently in the U.S. during the boycotts organized by ministers and civic leaders of the Black community. The example I focused on was the arrest of Mrs. Rosa Parks, who after taking her normal bus ride home each day after work, refused to give up her seat to a white person, as was required in those days if a white chose to sit there.

***

This event took place in Birmingham, Alabama, the heart of the deep South. Mrs. Parks said she was very tired that day, but more importantly, fed up with such demeaning treatment. She was thrown in jail for her boldness. After the news of Mrs. Parks' arrest spread, a group of black women asked ministers and civic community leaders to call a bus boycott to take place on December 5, 1955, the day of Mrs. Parks' trial. The leaders, who formed a committee to deal with this and other issues regarding the treatment of African Americans, included Ralph Abernathy, E.D. Nixon, and Rev. E.N. French. The group, which later called themselves the Freedom Movement chose the young Dr. Martin Luther King Jr. to lead them. And as had Ghana's freedom movement leader, Kwame Nkrumah, who used Mahatma Gandhi's (of India) strategy of non-violence, the boycott eventually proved a success.

Mr. Nkrumah advocated uniting all of his people (the illiterate masses, as well a the educated, and middle-class elite), including women organizations. He felt that this would present a more powerful force against their British colonizers, who only offered token concessions in the past, when the Ghana's citizens demanded better treatment. As had Africans throughout the continent, Ghanaians too finally began to understand that their European colonizers had no intentions of giving up, nor allowing them to share in the control of their own land and resources, as they expected. Through colonization, European powers controlled all the centers of power, including the government, the army, the schools, and most importantly, the economy in Ghana, as they did in other parts of Africa. After achieving his higher education pursuits in the U.S., and having learned how western governments worked, Mr. Nkrumah returned to his home country and organized Ghana's first political party, which he aptly named the Convention People's Party (CPP). The party's motto was "Self-government NOW."

CPP's tactics were to focus on "positive action", or nonviolent protest, similar to the passive resistance practiced by India's Mahatma Gandhi. The strategy of this theory was based on the idea that if the colonial government found all the stores and shops were closed, the offices empty, the buses on strike, and the Africans as a collective body refused to participate one day, the European powers would have no power. The tactics worked, and on March 6, 1957, without any bloody confrontations, Ghana became the first country in Africa to achieve independence. Mr. Kwame Nkrumah became Ghana's first prime minister. I had already made the group aware that I knew their country, the Federal Republic of Nigeria, also colonized by the British, achieved their independence on October 1, 1960.

During the ride to my place that evening, Basuye inquired about my current marital status since I was obviously not living in a married situation at the time. After explaining that my husband and I were currently separated, I made it clear that while I liked being with him and his friends, and that my goal was to get to where they were (to graduate school), I did plan to reunite with my husband. I was very impressed at how Basuye respectfully accepted my position. From that point, our platonic friendship flourished, and that summer's activities led to a new group of friends who were to be major participants in my life for years to come. Not only was I encouraged to continue and pursue higher education by this group, I also received lots of mentoring and moral support.

Me, after my graduation ceremony at Contra Costa C,ollege, 1972

From Parties to Pain

The weekend had finally come, and I could hardly wait for Janine and Bisi's party that Saturday night. The semester was over, and like my other schoolmates I'd planned to release all of my stored-up stress and strain by dancing until the wee hours of the morning. My daughters were visiting my parents in Chicago for the summer while I worked more hours and attended a summer class to upstart the next semester. Since meeting my new crowd, all students consisting mostly of Africans, partying during school breaks had become a routine for all of us.

The long separation from my husband had been very difficult, so I decided that the busier I was, the less time I would have worrying about when he might return. By now I was working on a Bachelor of Arts degree in Accounting and Marketing at San Francisco State University (SFSU). Although this was our third separation, it never occurred to me (nor to him, apparently) to seek a divorce, especially after my father's advice. I had gone to my father for guidance, and after reminding me that we were much too young when we got married, my father recommended that I give my still very young husband even more time. He predicted that Jimmy would eventually get over his need to "explore other pursuits" and return to his family.

Now, at 27 years old, I had not found many African Americans my age attending school and even fewer with children. There were many African students however, and like me, many had families. Additionally, like me, many worked while attending school. I was very encouraged by the dedication these students showed toward their endeavors, and when invited to participate in study groups, other school-related events, and social activities, I was happy to do so. Born and raised in the South, I found African hospitality both familiar and comfortable, especially the inclusion of the entire family during most social events and activities, since I was now living as a single parent. Unlike American parties, most African parties were not laced with alcohol and seductive music. Therefore, the attendees would often come with their children.

As observed by one of my close friends, African music, which usually tell stories of historical and current events and is generally upbeat, is very different from African American music, which often consist of sad topics, i.e., the blues and/or "somebody done somebody wrong songs." It was not long then, before the majority of my friends and associates consisted of Africans. The few American friends I had made, during this time, were either a friend of an African or was married to one, like Janine.

I had just finished cleaning my apartment and was removing the laundry from the dryer when the phone ranged. For some reason, my heart started pounding fast even before I picked up the receiver. By the time I heard my sister-in-law's voice, I could barely breathe. Gwen rarely made long distance calls, which cost extra during those days. Upon hearing her voice, I knew something was terribly wrong.

Gwen started the conversation with a blunt, "I thought I'd better be the one to call you since I talked to him last--Jimmy is dead," she blurted quickly, giving the impression that she could not bear to say it any other way. She went on to explain that he was shot at his girlfriend's house in Mississippi and that they (his family) were not sure if it was an accident or what. "I do know that they were on bad terms, because Jimmy told me they had argued when he revealed to her that he was going back to his family, so I just wanted you to know that" she continued solemnly. Minutes must have passed while I stood frozen in place trying to process this abrupt and harsh information. I realized I had not responded when suddenly I heard Gwen yelling my name and asking if I was okay. I do not recall what was said after that, or what I did the rest of that afternoon.

The next thing I knew, I was at the party, sitting on the floor in a corner, with uncontrollable tears streaming down my face. I looked up to notice that Janine had knelt down beside me and was urging me to tell her what was wrong. I recalled telling her that my husband was killed today, and I didn't know what to do. "He's somewhere in Mississippi, and I am here." Janine jumped up in horror and proceeded to run away. She returned shortly with her Nigerian husband Bisi, who rushed into a discussion with other friends, two of whom were instructed to take me home and stay with me until they could end the party. They would join us later and try to sort out what had taken place and figure out what action should be taken.

The word got around my small community of friends quickly and for the next month or so, I was not left alone for more than a few hours at a time. My friends all took turns cooking, cleaning, shopping for groceries, speaking on the phone with my parents, who decided to keep the children a while longer, and/or just sitting until they felt comfortable leaving me on my own.

In addition to my studies, by now, I was also working at the Consulate General of Nigeria, in San Francisco, and because it was an African tradition to allow adequate time for grieving, I was not pressured to return to work until I was ready. One particular friend, Rose, stood out among everyone, in demonstrating what it was like to be cared about and taken care of when one finds it hard to do so for oneself. Besides my children I had no other family in California, and I will never forget the nurturing and feeling of belonging Rose's family provided my family during our time of sorrow.

It turned out that, finally overcome by the ghosts that haunted him after his time in the military, and his resulting shattered life, my husband made the decision to end it all by shooting himself. It was revealed, during later conversations with my sister-in-law, that Jimmy confided that he left us in California because he did not want to continue imposing more stress on his family than that he already had. He'd also shared that since the lady in California seemed to understand what sailors (Black ones in particular) experienced during and after their military tours, and because he did not want me to see him as weak ("since I considered him my hero"), he'd found it easier to talk to her about his troubles (nightmares and flashbacks), which was the reason he allowed her to drive back to Chicago with him. Gwen, who had served in the military as well, said that her brother shared with her that he honestly did not think that the relationship would get out of hand as it eventually had.

It took months, after his death, before I finally accepted the fact that he was gone forever and that my girls and I were permanently on our own. I continued going to school, mostly to keep myself occupied so that I would not think about the tragedy that had suddenly imposed itself upon our lives. I also thought--so much for the son we were supposed to have.

By now, I had met and befriended Africans from all over the continent, and although they would turn out to be the most challenging, it was the Nigerian community that helped me through many of my early adulthood struggles. The Nigerians would also be there to help me celebrate, with my parents, when I received both my BA and MBA degrees. Although we remained friends, it was unfortunate that by the time I was free to start a romantic relationship with him, Basuye had found someone with whom he had fallen head over heels for and with all of his friends' blessing, including me, gotten married. After completing my MBA degree, I briefly considered returning to Chicago. However, while I missed being near my family, that thought quickly passed. Chicago still conjured up too many sad memories for me especially now.

Over the years I kept in touch with, and often tracked the success of the Gems. I learned that as they'd completed high school, each had gotten married, including Minnie Riperton, who had taken my place after I initially moved to California. Although several members remained in the music industry, the group finally dispersed, and as a result of our early introduction into the Chicago music industry, two of our members became well- known artists.

Before her transition in her early thirties, Minnie Riperton had become a huge solo singer boasting such hits as Loving you and Memory Lane. Raynard Minor became a famous song writer, composer and producer working with some of America's top recording artists, including Stevie Wonder. One of his most famous hits was Rescue me by Fontella Bass, on which the Gems and I did the background. Although the Gems remained a local group, performing mostly within the north central parts of the United States, our group was recognized in a book entitled "Chicago Soul." This book acknowledges all the musicians who contributed to Chicago's R&B culture during the 1960s. As for me, the fact that I started the group at such a young age not only gave me great pride; being among those who made a mark on the Chicago music industry, I also felt empowered to achieve any pursuit I desired. Look out world, I thought, here I come.

The Gems with Minnie Riperton as a permanent member, 1968

The Late James B. Philpott (1969)

Spiritual Enlightenment

While I was somewhat satisfied with how my life was going thus far, considering what I had learned during my search for personal understanding, my passion to understand Christianity even more eventually led me to want to know about how people in other lands worshiped the Creator. Well into my educational pursuits now, I had become confident in my ability to analyze written information. So, besides my academic studies, my focus now included learning more about those major religions--that I knew of at the time. Among others, these included Islam, Judaism, Buddhism, Taoism, Hinduism, Female Goddess worship, and of course, the various religions practiced throughout of Africa. I was curious to know why there were so many and why each one thought their own was the right one. Moreover, I wondered if God knew he was causing all this confusion when he allowed so many religions to exist at one time.

Additionally, after discovering that many of the major historical events in the world, significant enough to have been recorded, had indeed evolved around a religion, I read scores of history books, especially those that focused on the world's current conditions at the time said events occurred. To say that I found religion had a curiously huge impact on the development and structure of societies interesting is an understatement. And imagine my shock when I learned that my own religion (Baptist), which began in England, was born in the bosom of radicalism!

According to theologian and historian Dr. W.H. Whitsitt, "Baptists were not among the conservatives wanting to maintain the status-quo. They were not even among the 'avant-garde liberals' who wanted to tamper with the status-quo and change it a little. They were, instead, among the radicals who wanted to reverse the religious establishment." In fact, he says, "They were considered to be the chief culprits in the disorder of state and church and were seen as dangerous by the more established churches," that is, the conservative Anglicans (English Episcopalians) and the liberal Puritans. So, while I was disturbed after learning the eventual position of the Southern Baptists on slavery, I submitted to feeling a bit of admiration about the rebelliousness on the part of the founding Baptists, as well as their original position on slavery.

I also discovered that after the Baptist religion had been established in America in 1639 (by Roger Williams), and having gone through its metamorphosis, as did other religions transported from Europe, the opposing positions on slavery evolved between the Northern and Southern Baptists. This resulted in a split of the two; and because they all felt slavery was a transgression of "Divine Law," they wanted to denounce it. However, since the institution had become a means to an end for them, the South began to see slavery as an economic and social issue as opposed to a social or religious one, thus they became pro-slavery. With the North maintaining its position, these opposing views eventually caused a split between the two factions. Since an adequate discussion of my findings here would take this chapter into another direction, I have chosen to limit my comments on this subject, stop here, and discuss it further, only as it relates to my growth and understanding.

I had also come to believe that while indeed there are some on this earth who are more spiritually enlightened and therefore operate on higher spiritual frequencies then most of us, i.e., Jesus, Mohammad, Buddha, Martin Luther King Jr., and the Dalai Lama, because religion is man's interpretations of the spiritual law, and not that of the Creator's, these various interpretations are destined to be flawed, or at least, often too lofty for man to really achieve.

History has shown that when he falls short of these lofty rules and standards set by a particular religion, man will either revise, update, or justify his shortcomings. That is, he will come up with reasons and excuses such as "man is only human and therefore destined to sin." Alas, some claim, it is okay if one has fallen, because Jesus has already paid the price, and continue doing what pleases themselves, even at the expense of others.

Since how the law works is no mystery, it appears that we humans are the ones that have created the confusion and, as a result, we are the ones that perpetually suffer the consequences. If we could accept that like Imhotep (said to be the world's first multi-genius), Jesus (the miracle worker), Buddha (the enlightened one), Martin Luther King, Jr. (the dreamer), and scores of other highly spiritually developed individuals, why would it be such a stretch to believe that we all have access to this same spiritual source? If we could accept this as axiom, and live accordingly, is it possible that all the fighting over which one is the true religion will cease?

The enlightened ones seem to all understand that we live in a Spiritual Universe, governed by mental laws. Moses dubbed this law with the simple interpretation, "an eye for an eye": Jesus clarifies it more by stating that "As a man sows, so shall he reap." Jesus also revealed that behind all law is the Great Law giver or "God working out the great inner concepts of His own being in Harmony and in beauty, filled with peace, causing the sun to shine alike upon the just and the unjust." Today's religious scholars refer to it as the law of cause and effects.

One such scholar attempts to explain Jesus' actions by reasoning that he did not try to overcome the use of the law, but that he understood it and knew that the law was at His command -- if he cared to use it, as can we. "Jesus, therefore, did not break the law, but fulfilled it." Throughout my search, this spiritual law appeared to be a common theme in all the spiritual stories down through the ages, as well as all the religious dogma I've come across. This too made sense to me.

Through persistence prayer and practice, I began to understand how to comply with this spiritual principle (law), which seems to work for me better than the "fear of God" concept that I apparently rejected from the beginning. After learning that the Creator dwells

135

within each of us, I found that all one needs to do to tap into It, is to take a little time for solitary prayer, that is, talking with the Creator, asking for divine guidance, and meditation, or listening to that inner voice, which I call that of the Creator. Already aware that many of the Biblical and other world prophets did this very thing, I decided that perhaps I could too; and it worked!

As I began my daily ritual of praying and meditating (or going within), I discovered that prayer is, indeed, an activity of our consciousness--a gift of sort, that is always available to us as a response of conditions, situations, and circumstances and that, in its purest sense, meditation is like communing with the divine presence which, when we listen, offers guidance and direction. Perhaps this was why I had not taken religion seriously,

Besides the conflicting messages, my natural instincts did not permit me to respond to threats. Neither did being told things like if I didn't love God I was going to hell. For some reason, even as a child, my little brain immediately rejected these ideas. I didn't want to go anywhere and be with anyone who needed to force me into loving him or her through threats. So as this related to the religion I'd been first introduced, I refused a God that I had to be frightened into loving. Now, armed with knowledge of who and what the Creator was gave me the tools to make prudent and intelligent decisions, as well as better choices. More importantly, I could now love the Creator by choice, not by being threatened to do so. This, I proclaimed, works for me!

I concluded also that this spiritual law would probably work for everyone regardless of which religion one belongs to, and that when one learns how it works and how to use it, he/she might discover (like I had), that God (or the Creator) loves and works for each of us in the same manner and not something to be feared. Let me pause here to say that, indeed, I still go to church. But I do so now because I am no longer confused about how things work. Listening to the various forms of religious interpretations presented from pulpits every Sunday, or by observing how those who claimed to be religious intentionally hurt others then justified it, did not work for me in the past. Now that I understand, I can enjoy the camaraderie of congregating with fellow seekers, without using a lot of time wondering what is true.

My search for spiritual enlightenment would conclude with a belief that all religious systems rely on an unseen principle or spiritual law, within which there appear to be a consistent theme of personal empowerment, via one power to which everything and everyone is connected; and that we (as individuals) find our particular good only through unity with this power.

In an effort to fully understand how this works, however, it soon became apparent to me that, with the use of symbols, including statues, rituals, and doctrines that supported their understanding, the architects of each religious dogma sometimes interpret this principle to fit their own agenda. As a result, this power (principle) or spiritual law, has been given various names. Here in the West, we call it God. Since what It should be called has been so controversial, during the following discussion, when necessary, I will refer to It as the Creator.

Regardless of what a people choose to call It, I find that the Sacred Books of all people declare that indeed, there is only one Creator. And, as I discovered during my search, most also agree that within this One, there is a unity from which nothing can be excluded and to which nothing can be added. Additionally, all seem to be in agreement that this One is omnipotent (has all power), omniscient (is all-knowing) and omnipresent (is everywhere). It also seems to be understood, by them all, that this Creator is our Father as well as our Mother—and the source of our life here on earth. And it appears this source doesn't seem to care what one calls IT, as it seems to work for anyone who believes that IT does.

Armed with the guidance I received through prayer and meditation; I was now able to forgive myself for thinking that anything I had done so far in life was a mistake. I now believed that what occurred in the past was a result of the choices I'd made-- choices that presented opportunities for me to learn and grow. More importantly, I was now able to forgive those I thought had hurt me in the past. It had become clear to me that most of us do not hurt purposely, and while we will bear the consequences of our choices and behavior, when we acknowledge it and are remorseful enough to ask for forgiveness, we are indeed forgiven, and the consequences are not so hard to bear.

In terms of my questions on procreation, considering the biblical account, I surmised that the act of procreation in fact had little if anything to do with human love. If nothing else, it seemed that the act of "love making" had more to do with desire. Perhaps, this was all part of the Creator's plan as well. After all, when one considers the Creator's other earthly creatures, i.e., the birds and bees, and other animals, especially dogs, one has to wonder if they are "in love" when they engage or just responding to the call to

multiply. Perhaps when the time comes, I will incorporate all that I have learned about this process in the explanation to my children, when explaining life, and how it works.

Me after some time spent meditating during a relaxing boat ride on the Potomac.

Experiencing Nigeria in San Francisco

I guess I can call my position at the Consulate General of Nigeria, in San Francisco, my first real experience in the international arena. I had been hired as an assistant to Mr. Bartholomew, the Consulate's Accounting Officer. By now I was well on my way to completing my Master's in Business Administration (MBA), minoring in International Business, and although I'd initially found working at the Consulate very challenging, the experience turned out to be rewarding, as well as educational.

By age twenty-seven, I had worked in several industries and understood how to conduct myself in a professional work environment. Yet nothing I'd experienced thus far prepared me for the cultural shock of working with and for people who had an entirely different set of rules and work ethics from those that I had grown up with. I believe, however, that working in this environment is where I not only "grew up," it also played a major role in the universally thinking person that I would become.

Initially, having to adjust to this new environment on a daily basis, I'd jokingly tell my friends that entering the Consulate was like going to Nigeria each morning at 8:30, and returning to America each afternoon at 5:30. It is very difficult to put those first few months into words. Perhaps a recount of my hiring experience could provide an idea: It was the end of the spring semester at San Francisco State University (SFSU), where I was working on an MBA degree, and the end of my work-study job in the office of Ethnic Studies. I had given up one of my part-time department store jobs earlier, to allow time to attend more day classes.

Each morning, after dropping my girls off at school, I traveled by bus and train from Richmond, California to San Francisco (roughly forty-five miles) where I attended classes throughout the day. I also had two work-study jobs at SFSU were I worked between classes: during the mornings, in the office of the School of Business, and during the afternoons in the Ethnic Studies office. While this schedule was a bit rough, it allowed me the opportunity to work throughout the day, and to be home in time to make dinner for my children before we'd all take off for the library to do our homework (together), during the evenings. To supplement my small income, I also worked at various department stores on Friday evenings and during the day on Saturdays. I refused to work for anyone on Sundays, as that was church and family day.

My work-study positions at SFSU were about to end for the summer and knowing that my job at a retail store alone was not enough to sustain my family financially over the summer, I found myself sharing my concern with my fellow students/co-workers. That same afternoon, just as I'd finished lamenting, a Nigerian man, with whom I was not familiar, walked into the office and announced that the Consulate General of Nigeria in San Francisco was looking for an accounting assistant.

After his announcement, I could hear the jaws of everyone in the office as they literally dropped. Everyone looked in my direction and said in -unison, "There's your job Van." The young man took the cue, walked over to my desk, and handed me the written details on the position. He then requested my name, directed me to show up the next morning for an interview, "at 8:30 A.M." and departed. While I was very flattered by this bizarre event, I proclaimed that I did not feel qualified for such a job.

Joking about my ability to get along with anyone, my peers began conducting an office lottery, in which they agreed to put up five dollars each, all betting that I would get the job if I went on the interview. The total collected amounted to thirty dollars. They agreed further, that if I got the job I would have to add another thirty dollars, doubling the five dollars that each had contributed, which they would divide among themselves. If, on the other hand,

I did not get the job, as I predicted, the thirty dollars collected from them would be mine. Although I was not a gambler, considering that I stood a chance to add thirty dollars more to our weekly food budget, I accepted the challenge.

I arrived at the Consulate the next day before eight thirty in the morning as instructed, only to learn that the office did not open until nine in the morning, and as told to me later, "besides the receptionist and, at times, the Counsel General, absolutely no one came to work earlier than that." So, I waited outside in the hallway. Finally, a young African American lady, who identified herself as the receptionist, showed up. When I told her, I was there for an interview, she invited me inside and instructed me where to sit.

Gradually, others started arriving, including Cordelia, whom, I'd learn later, was the Counsel General's secretary and also wife of the young man that came to our office. It was she who requested that her husband search SFSU for possible candidates. When Mona, the receptionist, thought Cordelia had settled in her office, she called to inform her that I had arrived for the interview.

As I sat waiting, I soon became aware that several of the gentlemen, who'd arrived earlier, began filing out of what turned out to be an inner office, one at a time. I also observed that each one would take a quick glance in my direction, then go out into the hallway. Upon re- entering seconds later, each would pretend to have some business at the receptionist desk while stealing glances at me before going back into the inner office area. After about two hours of this dance, it became blatantly obvious that they were checking me out.

Having waited three and a half hours now, I began to get a bit annoyed. Hoping for some explanation, I looked over at Mona, who had long stopped pretending to be busy, but all she would offer was a smile. It was only after Mona announced that she was going to lunch that I mustered up enough courage to ask, "What about me--is anyone coming to interview me? Should I just go home?" Mona shrugged, indicating that she didn't know, and dialed

Cordelia's number.

After conveying my concern to Cordelia, Mona informed her that she was going to lunch. Upon replacing the receiver, she gave me Cordelia's message, which was simply that she would be out for me shortly. After I gave her a "you must be kidding look" Mona told me not to worry. After enjoying a good laugh with herself, she explained that everyone had checked me out, thoroughly, and the fact that I was still there was a good sign. I was not impressed. Soon, most of the people who'd come in earlier strolled passed me again, apparently going to lunch.

Finally, around a quarter past noon., Cordelia came out and escorted me back into her office. She asked if I could type and a few other clerically related questions. She then directed me to follow her, as she guided me to a larger office that connected to her own. There, I was instructed to have a seat at a large table where three of the same gentlemen that had carefully scrutinized me throughout the morning sat with a fourth, more important looking, one. They all sat in silence for a few minutes--long enough to make me a bit nervous. By the time Mr. Nochiri, who turned out to be Consul General, broke the silence by thanking me for coming to the interview, I had already decided that I did not want the job. I'd begun silently formulating a thanks-but-no-thanks speech, that included a short, though polite, lecture about how rude it was to make a person wait all morning. Then, suddenly the questions began.

"How old are you?" "Are you married?" "Do you have children--how many?" Do you live with your husband--most Americans do not," one said jokingly? After recovering from an initial state of shock from such personal scrutiny, I somehow calmly managed to answer each question while noting that one of the gentlemen never opened his mouth. As abruptly as it began the interview was over, and I was directed to go back into the reception area and wait.

Not sure what to think, do, or say, I moved slowly out of the

Consul General's office toward the first door but picked up the pace and almost ran through the next. I was just about to head out of the reception area into the hallway and dash right out of that building, when my inner voice spoke, "HOLD UP, MISS INTERNATIONAL!" The voice was so loud and clear it almost startled me. It went on to whisper, "Why not stick around, you might learn something here." I obeyed and sat down. My curiosity has gotten the best of me again, I warned myself as I sat.

It was now about 1:30 pm and the staff had begun returning from their lunch break. When they saw that I was still there, I noted that each would smile as they passed me, and disappear, once again, into the inner office door. And, although she didn't reveal much, Mona began to talk to me.

At three in the afternoon., I announced that I'd had enough, and that I was leaving. Mona begged me to wait as she quickly began dialing Cordelia's number. She pleaded that she must let her know that I was going. While she was still on the phone, Ester, whom, I would learn, was the secretary to the Passport Officer, came rushing out, and softly asked that I follow her. Too polite to say, "No, I won't," I followed her, silently thinking about something I observed about both her and Cordelia--something I had observed earlier about African women in general, namely how they could maintain their composure, as well as an air of gentleness in the face of the most obvious chaos. After arriving at her desk, Ester revealed that she was told to give me a typing test.

During the typing test Mr. Orupabo, Ester's boss, who was also the gentleman that asked questions about my marital status during the interview, came out of his office. As he stood behind me, I instantly became aware of his nearly seven-foot statue peering over my shoulders. Once he noted my annoyance, he jokingly told me how slowly I typed. I was very pleased, as well as surprised, when I heard myself tell him that I was not applying for a typing job. He laughed and said, "Oh, so you can talk!" Apparently, I was so stunned during the interview, I'd left the impression that I was timid. I wasn't. It turned out that Mr. Orupabo had the best sense of humor in the Consulate, took few things seriously, and kept everybody cool whenever there was a crisis.

I made it through the test, in spite of being interrupted by several other people. By now I had figured out that they were looking for accuracy as opposed to speed--or were they still testing my patience, I wondered. When I was done, Ester directed me to wait again in the reception area. This time I said an emphatic no, and politely explained that it was nearly 4:00, and that I had to get across the Bay Bridge to pick up my children from school. Just as politely, I also told her that if I did not have the job by now, I did not want it. She begged me to hold on as she dashed down the hall and into Cordelia's office. When Ester returned, she escorted me to Mr. Nochiri's office again, where all the same gentlemen were waiting. Mr. Nochiri congratulated me on getting the job and introduced me to my boss, Mr. Bartholmew, who turned out to be that person who did not ask a question during the entire interview. After welcoming me on staff, he assured me that I would be paid for the day.

Before starting my new job, I called my old office mates at SFSU to inform them that I had gotten it, and to let them know that I would bring them my $30 on my first payday. Carmella, the office manager, said she knew that I would get the job, and wished me success. She also told me to keep the $30 as a going away gift from my office mates. Not long after I started working at the Consulate, Mona informed me later that eighteen people had shown up for my job. Most, she said, were turned away after the reception room scrutiny, without even the benefit of an interview. Others were rejected by Mr. Bartholomew after he'd sat and quietly observed their behavior during interviews.

While, initially, I found it a challenge to work outside of my own familiar environment, my desire to learn about the work ethics of other cultures (a topic recently explored during one of my international management classes), I persevered, and it paid off. Not only had I gotten the opportunity to witness, first-hand, the proverbial pecking order, the chain of command, the division of labor, and how the reverence given to persons at the top played out in this particular culture, I was also exposed to the international diplomatic aspect of this industry.

My job at the Consulate presented me the privilege of meeting both American and foreign dignitaries and, as a result, I learned what I would eventually need to know about diplomatic protocol. I was also pleased to be able to invite some of my professors, including Professor Lacy, to some of the activities and events hosted by the Consulate. This experience pretty much solidified my desire to work in the greater international area someday.

During the two years I worked with the Nigerians, I also witnessed a high turnover among the Americans who tried very hard to work in this environment. I found, however, that as challenging as it may have been, by giving oneself time to settle in, one would begin to see that even though many of the techniques practiced by others where different from those to which we are accustomed (especially how employees are managed), the end result turned out the same or even more efficient--not to mention more compassionate. For example, I observed how loyal a Nigerian employee was to his/her employer. This was most demonstrated when Murtula Mohammed, president of Nigeria, who was assassinated during my tenure. As a result of his death, Nigeria went through a period of political and economic instability. In fact, all the African employees, several of whom were from other countries, did not get paid for nearly one year, (while we Americans did) yet they all remained on their jobs.

Fortunately, most of the workers had spouses whose jobs kept them going. For those who needed it, however, Mr. Umoren was instructed to pay monies to cover rents only, and they all continued working until money finally arrived to pay their back and current salaries. I was also awed by the concern that the now mostly foreign staff had, not for themselves, but for the plight of the Nigerians, as well as for their people back home in Nigeria. As peculiar as it may have appeared, staff members from other countries, namely, The Philippines, India, Cameroon, and Bermuda understood the crisis, and shared what resources they could with the Nigerians.

Additionally, my attitude increasingly metamorphosed into a high level of comfort in this environment. The best example I can give here is to refer back to my husband's death. I could not ask for more understanding, consideration, and kindness during a time I was totally immobilized. As a result of the efforts by the Consulate's Directors, my children and I were totally embraced by those that constituted the entire Bay Area Nigerian community at the time. And it was Mr. Orupabo (the one that gave me the hardest time during my interview) and his wife, who were the first to come to my aid during my personal crisis, and it was he who insisted I take as much time off as I thought necessary.

At one point, during my tenure at the Consulate, I was offered a job in Nigeria. Considering that I was well into my MBA program, however, I turned the offer down. As if it was already destined that I go to Africa however, at the completion of my graduate studies, another opportunity presented itself.

During my graduate studies, I was also presented with the opportunity to participate in several international student clubs and many internationally oriented activities. It was during this time that I became aware of a disturbing lack. I observed that while many African students came to American to learn how to function in American business and economic environments, few American students had the same opportunity to go to Africa. This observation would become the focus of my master's thesis.

Upon completing the course work for my master's degree, I chose to present this lack as the subject of my thesis project to the School of International Business. Reasoning that a student exchange program in business should be established between

American and African universities, I argued that having such a program in our school system would be of benefit to both the students and the business industry. Shortly after presenting my hypothesis (the justification for my study) to my Thesis Committee, miracles began to happen, and shortly thereafter, I was offered a one-year Fulbright Scholarship that would allow me to go to Africa and research the possibilities for the exchange program I proposed. In addition to funding my research, the fellowship would also pay for my trip and tuition at Legon University in Ghana, West Africa. After the initial excitement of such an opportunity subsided a bit, however, it occurred to me that I could not leave my children for an entire year. After all their father had died only a short while earlier.

Somehow, the word had gotten to Professor Lacy that I had turned down the Fulbright Fellowship, and thus the opportunity to study at Legon, where he once taught. After my explanation for why I could not leave my children for an entire year, Professor Lacy recommended that perhaps I could go for a shorter period of time. He informed me of a program offered by the African

Me with friends at a reception given by the Consulate in San Francisco, 1976

American Institute (AAI) that provided summer research opportunities to Educators. This program also offered a few slots to deserving graduate students interested in African Studies.

He pointed out also that although the AAI program was shorter (two months), I would at least be exposed to more of the continent. Not only would it provide time at several universities in West Africa, it also provided the opportunity to study and observed the business industries in each of its five-country study tour. He was sure that since my research involved examining the educational systems in West Africa, a written proposal explaining what I wished to accomplish would be accepted, and it was. The remaining problem now was finance, and once again Professor Lacy stepped in and helped secure funding through a local community financial institution that provided loans for student projects such as mine. And, that very same year, 1977. I was on my way to Africa! Now that it was confirmed I would finally be going to Africa, there was something I had to do first. It was imperative that I go to Mississippi to let my grand Aunt Mariah know that I was going, just as I had promised. I arranged for my two daughters to spend the summer at our farm, where both their grandmother and I had lived in Egypt, and where their great-grand Aunt Mariah, now about one hundred and four years old, was born and still resided.

It had been more than twenty years since I'd last seen Egypt, Mississippi. Yet, with the exception of a few additional mobile homes on our property, in which some of my Aunt Evelyn's now adult children lived, the place seemed just as it was when I left. For my children, however, Egypt was like a foreign country. Not only were they able to meet scores of relatives they'd only heard about, but they were also "finally going to see this Aunt Mariah," whom they'd heard so much about.

Standing under "the old shade tree" from left to right is Janie, Denise, and Aunt Mariah, 1977

Me, shortly before departing on my first trip to Africa, 1977.

Summer

Africa at Last

Our flight from New York to Senegal was long and uneventful, but very exciting. The airplane was full of scholars from throughout the United States. I met many interesting people; among them were several who, like myself, graduate students with whom I was to study, and also become life-long friends. Everyone on the entire plane, including the African stewardesses, literally partied all the way to Senegal, West Africa, where we would stop for a short layover before proceeding to Ghana, the first stop on our study tour.

We were all so excited I don't believe anyone slept throughout the entire twelve-hour flight. At any given time, many were out of their seats visiting, while others were literally singing and/or dancing in the aisles. And although the atmosphere was very intoxicating, it briefly crossed my mind that we were in fact in an airplane, and considering what was going on, it could go down at any time. In fact, with all the jumping around during this long flight, I felt that the plane had every right to crash. But, like others, I somehow knew that it would not, or didn't care. At least, I thought to myself, we would all go down happy.

We finally landed in Senegal, and although we did not go outside the airport, one clearly got the sense that this country, which had been colonized by France and thus French speaking, would be different from Ghana, which had been colonized by the English-speaking British. After waiting a short time, I was approached by several Senegalese who were accompanied by one I had responded to when he greeted me earlier. Apparently, since I had responded in French, he thought I could speak the language fluently, and chose me to be the interpreter for my group and his. When they realized that although I was trying hard, I could barely understand them, and carried on anyway. Seeming to be just as excited to communicate with us as we were with them, we laboriously continued our feeble exchange until it was time to re-board.

We arrived in Ghana on July 7, 1977 or 7/7/77. Considering it was my mother's birthday, this was very special for me. Born on July 7, 1914, had she lived she would have been 63 years old. Upon deplaning unto the tarmac, I watched in wonderment as my fellow travelers bowed down to kiss the ground. I guess I was so sleep-deprived from the long trip I wasn't sure if I was dreaming that we'd arrived, or that the plane had actually crashed, and we were all now in heaven. Once I realized we were still on planet earth, although I did not kiss the ground, I did gather up some soil and packed it away in an empty film container that I was carrying. Admittedly, I did this partly to convince myself that we were indeed on earth. This soil remains with me today.

Some three hours had passed before I realized we were still sitting in the passenger lounge of Ghana's International, waiting to exit the airport and get on with our trip to Legon University. Many of the people who had kissed the ground earlier were now complaining and questioning why it was taking so long for us to leave the airport. I, on the other hand, had been so caught up in my observations that I had not noticed the long delay. Never in my life had I witnessed such a scene. Everyone running the airport facility was of African descent or what we call Black in America. Besides studying the airport's operations, I was literally mesmerized by what I was witnessing.

It turned out that, due to a current political and economic development issue, most of Ghana's university campuses were in the middle of a major student protest. And, when the airport officials learned that an airplane, loaded with what they thought was full of American students had landed, were concerned that allowing us entry might further ignite the situation, and that they would be held responsible for the imminent unrest. So, when Kobina Annan, (our Ghanaian group leader) could not convince these officials that we would not cause any problems, he had literally flown to Lagos, Nigeria (less than a two-hour flight away) to reorganize our stay with the Nigerian universities scheduled for later on our itinerary, making them first in lieu of Ghana.

Me after arriving at Kotoka International Airport in Ghana, 1977

***

We would learn later, when some of us were treated to a reception at their family home in Kumasi, that Kobina was the junior brother to the Honorable Kofi Annan, who at the time, was a United Nations diplomat, stationed in Geneva, Switzerland. Mr. Kofi Annan would eventually become the Secretary General of the United Nations.

Kobina was successful on his short trip to Nigeria, and our tour was re-arranged accordingly. By the time he returned to Ghana I had made several local friends at the airport, one of whom was on his way to London to participate in a tennis tournament. Kwako would visit my family in California, a few years later, during one of his tournaments in the United States.

The first stop on our tour in Nigeria was the University of Lagos, where after daily doses of very informative lectures about the history, tradition, and economy of West Africa in general and Nigeria in particular, the American students would be bused to the Universities of Ife in Ibadan, and Amadu Bello, in Zaria where even more enlightenment took place. Two weeks later, we participated in further stimulating conversations with Nigerian students.

Ahmadu Bello University Main Campus, Zaria, Nigeria

For a more in-depth travel description on countries in Africa, I strongly recommend reading *Reflections on Africa,* by Grace Chavis, an African American educator who took a similar study tour but covered more countries. A historian, Ms. Chavis wrote in detail about each of the 13 countries to which she traveled. Among other things her analysis included information on tourist attractions and a brief history of each country. Her short book is an excellent guide for those who wish to travel in Africa, and for those just wanting to know more about the continent without having to take a course on the subject.

Our studies included visits to a various art galleries and museums where thousands of years of historical pictures, paintings, and artifacts still remained, confirming the information we had been taught. And for those like me who had special interest, time was permitted to pursue that as well. We also spent time at Oshogbu, an ancient religious shrine near Ibadan, as well as the Imire Shrine in Kano.

A little girl who reluctantly posed for me at the Museum of Antiquities in Kano

University of Ife, at Ibadan, Nigeria

Before finally leaving Nigeria, some in our group had become frustrated while trying to purchase items they wanted and/or needed from the markets. Since they were not familiar with the bargaining techniques practiced throughout much of Africa, they gave up. They had not done much better at the banks where there was no such thing as a line. When the word got around that I was an "expert" at bargaining with the Market women, and that I actually enjoyed it, I was constantly asked, from the many friends I had made, to accompany them to the market and/or bank to assist with their negotiations. Others waited until they heard I was going to one of these places before venturing out on their own.

Members of the Educators to African. 1 am seated on the front row, the eighth from left to right.

While my ability to interact with Nigerians could have been attributed to my long association with them back home in California, it was more likely due to my desire to understand how African businesses and other institutions worked, as well as the knowledge I had gained by observing how people functioned

158

within these institutions. When things did not happen as I had expected or did so in a manner in which I was not familiar, I would neither panic nor get upset, but make a mental note of what happened before trying another approach. Consequently, I learned that long before a decision was made regarding the final cost of a particular item, one must be prepared to participate in what could turn out to be an encounter that included a matching of wits with the seller. It was also necessary to have a sense of humor during this bargaining process as well as significant amount of patience.

After fully participating in these encounters, I would spend time, in my dorm room each night, recalling and recording my observations for later use, and for my Masters' thesis. Unlike most in our group, I had also spent a great deal of time observing the purchasing process. As a result, I had become good at bargaining and enjoyed it.

Bargaining at the Market in Nigeria, 1977

After about four weeks of traveling throughout Nigeria, we finally left, by bus, for the Republic of Benin, the next country on our itinerary. Although it was just across the border from Nigeria, this quaint little country was entirely different.

Me about to board the University of Lagos bus that would take our group to the Republic of Benin.

Colonized by France, French had become Benin's official language as well. The atmosphere in this small republic was much more relaxed; the people appeared calmer than in Nigeria. And, while I thoroughly enjoyed Nigeria, I was ready for and really appreciated the rest and relaxation we experienced in Benin. Benin was also where I would meet Sean (pronounced John), an ocean navigator for the country's shipping industry.

One evening during our hiatus in the Republic of Benin, two friends and I were sitting in the lounge of our hotel in Cotonou when I noticed we were being intensely watched by two very handsome young men. Noting that one was unyieldingly staring at me, I intentionally avoided eye contact with him. After letting my guard down for a split second to sneak a peek, he, determined to catch my glance, smiled, and immediately headed toward our table.

Having suspected that we were Americans, Sean tried his best to communicate with us in English. I conjured up some of the

French I'd taken at school, and while I did not understand everything he was trying to say, it was clear he was asking if he and his friends could join us. After I explained what was being requested to my friends, we agreed to accept the offer. By the time the evening ended, Sean was speaking English and interpreting for his friends very well. I wondered if his initially shy approach was on purpose or if, like my own, his fluency in English became better after he'd gotten used to us, or maybe our accent. In any case, we had fun figuring things out as a group, and as a result, my friends and I accepted an invitation to allow them to take us sight-seeing the next day. It was during our outing I learned that Sean had traveled to many parts of the world taking export goods out and imports back to Benin. I couldn't help but think to myself how amazing it is that people who have much in common are instinctively attracted to each other.

While lying across my bed later that night, recording mental notes, my thoughts continued to wander. How ironic was it that not only was Sean and I in the same field (international business), but his career was also in the same area as that of my great-grandfather, who had been in the international shipping industry out of West Africa over a century earlier. Sean and I had exchanged addresses and promised to keep in touch with each other.

***

Our next stop was the Republic of Togo, an even smaller country sandwiched between Benin and Ghana. Togo is also a French-speaking country. Just before entering Togo, the driver was instructed to stop in a small village, near the border between the two counties, to allow us to stretch and meet some of the inhabitants, who had set up small stalls to sell various goods and refreshments to travelers. I had remained on the bus and was going over the notes I'd written the night before when several of my friends came rushing back, calling for me to come out. While they were mingling among the villagers, my friends had come across a young woman "who could pass for my twin." By the time I descended the bus and arrived at the spot where this young lady was waiting, apparently after being instructed by someone in our group who had managed to communicate with her group, a crowd had gathered to find out what the excitement was about.

Upon my arrival, the villagers all gasped in amazement, at about the same time I did. I was stunned to discover that the young lady and I did have an uncanny resemblance complete with the same gap in our upper front teeth. By the way she looked at me, I was sure she was thinking the same thing. Unfortunately, she and everyone else in the village spoke a dialect of French that I could not understand, and we could not verbally communicate very well. However, while we were hugging to communicate our consensus regarding our similar imagery, Kobina arrived and managed enough French for us to exchange addresses. When the time came for us to leave, we reluctantly said goodbye. I promised myself that I would take French lessons (again) as soon as I returned home, and that I would write my twin sister. While I did keep my promise to take French, by the time I'd learned enough to compose a letter, about a year and a half later, I was well into another phase of life and never wrote her.

Me and my Beninese twin sister in her village in Togo, West Africa, 1977

The Republic of Togo was pretty much like Benin--French in every way. We had one week of lectures at the University of Lome (in English), and then spent the next two days relaxing at the Hotel Le Benin, in the city of Lome (pronounced low may) Like Cotonou, in the Republic of Benin, this capital city sits right at the edge of the Atlantic Ocean. The palm trees and white sanded beaches are reminiscent of a resort. And while we were allowed to walk and/or relax on these beaches, we were advised against swimming in the ocean due to the strong under currents. In Lome (Togo's capital city), we would have the added bonus of being the special guest of America's current Ambassador to Togo, Ambassador Ronald Palmer, who had planned a reception for our group.

Overlooking the courtyard at Hotel La Benin, our residence while in Lome,

Shortly before our time in Togo was to conclude someone noticed that we had not seen Kobina for several days, and some in the group almost went into a state of panic again. Since two of our group members had gotten ill, apparently from eating food sold on the street of Lagos and ended up near death in a hospital in Lagos, that did not resemble anything we had ever seen, the entire group had become depended on Kobina for knowing how to fix any circumstance and/or soothe our now fragile nerves, upon any situation.

L'Ambassadeur des Etats-Unis d'Amérique

M. Ronald Dewayne Palmer

prie **Mr. V. PHILPOTT**

de lui faire l'honneur d'assister **COCKTAIL PARTY**

qu'il donnera le **4th AUGUST 1977**

à sa résidence **AT 7.30 p.m.**

Venant de différents états des Etats-Unis, ils se sont cé

Les enseignants avec quelques invités

The group of us invited to a reception at Ambassador Palmer's residents in Lome, Togo August 1977

Despite the fact that Kobina had advised us against eating food from street vendors and any other cold or uncooked foods, such as salads until our immune systems had time to adjust to our environments, some of us ignored his warnings. The street foods looked and smelled so good; one could almost taste a morsel without even eating it. It took the systems of most people more than a couple of months to adjust, and because our schedule was often so rushed, we, of course, did not have the time. Those who did not take these warnings to heart, and submitted to their desire to take a bite, ended up spending the night at the hospital.

Having traveled throughout West Africa with American groups he had taken there for years, Kobina seemed to always know what to do whenever there were problems of any kind or nature. More importantly, he understood how to deal, diplomatically, with the adventurous traveler, who "would start out on a trip to a foreign country strong, eager, and even sometimes stubborn, but by mid-way behave like a dependent child." There were times when I was sure we had worn the poor man completely out. It seemed that Kobina was attending to our needs twenty-four hours a day; so much so, I had begun to secretly pray each day, "Please don't let him become frustrated and abandon us now."

It turned out that Kobina had gone ahead to Ghana to make sure it was okay for us to finally enter the country. The situation that had caused the university students to react in protest weeks earlier had been settled and we were allowed entry. The student unrest involved an ongoing battle that began when Ghana gained its independence from Britain in 1967. Since Ghana was the first African country to achieve independence, I thought it fitting to discuss this subject more fully, which I will in a chapter I've dedicated to colonialism in Africa.

***

Although both Benin and Togo were quite nice, we all were very happy to be in a country where we could easily communicate with its people. Despite our initial introduction, we found the people of Ghana very kind and hospitable. Our first set of lectures took place at the University of Legon, in Accra. We would later attend lectures at the Gold Coast University, and finally participate in one or more of several student-guided field trips that had been previously planned for us. As was the case in the other countries we'd visited, our tours included the centers of production, markets, museums, and galleries.

It soon became apparent though that, while not unlike Nigeria, Ghana being English-speaking, the two countries were very different. For example, in comparing Lagos, Nigeria's capital at that time, to Accra, Ghana's capital city, I felt that Accra had more of a small city feel to it. Lagos, on the other hand, abounded in expensive high-rise apartment buildings, and luxury cars such as BMW and Mercedes on every street. Although both these capitals boasted modem areas containing fine restaurants, and centers containing department, grocery, and drug stores, which on any given day seemed more crowded than those in some of America's major cities, especially during the tourist season, Accra's market activities and other business institutions appeared much calmer than those in Lagos.

In terms of the pace in each city, discussions with others revealed that, like me, they too associated Lagos with New York and Accra with San Francisco. Considering that comparison, and with Kobina's blessings, by our second weekend in Ghana, many of us had begun to venture out on our own, to do everything from night clubbing to visiting the families of our African friends at home, who lived in the smaller towns surrounding Accra.

Scenes around Accra, Ghana 1977

166

Scenes around Accra, Ghana 1977

Photo at Legon University, 1977

Balme Library-University of Ghana, Legon

Kofi, a friend I met years earlier in California, had given me the names and addresses of several of his family members and asked that I visit them. He'd also given directions on how to get to Winneba, where they resided, as well as instructions on how to get transportation from Accra. I was surprised at how easy this was to do. Once I found the "nanny bus" (the local transportation that took passengers to the outer city areas), with the sign Winneba on it, I climbed aboard with the other passengers. These passengers carried everything from live chickens to large pieces of furniture, that the driver would patiently help secure on the top of the bus.

I figured out later that because I was kind of dressed up, or maybe even a bit over-dressed for a bus ride (in a new dress I'd purchased at the garment market earlier), the driver beckoned me to sit in the front seat, beside another well-dressed lady. Knowing I could easily pass as a local African, and because I was not ready to let anyone on the bus know that I was an American, I merely nodded and followed the driver's instructions. It really never occurred to me that most of the people on the bus already knew one another. None-the-less, the lady, with whom I was sitting, curiously greeted me and politely introduced herself as Adjua. I nodded with a smile without introducing myself. Soon the bus was noisy with all kinds of conversations, mostly jokes, and news about people the passengers knew in common.

Finally, wondering why I would just smile and never spoke, the lady who had curiously inspected me earlier, asked where I was going. When I spoke, I could hear a quiet gasp flow throughout the bus and for a brief moment one could hear a pin drop. For only the second time, in my entire life (that I could recall) I wasn't sure of exactly what to do or say.

Suddenly, Adjua busted into laughter and announced, "You are an American! That's why you're so quiet" As though they were instructed to do so, everyone repeated in unison, "An American!"

Photo with Ghanaian Students on Campus Lagon, 1977

Then someone questioningly said, "But you look just like us!" I spontaneously replied, "But I am one of you, it's just that I am from America." Everyone clapped with joy. Finally, one man said, "And you are not afraid to ride on a nanny bus?" I replied, "of course not," and emphatically asked, "why should I be afraid to ride with my own people?" From that point we all laughed and joked together. I didn't bother to explain what it was like to ride the local buses on the West side of Chicago, where I spent my teen years. I smiled as I briefly reflected and satisfied myself with the feeling that since I had survived that experience, I could ride public transportation anywhere in the world.

Chatting with fellow Ghanaian Students on Campus at Lagon, 1977

Shortly after my identity was exposed, I was asked scores of questions about America throughout the remainder of the trip, and why I came back to Africa. Adjua asked on what day I was born. When I replied Wednesday, she explained that in Ghana, certain names are assigned to a particular day of the week and that a child was initially named according to the day on which he/she was born. For example, until the newborn's naming ceremony takes place, normally about six months to a year after birth, at which time she/he is given a name the suits her personality, a child is given that name assigned to the day of the week on which he/she is born. Since I was born on a Wednesday, I would automatically be called Akua. A male child, born on a Wednesday is called Kwaku[6].

As some of my travel companions arrived at their destination, they'd remind the driver to take good care of their American sister and make sure she got to her destination safely. This experience pretty much describes my entire stay in Ghana, save my experience at the slave castle. During our final week in Ghana, we visited the Slave Castle at Elmina, which had now been turned into a museum. Upon entering what was now considered the introductory lobby, I began experiencing an odd feeling; and upon entering the castle's courtyard, I found difficulty going any further. I recognized that this feeling was similar to the one I'd had previously, while walking with my fellow student friends on the beach at Cotonou in the Republic of Benin; I felt like I had been there before. This time, however, the feeling was more intense.

---

[6] Find your Ghanaian name on the chart at the back of this book. Remember you need to know the day on which you were born.

Photo of me at Elmina Castle at Cape Coast, Ghana West Africa, 1977

***

While strolling on the beach one day in Cotonou, the month before, I'd urged my friends to wander beyond the boundaries of a sign that clearly warned us not to. While I had not explained it to them in detail yet, I wanted to see if the bizarre feelings I'd began experiencing during our walk (about something still being where I remembered). Having already labeled me "the weird one of the group," after hearing my strange request they looked at each other as if to think, in unison, yeah, she's losing it. They followed me anyway. Actually, the request I made surprised me even. After all, I had never been to Benin before, much less on that beach, so I had no idea where my suspicion came from.

In an attempt to justify my declaration, I began to describe a natural rock formation that I somehow knew was just a short distance ahead of us. Then suddenly, there it was I shouted a loud, "My goodness, it's still here!" Could this be a figment of my imagination, based on what I knew about the slave trade from Aunt Mariah's stories, I wondered silently while everyone else just stood there in amazement, or perhaps something I'd come across during my more formal education about Africa?

My African studies classes had indeed confirmed a lot of what Aunt Mariah had already taught me. While she had focused mostly on why the Europeans desired Africans as opposed to other races, the more formal historical studies only refined my knowledge, and validated my aunt's stories. After telling us of their mental and physical strength, as well as their intuitive and creative skills, asserting that they [Europeans] already knew that the Africans were superior in these areas, "Why else would the white man risk his life, limb and money going all the way [across turbulent seas] to bring Africans to help build their economies," she'd reason. Inadvertently or otherwise, apparently written history has backed her assertions. Now, I wondered if Aunt Mariah's stories had been so vivid that I'd actually imagined being on that beach. If so, what did this rock formation have to do with anything? At any rate, while we all stood staring at the rock formation, I found myself completely mesmerized by it. And my having described the formation before we actually saw it, left us all too shocked to say any more.

I was shocked out of my thoughts when one of my student friends nervously warned that we should turn back. Apparently, she could see approaching soldiers, who controlled the protected beach areas on which civilians were not allowed, before the rest of us. Having half ignored her warnings however, I was now quickly brought back to reality when I heard voices shouting, "arretez!" In harmony with the others, I turned and witnessed about ten soldiers aiming machine guns in our direction. Knowing this could be the end of us, the two other women in our small ensemble both started crying, while the one guy with us just stood frozen, with his hands up in the air. We all were a mess with fright. I knew that arretez meant stop, but I could not decipher what the soldiers were saying further. Yet, I found myself rapidly explaining, in English (I could not think of any French), that I was the one at fault; that it was I who wanted to know if the rock formation was still where I remembered. I begged them to please forgive us. While I was not sure they understood my words, my actions left no doubt. Anyone could see that I was scared to death. The soldiers did not relax, however, until their leader spoke, after which they all started laughing and, with their guns, pointed us back in the direction from which we came.

Later that evening, we related our experience to the others in the group. In an obvious state of annoyance, Kobina (our guide), told us how lucky we were. He went on to explain that the reason we were warned not to go beyond that certain point on the beach was because that part (on which we so boldly trespassed) was part of a military base, and that soldiers could shoot intruders without consequences. He wondered, out loud, why the rest listened to and followed me. Kobina was so upset with us he dismissed my intuitive experience, which I'd rapidly tried to explain. So, did we, after witnessing such an elegant dismissal.

***

While standing there in the court of the museum however, my thoughts continued. I wondered if, in another life, I had been captured on that beach and brought to a place like this. Even though it was miles away from Benin, I seemed to be having the same feeling at Elmina, (one of the twelve slave castles situated along Ghana's coastline), I'd had on the beach. The fact that this castle was now a museum, and thus a tourist site, did not diminish the feeling that I had been there, or one like it, before. So, when we first approached the entrance, I was finding it hard to go inside. Noting something peculiar about me Sheila, my travel partner, asked what was bothering me. After hearing my explanation (which included that it was one thing to pose for pictures outside the castle, it was quite another to go inside), she reasoned that if I didn't go, I would be missing an experience of a lifetime.

Sheila continued defending her position by reasoning that not many African Americans would have the opportunity to come back to Africa, as had we, to see how our ancestors were treated after being captured and held at such ports until the ships came to take them away from their homeland. And, since I was lucky enough to have this opportunity, she argued I should go in, "Not only for the privilege of sharing [my] experience," but that I was "obligated" to do so.

I had long discovered that one of the most important slave ports along the West Africa coast was established at Whydah, in Dahomey (currently called the Republic of Benin). Dahomian kings and chiefs, who seldom if ever left slave ports, all of which were located on the beaches, had become notorious for sending out raiders to enemy or competing villages to capture its inhabitants to sell to slave traders. These captured inhabitants were exchanged for goods the traders supplied, including weapons to either attack their neighbors or to protect themselves from their own enemies. This process is vividly explained by the Dutch writer, William Bosman's in his book entitled *Description of Guinea*, London, 1705, who himself was a slave trader, working along the coast of West Africa.

Having observed that she still had not convinced me, Sheila continued by questioning how I was going to explain what I saw or describe how I felt, if I did not take this rare opportunity to go further. Although I did not say it out loud, I could hear a silent reply within myself asserting that I already knew. With such a convincing argument however, I submitted and went with her into the castle's courtyard. Upon entering, we followed the tour guide around, listening to his account of how the captured were treated. As were practically everyone else, I was having my own unsettling experience. I could almost see myself being "handled."

By the time we were directed to follow the guide down into the dungeons, where the captured slaves were kept, unable to breathe now, I began hyperventilating and I refused to go in. It was only then Sheila understood that indeed, something serious was going on with me and stopped insisting. Without going any further, I could still feel the cold atmosphere and smell the scents of the sick and suffering; I could still feel the pain of being trapped in a deep dark pit with my hands and legs bound, in cold hard chains, with little to no air--I could not and did not go any further. Even today, I remain haunted by the experience. Consequently, I am not sure if I did the right thing by even entering the courtyard.

***

All too soon, it was time to leave the African continent, and all I could think about during our return trip to the States, which seemed longer than our journey there, was that I must come back. Besides a student exchange program in business and economics, I decided that American students, particularly those of African descent, interested in these areas, deserved such a program that allowed them to learn more about Africa. Perhaps I could develop one, I thought.

The entrance to where the captured were kept at Elmina Castle at Cape Coast, Ghana, 1977

Due to the importance of this subject and its effect on African American life, as well as those Africans in other Diasporas, I felt that a discussion about slavery deserved a chapter of its own.

Although the chapter that follows does not cover the history of slavery in its entirety, this overview, I believe will provide enough to support a few of the personal experiences I have had to deal with.

The Slave Trade

Recorded history tells us that the Portuguese were the first of the modern Europeans to explore Africa. This, however, does not acknowledge ancient history which records the Greeks who traveled there, nor the Romans who finally recaptured the land of the Africans from places like Carthage (today's Tunisia), after Hannibal, his father before him, and his brothers conquered and ruled much of Italy between 264 and 149 BC). After many years of African rule in a large part of the Mediterranean, and after many failed attempts, the Romans finally conquered and ruled the people of Carthage. Perhaps recent history focuses on the Portuguese because they were the first Europeans to carry Africans to be sold in European markets for labor purposes.

While we know that this did not mark the beginning of slavery in Africa, since enslavement had been practiced within the Continent for many hundreds of years before the Europeans arrived (as did others including Europeans around the world enslaved their own people), recent history explains that the institution practiced on the African continent could not be considered slavery at all, but rather, a form of servitude imposed on those who were either captured in war or loaned out to pay off a debt. This included a kind of servitude that could keep a person within his/her own family. And while this kind of slavery may not be justified either, when compared to that which would later be practiced by Europeans against Africans, one must admit that the former form was quite humane.

The African "slaves" were more often allowed to earn money to pay off their servitude or debt, buy land, and/or eventually integrate into the local population—in other words, they had rights. They could even intermarry within the population in which they served! In *The Chronicle of the Discovery* and *Conquest of Guinea*, 1441-1448, Chapter 36, entitled "*Booty for the King*,"

Portuguese historian/writer Gomes Eannes de Azurara describes how the Portuguese practice of taking slaves began in the year 1446. According to Eannes de Azuara, "rumors had abounded for years about the abundance of gold and ivory on Africa's southwestern coast, and persons like Captain Antam Goncalvez wanted to exploit these riches." Having already traveled to Cape Blanco, located at the most northern coast of Mauritania (just a few days sail from Portugal), Captain Goncalvez designed a plan to capture a few Africans to hold for ransom in exchange for the resources needed for him and his crew to continue further south, in western Africa, where these riches were located. While in captivity these Africans would serve as laborers in Portugal. It was during this time, he says, that the Portuguese took note of the African's attitude towards work, their respectful and mild disposition towards their masters, and their strength or endurance.

Although it has been well documented that the first slave raids were orchestrated and conducted through surprised attacks aimed at the Moors (Blacks) living at Cape Blanco, I also knew and understood that the later European slavers could not have captured African slaves without the assistance of Africans. Given that a slave system "of sort" already existed on the continent, it was not unusual for a servant to be traded to others, which is how it appears, the trading of Africans to Europeans began.

Eventually the Portuguese made it to western Africa, and by 1448 had set up trading forts. It wasn't long however, that these Europeans had expanded their plans. Besides their insatiable commercial interests, they soon begun establishing permanent settlements. After discovering that the West Africans were not easy participants in their new plans, to assist in this area, the Europeans began embarking on a mission to save souls. While I do not wish a lengthy discussion on how religion was used to subdue the Africans here, I am compelled to mention how one Prince Henry of Portugal, a devout Catholic as well as a sailor and Christian crusader, took as his personal mission to "take the word of God to the African heathens[7]." For those who wish to read more on the importation of religion to Africa I recommend Basil Davidson's book entitled, *A History of West Africa,* 1000-1800.

I recall posing the question to one of my history professors, when I could not understand that, considering the size of the African continent compared to that of Europe, how could so few explorers from the European continent, which is substantially smaller, impose such a disastrous blow to the many people of Africa? His explanation compared Africa with other continents on earth that had a vast diversity of people. "Many of them, [Africans] didn't always get along with each other." He continued by using the Biblical example of how nationalities such as the Romans and Greeks behaved toward each other, explaining "that although people lived on the same continent or were from the same ethnic group, they were sometimes lifelong enemies. And, not unlike other places in this world, Africa too had its share of greedy people, including rulers who, at the expense of their own people, cared only about themselves." I would eventually learn that many history books on Africa's history, including Basil Davidson's, backs the professor's views. Davidson does an excellent job explaining how the already established slave system in Africa supported the European slave trade and may have even prolonged it.

I recommend Davidson also for those interested in learning about the African/European slave trade in West Africa in its entirety. Not only does he provide in depth accounts of how it took place, but he also explains why, although a region may have become poorer (due to the many raids), the chiefs and kings that participated in this catastrophe found it difficult to end it. "Some had begun depending entirely on the selling of people for their

---

[7] Historical Account of Discoveries and Travels in Africa, Vol. I, Edinburgh, Archibald Constable & Co. 1817, pp.65-75

subsistence. Others [for whatever reason] were compelled to maintain power," he states. Davidson suggested that even if he were not a tyrant such rulers, who only cared about their own gain never mind his own greed, once they'd begun trading in this manner, had to continue supplying their foreign partners; that without doing so, the ruler would be ousted from power, or worst, taken into slavery himself.

Against this backdrop, I had to accept that while the slave trade may have been created by forces outside of Africa, were it not for some African rulers this barbarous system may not have been as successful as it was, nor would it have lasted as long as it did --over four-hundred-years.

Once Was Not Enough

Reflecting on my experiences of my time on the Continent, I noted that much of my conversations with the African students I'd met revealed that they harbored the same kinds of misinformation about African Americans that African Americans had about them. Additionally, I observed that much of this misinformation came from the media to and from both Continents. Intentional or not, it became clear that the same kinds of images shown in the American media to denigrate Africans were being shown in Africa, to denigrate African Americans.

For example, among others, the movie "Super Fly" was being featured on the campus at Legon University when we arrived there in 1977. This movie, and others like it, depicted African American males as pimps who sold drugs to neighborhood children and exploited African American females by making them sell their bodies. Movies such as this (appropriately called Black Exploitation movies in protest), were released in mass during the early 1970's, and gave the impression that this lifestyle was the norm for all African Americans.

Alas, I was even asked, by some of the African students, why African Americans preferred this kind of life over taking advantage of "all the educational opportunities" offered them in America! Consequently, I began to understand Sheila's point about sharing the Elmina Castle experience and decided it more important to make sure that all Americans understood the full dynamics of Africa, than my fears. Likewise, Africans must understand the realities of life for the African American.

An example is how the limited view Americans have about Africa constantly shows up during any conversation two or more might have about the continent and its people. Much like my own initial perceptions, most Americans think of Africa as just one country containing one kind of people ("black skinned people"), as opposed to it being a continent, containing fifty-three different countries, each containing an enormous diversity of peoples.

Most countries on Africa's continent are inhabited by hundreds of different ethnic groups (of many skin hues), much like the continent of Europe, only much, much bigger. For the most part, skin color in Africa is mainly dictated by how close one lives to the equator, which passes right through the middle of the continent. Those who live closest to the equator appear to have darker skin tones. The further one lives away from the equator the lighter one's skin tone tends to be.

People with darker hues are said to have more melanin in their skin, a substance that protects it from harmful rays produced by the sun. Note the skin tones of other people living on continents through which the equator passes, i.e., the South Sea Islands, parts of Southern Asia, the Caribbean, and South and Central America. These populations have varying shades of darker skin tones as well. Could it be then that maybe our proximity to the suns helps determine this element in the skins of those most exposed to the sun?

As a product of those Americans who lack understanding about many parts of a world outside of our own, I understood our ignorance. Even though I had learned about Africa (via my Aunt Mariah) early on in life and had studied the continent intensely during my college years, it was not until I actually went there that my initial ideas and perceptions about Africa changed. Besides, regardless of one's learning, the media can do some serious damage to one's reality. This research tour in West Africa clearly revealed my own ignorance. It also launched my desire to better understand this diverse and dynamic place. That understanding would happen only after I'd had the opportunity to live in and/or travel to other regions on the continent. As a result of my current travel experience however, I discovered that there were parts of Africa that I loved intuitively, and other parts I did not care for at all. Whatever the case, I could no longer lump my opinions about

Africa into one.

Finally getting it myself, my next quest became that of educating my fellow Americans about the continent of our heritage. A good starting point, I felt, was getting people to understand that while those countries that are situated in the same region, on this vast continent, may have some things in common, each has its own culture, own set of traditions, own languages, own customs, and own currency even. Furthermore, like the United States, each country has within it: states, cities (including its capital city), towns, and villages, complete with small and large farms. Moreover, not unlike countries on the European continent where, for example, there are major differences between the British and the French; the Germans and the Italians, the Spanish, and the Irish, etc., so are there differences between the Ghanaian and the Nigerians; the Beninese and the Kenyans; the Ugandans and the Ethiopians, the Egyptians, and the Tunisians, the Zimbabweans and the Ivorians, etc. One can continue this comparison with continents such as Asia, which contains its own diversity and includes (but not limited to) the Chinese, Japanese, Indonesians, Koreans, Philippians, Singaporeans, Vietnamese; while they all are Asians, they are different. Likewise, the different groups in the Middle East and Mediterranean's, which includes the Arabs, Jews, Philistines, and/or Persia, containing the Syrians, Iraqis, Iranians, to name a few. In fact, in most cases, the only thing people on each of these continents have in common is the colorings of their skin, which more often than not is dictated by their environment--that is, where they are located on the globe.

While my travels were indeed enlightening, it still remains unclear to me, why it is that Africa continues to be depicted in the American media as a poor "country" full of starving people (with flies swarming their faces). Surely, the well-traveled producers in the media industry must know better. And, while it is not my intentions to minimize the needs of the people in those countries that are poor, nor those areas within countries that are not (remember, AFRICA IS MASSIVE), I feel compelled to point out that it was only when I was in an African country that I experienced belonging to a private Country Club; of flying in a private jet; and of playing on the waters aboard a private yacht! I can only console myself with the idea that perhaps these depictions are the behavior of innocent documentary film makers, who only find it worthwhile to produce films about the world's poor and suffering. Perhaps it is up to us, individually, to read and learn more about a subject before pretending to be an expert on a place as massive and diverse as Africa.

A few more observations about the media may not be out of place at this point. So, while I am on this subject, perhaps if I put it out there, someone will explain to me the following, as I have been puzzled by this phenomenon most of my adult life. Why is that America's major television networks (NBC, ABC, CBS and Fox), all allow only one African American to appear at a time. This includes sitcoms, movies, talk shows, game shows, and commercials even. Take Wheel of Fortune as an example. In all the years that I watch this show (one of my favorite shows), save for the athletes that appear from time to time, I have never seen more than one African America player at a time. Why aren't there ever two or more of any the "minorities" in America at any given time; or three even?

Likewise, talk shows like the political analysis forums such as Fox News Sunday, where there are always three to four panelists, but never more than one African American, or Asian, or Hispanic not to mention the absence of Native Americans! Issues or questions are often raised on these shows where this one person is asked to speak for his or her entire race of people, whether educated or not, rich or poor, from the city or the farm. If by chance this lone soul is brave enough to offer his/her honest opinion, which is likely based on his/her own personal experience and/or perspective on the subject, he/she is often attacked by the head honcho, if not the entire panel for "feeling that way". Why is that? As I set through these talk shows I often wonder if the producers fear that the "strength in numbers" axiom may occur, and therefore refuse to take the chance of having more than one at a time, or if by having only one, with no support, the opinions of the majority on the panel prevails or are more easily proven, and that this, therefore, relieves the majority from having to accept the truth or acknowledge how others really feel. Please forgive the digression. I've calm down.

In any case, the urgency for my sharing what I have learned, both about the continent of Africa and my other travels, was due to my belief that, as innocent as such ignorance may appear, this lack, which tends to manifest itself in other parts of the world as being self-centered and/or arrogant, is very harmful to America's overall image. It is also a precursor to how the rest of the world may feel about Americans as a whole, not just one group. During my world odyssey, it seemed everyone else on this planet understood Africa and other world cultures except Americans--My goodness, I thought to myself, once was not enough.

Discussions with students at University of Zaire in Nigeria, 1977

Her(story) vs His(story)

Now, at thirty-five years of age, I had reached full maturity, and was about to embark on a new experience; one that did not include school--in the corporate world. For the first time in a long time, I no longer felt the need to prove (mostly to myself) that I was not destined to be the failure that I thought everyone expected I would be. It was time, I decided, to concentrate on my personal life--something I had neglected thus far.

Having intentionally passed on several opportunities to pursue and/or develop personal relationships before, and with my girls at a point where I did not have to direct the majority of my attention on them, I often found myself feeling the effects loneliness brings. And, like every other goal I pursued in the past, I decided to go forth, and find myself a mate.

After several failed attempts to hold on to a romantic interest for any significant amount of time, I decided to bluntly ask one of my suitors what the problem was. I was equally bluntly told that most men were afraid of me. "Why?" I asked the person to whom I was currently making the inquiry, and a few others as well. I was told everything from my being too independent and/or self-sufficient, to being too intelligent and/or worldly.

I was a bit floored when one guy I really liked painstakingly explained that, while I was a nice lady, he was looking for a woman who would be satisfied with what he had to offer her and not expect anything more. When I asked if I had made any demands on him, he defended himself with an emphatic no, but added that because of my lifestyle, he knew that I eventually would. Considering that I received this kind of feedback from several sources before, I decided it must be true. I therefore decided that it was up to me to tone things down a bit if I wanted a man. So true to who I am, I began my normal quest to find out what I needed to change; well, not change (I kind of liked who I was at this point) but rather, learn what I needed to do to comply (or at least compromise) with the current social norms of my society--the ones that would help to achieve my goal.

My love for reading "about it" kicked in. And read I did. I also made it a point to observe how other sisters, with mates, behaved. Admittedly, more times than I cared to acknowledge, I did not like what I saw. In the meantime, in wonderment of this new challenge before me, I could not help being puzzled that despite the spiritual enlightenment I had worked so hard to achieve, I was still at a lost when it came to understanding the behavior of males toward females in our society.

Why, for example, did women act like meek little humble and helpless kittens, with or around men, but act themselves when in the company of other women? More importantly, why did men condone and/or need this kind of behavior from women in order to feel important or in charge? Why couldn't men want a woman who genuinely wanted to be with them, and not because they needed something from them--mainly to be taken care of? I also wondered why most men could not deal with an equal partnership situation. Even more disturbing, why had I not noticed this in the past. Who, I pondered, was it that told me that men and women are to be complementary to each other? Although I will be jumping ahead, before sharing some of my findings, I believe this is the perfect place at which to pause and offer views (from others) on why the world, affecting women and children, is as it is today. One perspective was shared during a gathering of women, to which I was invited while living in Africa.

During this gathering, the conversation eventually turned to marriage and how difficult it was to maintain. After all the younger women had offered their opinions, which focused mostly on its ultimate lack of benefits to women, an elderly woman offered an interesting explanation for why and how the institution of marriage was created in the first place. I was surprised when some of her views reflected some of those, I came across during my search for answers earlier; only hers were more graphic. This wise older woman, who said that she was the product of polygamous marriage, began with a position (and I paraphrase) that humankind is no different than any other of God's creatures; all of which were put on earth to, basically, keep it populated. "This was God's original plan," she stated emphatically. "In His infinite wisdom," she continued, "God created male and female of each species and designed their reproduction systems with this same purpose in mind; that is why, for a certain set period in their lifetime (during youth) the male is inherently wired to pursue the female. The human animal was included in this divine plan."

To substantiate her position, she went on to tell the following story: Inviting us to take note of the animals, she cited dogs in particular "because they exemplified this theory so perfectly." When the male dogs' instinctive urge to procreate occurs, he will approach any female dog it runs into to satisfy this natural desire. This compelling urge remains throughout the animal's reproductive years. In contrast, rarely, if ever, will one observe a female dog pursuing a male dog, she continued, confident that we understood-- this, too, was by design. Except in the case of lions where the female lion goes among her sisters who protect her during the gestation period, when the female dog has become impregnated, she goes on her way, alone, to have her litter. In the meantime, now that his immediate need (that natural urge) has been satisfied, the male dog goes on his way, not even realizing he had anything to do with this reproduction process.

According to this wise woman, when man took control of the earth, he decided to change the rules to fit his now more socially evolved needs. Among other things, man instituted marriage, complete with terms and conditions that catered mostly to his own desires. For example, a woman must pledge to love and obey him (her husband) only, for the rest of her life. Conversely, the woman was given many rules and restrictions. In many cultures established around that time, women were not even allowed to show their faces to anyone other than her husband, nor wear comfortable clothing; to do so constituted a public offense for which she could be severely punished."

Observing the looks of depression on the faces in her audience, our elder pointed out that a few provisions were thrown into these rules and laws to appease women; perhaps to make their new plight more palatable or to encourage them to remain in the marriage. She added that the husband was to protect and provide for his wife and the children she produced for him. Finding it difficult to honor his own rules, however, considering his inherent, natural instincts, man has severely fallen short of following his own rules. She went on to poke fun at men in Africa, whom she says, took the institution of marriage a bit further. After observing the king of the jungle (the male lion) and thinking how sweet it would be to have an entire harem of females at his disposal like the lion, African men created polygamy.

When the laughter subsided, one woman asked, "What could women today do about their situation?" to which the elder shrugged her shoulders and responded, "Not much, it is their [man's] time to rule the earth. Each woman must find her own way of dealing with it." She joked that although most women already knew how, she pointed out that it all depends on a woman's character type. When asked what she meant by this, she explained that there are basically two types of women, the smart ones and the greedy ones.

According to our more experienced sister, when smart women find themselves in a polygamous marriage, they bond with their sister wives to build a system that will care for them and their children should the husband become unable to contribute or dies. Although the men do not seem to get this, the women all know that because of the heavy burdens placed on a man with many wives and the inevitable large number of children he'll have to feed, his wives are likely to out-live him. The system these smart women create together then, is designed to take care of them in any event, including old age.

Contrastingly, caring for herself only, the greedy wife usually tries to get as much as she can for herself and her children. Since the apple doesn't fall far from the tree, however, and she is too selfish to foresee this, her children will probably inherit her selfishness and do the same, that is, look out for themselves only, forgetting about her. Even though she risks being left all alone in her old age, however, she will still fair better than her self-indulging polygamist husband." Before ending her session our elder cautioned us not to let this secret out. "Because, ultimately, the joke is on the male."

While we all found our elder sister's account humorous, we also agreed that considering our current situations, it had great validity. Yet, I remained unclear about how to conduct myself in a society where the odds seemed stacked against women who, like myself, live in a non-polygamous society, and choose to better herself until her mate comes along. Why is it that a woman runs the risk of being considered "too independent" and therefore doesn't need (or deserve) a man if or when she is successful? By now I was beginning to wonder if it were even possible for men in general, and African American men in particular, to behave in any way other than what the society in which we lived had historically imposed on them. If this self-indulging theory is true, or given what I'd experienced so far is true, how shall I pursue in such a hostile environment, without giving up who I am and still be desirable to the opposite sex, I wondered?

Interestingly enough, it was during this time that the women movement, which began in the early seventies with demonstrations of women burning their bras, aired on prime-time television, was now gathering momentum. Observing that some of these issues coincided with those of present concern to me; I decided this was a good time to expand my understanding. Inevitably my readings began to focus on the role's women played throughout history. During my search I discovered several books on women and religion. These included books like, "When God was a Woman," by Merlin Stone, and "The Language of the Goddess" by Marija Gimbutas. Both these books traced a peace-loving culture headed by females that flourished as far back as 25,000 BC.

Ms. Stone's research on the subject revealed that in prehistoric and early historic periods of human development, religions existed in which people revered their supreme creator as female. She argues that events in the Bible, which we are generally taught to think of as taking place "in the beginning of time," actually occurred during these historic periods. She argues further that for thousands of years both religious (female and male) deities existed simultaneously. She goes on to cite evidence which proves that the female religions did not just fade away, but were in fact, the victims of centuries of continual persecution and suppression by the advocates of the newer religions which held male deities as supreme.

According to Ms. Stone, from these new religions came the creation myth of Adam and Eve, and the tale of the loss of a paradise that put the blame on women. She notes authorities in the fields of anthropology, archeology, and ancient history who have unearthed evidence which extends from the beginnings of the Upper Paleolithic age that supports her findings.

Ms. Gimbutas's research and writings seem to agree with that of Ms. Stone. In her description of life before the Indo-European conquests, around 7,000 BC, Ms. Gimbutas discusses how female deities, "which no male could equal," had been eroticized and changed into wives and daughters and made subservient to male gods. She goes on to explain that during the time of female goddess worshiping, "people did not produce lethal weapons or build forts in inaccessible places as did their successors, [who worshiped male deities]." "Instead," she continues, "they built magnificent tomb-shrines and temples, comfortable houses in moderately-sized villages and towns, and created superb pottery and sculptures." "This," she continues, "was a long-lasting period of remarkable creativity and stability, an age free of strife," and that "little by little societies became patriarchal and war-oriented."

Surprisingly enough, one of the most renowned tribes in Africa tells a similar story of women as the first rulers. In his book, Facing Mount Kenya, pp 5-8, former president Jomo Kenyatta, of Kenya, gives the following account about the origin of his tribe, the Gikuyu:

...in the beginning of things, when mankind started to populate the earth, the man Gikuyu. the founder of the tribe was called by the Mogai, the Divider of the Universe, and was given as his share, the land with ravines, the rivers, the forests, the game and all the gifts that the Lord of Nature (Mogai) bestowed on mankind. ...Before they departed Mogai told Gikuyu that whenever he was in need, he should make a sacrifice and raise his hands toward Kere-Nyaga (the mountain of mystery), and the Lord of Nature will come to his assistance. Gikuyu vowed to do what was commanded by the Mogia, and when he reached the spot [to where he was directed], he found that the Mogai had provided him with a beautiful wife whom Gikuyu named Moombi (creator or moulder). Both lived happily and had nine daughters."

The story goes on to narrate how Gikuyu was disturbed at not having a male heir, and how he called on the Mogai for assistance, after which nine young suitors were provided to marry Gikuyu's daughters. Gikuyu would only give the young men his consent, however, on the condition they agreed to live at his homestead under the matriarchal (controlled by women) system established by Mogai. The young men agreed to this condition, "for they could not resist the beauty of the Gikuyu daughters, nor the kindness which the family had shown them."

The families eventually increased into large groups and were given the ancestral collective name of Rorere raw Mbari ya Moombi (the children of Moombi or Moombi's tribe). But, after Gikuyu and Moombi passed away, the males decided that the matriarchal system should be changed to patriarchal (controlled by men). Kenyatta offers the following for this sudden change, which is the complete opposite from both Ms. Stone and Ms. Gimbutas's accounts of the change in gender rule:

"it is said that while holding superior position in the community the women

193

became domineering and ruthless fighters. They also practiced polyandry [multiple husbands], and through sexual jealousy, many men were put to death for committing adultery or other minor offenses. Besides the capital punishment, the men were subjected to all kinds of humiliation and injustice. Men were indignant at the way in which the women treated them, and in their indignation, they planned a revolt against the ruthless women administration of justice. But as the women were physically stronger than the men of that time, and also better fighters, it was during the time when the majority of women, especially their leaders, were in pregnancy."

Although Kenyatta's account on the manner in which women ruled appears the opposite of that of the two female writers, both accounts speak to the idea that the original ruling system was matriarchal.

Perhaps the most intriguing reason for the breakdown in male/ female relationships is that of Ayi Kwei Armah's where, in his book, Two Thousand Seasons, he explains the theory of reciprocity. Although his views focused on slavery, he provides his views on how man got to this "disastrous state in which we all live today."

Armah explains that reciprocity (the giving and the receiving) was originally "The Way" humans were meant to live, "Giving, but only from whom we receive in equal measure. Receiving, but not only from those to whom we give in reciprocal measure." He goes on to explains that "one should not merely take, nor merely offer, and that although this law was devised when women ruled the earth, it was not meant that women should rule over men, but rather to create abundance and harmony without one taking advantage of another."

In addressing the plight of the African, he contends that "slavery, where one's very mind would be taken away from him, was a lesson for man's greed and warlike ways, but also descending to laziness, unjust, and harshness against his woman." "This punishment," he predicts, "which consists of the African losing his country, identity, and self-dignity would last two thousand seasons." I highly recommend reading this book to get a fuller understanding of Armah's views.

Scientist traces all humans back to African woman

BERKELEY (AP) — All humans descended from one African woman who lived 140,000 to 280,000 years ago, according to a biochemist who based his theory on the estimated rate of mutation of a type of DNA.

The study by Allan C. Wilson, a professor at the University of California at Berkeley, suggests that modern humankind emerged just once from earlier species somewhere in Africa.

The study also indicates that preceding species from Indonesia, China or Greece may have been swept aside by the "African Eve" in subsequent years, and bolsters the contention that Africa is the sole nursery for modern Homo sapiens and more distant ancestors.

"We are probably talking here about less than 200,000 years since the common ancestor of us all," Wilson said.

Wilson, along with the study's co-authors Rebecca L. Cann and Mark Stoneking, used new methods of biotechnology to separate and catalog microscopic genes from tissues in placentas of women of various racial groups.

Most of the specimens were obtained in the maternity wards of American hospitals and some were sent from the highlands of New Guinea and Australian hospitals where aborigine women bore children.

A peculiarity in cell structure permits only women to pass one class of genes to offspring. These genes occupy tiny suborgans called mitochondria, which are located within cells but outside the nucleus. They are critical to liberating metabolic energy.

"Each of us, men and women, got our mitochondrial DNA only from our mothers, and she from her mother, and her mother from her mother, all the way back," Wilson said.

Accepting What Is and Pushing On

As I reflected on how I was brought up and how I had been introduced into adult life, I was forced to acknowledge and accept that the rules established for the behavior of men and women were different during my youth and to some degree, still are. In fact, in many places, from adolescence on, boys continue to be encouraged to have as many intimate encounters as they can, while girls are warned to maintain their chastity. As these boys grow into men, to prove his "manhood", the urgency to score appear to become even greater. If females are to remain virtuous, one wonders with whom then would boy/males have these encounters? I am forced to accept that one is lucky to reach maturity without falling victim to this double standard. The consequences of such behavior have had devasting effects on African American communities.

While instituted slavery may have ended, the behavior toward women and the children it produced continues especially for the African American female, the resulting family that is still forced upon her. To the indulger, it doesn't seem to matter if the female is a stranger, friend, or relative. Nor does it matter if she is a naive virgin, a saint, or a prostitute. The goal appears to be the same, and that is, to score. Once success is achieved, as long as it cannot be classified as rape, the male is allowed to go on with his life, which often involves pursuing his next challenge.

In some circles, those who could boast of having the most conquests are often admired even more by their peers. If his targeted female is left with a child, the problem is often hers alone. Contrastingly, once a girl has fallen victim to a fellow's charm or force, and gets pregnant in the process, she becomes a "fallen angel" and suffers the scorn of the entire society for her sins (permissiveness), whether she agreed to it or not. Such scorn can include everything from being forced to drop out of school and, thus, experience all the problems that come therewith (i.e., low-paying jobs, the inability to provide affordable housing for her child(ren), stealing in order to feed them--the list goes on).

More importantly, the young girl misses the very necessary experience of growing up and getting to know herself before becoming responsible for the life of another human being, which compounds a fate of limited future choices in life. Once a female has fallen victim, it matters little that this child-mother knows little to nothing about raising a child. As far as society is concerned, once she becomes a mother, if and when she fails at this very important job, it is her fault after which she is labeled an unfit mother.

On the other hand, in western societies, even if the girl/woman is lucky enough to win her man, if or when at some later date he tires of her, he still has the option of walking away and leaving her with the products of their union, and all the responsibilities that comes with it. The male easily moves forward with his future, often without any "baggage," suffering little to none of society's scorn.

Although I had never bought into the Adam and Eve story, I still wondered how God could create a world in which the one bearing the greater responsibility (the nine-month body metamorphosis and labor process) for peopling his earth, be allowed to be treated so unjustly. Could it really be true that this all came about because Adam was foolish enough to accept and eat an apple offered to him by Eve who, according to the Bible, was the lesser of the two? More alarming is the fact that it was this same foolish person (Adam) that was given dominion over the earth! Wasn't he smart enough not to accept the apple? No wonder the world has been at war since. As a young person trying to understand, I wondered, in alarm, what was God thinking!

By now I had deduced that Willie (the father of my first child) did not set out to hurt me, nor do I believe he intended to have all those children before he was twenty. Rather, he and those like him can also be seen as victims. Perhaps they too are innocent, unconscious products of the rules established by a society that offers one-sided privileges that will inevitably work against them as well. After all, having been taught, via the Bible, historical events and other societal influences or encouragements, not to mention slavery and its teachings, most men see nothing wrong with seeking self-gratification at the expense of women. In fact, some societies are convinced that women ("made from man's ribs") were made purely for the satisfaction of mankind like those who believed that blacks were put on earth to serve the whites.

Since such behaviors had long been established and condoned as okay by society, most men never even consider the final impact it would have on them. Nor do they consider how such behavior affects the future survival of their immediate family, their entire community, and their race. Unfortunately, society does not prepare those who choose such indulgence for the moral and/or mental consequences they too will inevitably face. Whether their actions were innocent or not, such individuals often end up more wounded than their victims.

Nevertheless, as I reflected on my growth, I now realized that I may have played a role in what happened between Willie and me that fateful night during my youth and must take some of the responsibility. After all, I was seventeen and should have been able to use my budding analytical skills to reason the situation out, as I had done many other times before in my young life. The choice I made, be it out of curiosity (about this strange, new and wonderful feeling I was experiencing that night) or otherwise, the decision not to stop before it was too late was my own. Willie had not forced me--at least not in the beginning. Because I did not demand that he stop in time, perhaps I sent the wrong message and he pursued. I, therefore, had to suffer the natural consequences of my own actions, as naive as they may have been at the time.

My reason for acknowledging this is to show that even when a woman is young, naive or weaker, in cases such as my own, she always has a choice. However, because I made that choice and became a mother too young, at some point during my life's journey, I must have realized that I did not have to continue along that path, so I did not. And, while it may not turn out this way for some young mothers, the beautiful child resulting from the choice I made that night turned out to be one of the best things that would happen to me. I now believe that this is because I was determined to make better future choices.

On the other hand, it must be a lonely state in which a male finds himself, after having matured enough to reflect on his past; knowing he has fathered several children but does not know who or where they might be. Not only will he be unable to reap the benefits resulting from participating in the proverbial cycle of life, which happens after one has done his part in helping to raise and provide for the children he helped to create as he grows older, he also risks not having anyone to care for him during those inevitable winter years of his life (see chart at the end of this book). I believe that this was the intended benefit for both the male and female when our marriage rules and laws were established.

More importantly, not having the male half in their lives, as a role model, the sons a man fathers runs a greater risk for repeating the same behavior, and suffering the same consequences as he, thus perpetuating the same negative effects on and in society. Likewise, unless the mother is fortunate enough to secure a relationship with another willing to father her fatherless children, the daughters produced by the absent biological father will grow up not knowing what to expect from a male figure.

While such behaviors (stud ism) have negative effects on the larger society, for the African American community, the impact is even greater, since it is compounded with years of other mentalities residual from slavery times. After generations of living with the double standards described earlier, what began as forced behavior--that is, siring many children, metamorphosed into established beliefs or norms, and eventually became a sign of manhood, especially among African American men.

Unfortunately, today, it still appears not to matter if men do not help raise or, at least, participate in the lives of their offspring.

Equipped with the knowledge that, while I may have been a product of a social system in which I had no part in establishing, but one in which I do have the choice of not accepting an ultimate defeat, I now had a better perspective about my life and how I was going to live the remainder of it. Indeed, I understood by now that true relationships should be complementary, not deceitful, dependent, nor competitive and, that when the right person shows up, I will not have to give up anything to get him.

Thus, I decided to not change who I was just to have a relationship. And while I will keep myself open to the possibility that someday someone may come along who will accept me for who I am, if that does not happen, I will remain committed to living the best life I always have; that is, of going it alone but totally fulfilled.

My father and stepmother at MBA Graduation, 1977

San Francisco State University

GRADUATE DIVISION
OFFICE OF THE DEAN

1600 HOLLOWAY AVENUE • SAN FRANCISCO, CALIFORNIA 94132

May 15, 1978

Vandean Philpott
5307 Crosly Avenue
Richmond, CA 94804

Dear Ms. Philpott:

I am pleased to advise you that your recently completed thesis/creative work has been officially accepted by this office (approval Master's Thesis Receipt enclosed). Accordingly, a Credit (CR) grade has been forwarded to the Registrar's Office for recording on your permanent academic record.

Your thesis/creative work will be received in this office only briefly and will then be forwarded to the University Library which is responsible for further processing (including binding, cataloging and shelving). This latter process may involve several weeks time. If you requested and paid for more than the two copies required for the Library, the extra bound copies will be returned to you (or distributed according to your previous instructions) by the Library.

Congratulations on completing this particular requirement for the master's degree! If we in this office can be of assistance to you at any time, please feel free to call upon us.

Sincerely yours,

Donald E. Garrison
Dean, Graduate Division

DEG:kr

Enclosure

San Francisco State University

The Trustees of The California State University and Colleges

on recommendation of the faculty

have conferred upon

Vandean Philpott

the degree of

Master of Business Administration

Next Stop: Los Angeles, California

For years after my first trip to the continent of Africa, I could hardly think of anything else besides getting back there. The five-year plan I had developed included becoming fluent in French and reading everything I could about the different countries I wanted to explore next. I became so passionate about returning to Africa, my small family which, besides my two daughters, now included my cousin Barbara (the daughter of my father's younger sister), thought I was losing my mind. Barbara had joined us in California to attend college. Because of my obsession, Barbara and my girls had jokingly began comparing me to the lead character in Close Encounters, a popular movie out during that time.

After learning of the arrival of aliens from outer space, an earthling (the movie's lead character) convinced himself that they were looking for candidates to take back to their planet. Believing that they were good and that he could be one of the chosen few, he became so obsessed about leaving earth he began focusing his whole life on his eminent departure. In an attempt to convince his unbelieving family that the aliens would come for him, he began building a replica of the mountain on which their spaceship had landed {in the middle of his living room) to prove that he knew what he was talking about. At that point, his family thought he had gone completely mad. Although it would be nearly ten years before my dream of going back to Africa would be realized, like the movie character, I had begun preparing myself, including buying things I thought I'd need, for living there.

Having already visited five different countries in Africa, I was aware that these were all located in the same region on the continent, and while they had many things in common, they were all different. I, therefore, wanted to experience other regions--if for no other reason than to measure their differences. Additionally, considering my background with Africans (both here in the states and in Africa), I knew that while I had acquired more knowledge than most Americans, considering the vastness of the continent, I also knew there was much more to learn. It was at this juncture the idea came that even though I had only acquired a fragment of what was needed, to better achieve a future goal of establishing an African/African American Cultural Center in which I could share my knowledge, it was necessary that I experience other African countries.

After successfully arguing the hypothesis for my Masters' thesis, I presented the materials collected during my research in West Africa to my thesis committee. Once my research data was accepted, I spent the next six months writing my thesis, entitled *"Inter-University Exchange in Business"* I received my MBA degree in International Business shortly thereafter.

While collecting a significant amount of primary data in West Africa for my proposed exchange program and having met many in academia eager to assist with it, I also met several individuals committed to helping me with my dream of establishing an African/Africa-American cultural center as well. Unfortunately, by the time officials at San Francisco State invited me to remain at the University to create and establish the exchange program, given the fact that I had already spent so much time in academia, and that it would take time to find the kind of funds necessary to establish and sustain such a project, I decided to accept what I concluded was the best of several other job offers, and went forth into the world of Corporate America. And, although it was put off as a future endeavor, I remained committed to my dream for the center.

While working in the corporate world, I decided to write a proposal seeking the necessary assistance to establish the cultural center I'd envisioned. The proposed center would provide an environment where Africans currently residing in America could interact with African Americans in an environment conducive to cultural sharing and understanding. From these personal interactions, I believed that both groups would get to re-acquaint themselves, achieve a better understanding of each other, and thus build better relationships. I believed that ultimately, the myths and misinformation passed on to us by others about us, would soon dissipate since we would then, know better.

More importantly, the center would be a place where all interested Americans could learn about the African continent via the various programs, activities, and exhibits it would offer on an ongoing basis. Knowing that while my vision was grand, I was confident it would happen someday. I also knew that one could never visit just a few places on a continent as vast as Africa and learn all there was to know about its entirety in one lifetime. Thus, my current proposal was entitled *"Fragments of Africa."*

After presenting the proposal to various prominent individuals, organizations, and institutions around the San Francisco Bay area, many felt that "while the idea was great, it was undo-able [for them] at this time." I would get the same response later in Los Angeles when, after the job I accepted I relocated my family there. Fortunately, these attitudes did little to discourage me.

***

I had been hired as a Market Developer for an International Insurance company located in Los Angeles. Besides developing markets, my job also included underwriting commercial insurance coverage on our client's overseas operations. While this two-prong assignment presented a great challenge for a new graduate like myself, I realized that the experience would provide me the opportunity to learn every aspect of doing business abroad. It also offered a vast amount of knowledge on the economic structure of the countries in which the organizations in my portfolio conducted their operations. I knew, even then, that this knowledge would someday be invaluable to my career development. An additional bonus was that it allowed me the opportunity to inter-mingle with a vast array of people, something I truly enjoyed. While in Los Angeles I also looked for opportunities that would ensure my continued participation in Africa.

***

Such an opportunity presented itself during an event at Los Angeles' City Hall, where I was introduced to one of Mayor Bradley's staff members. This person happened to be in the process of recruiting volunteers to assist the Mayor's office with developing events to host a group of visiting African dignitaries from Ghana. Already aware that I had worked for the Nigerian Consulate and was familiar with African protocol, he asked me to assist with the visit. After the success of that event, I was informed that Mayor Bradley was interested in developing a better relationship with other African countries and having become aware that I had done extensive research in West Africa, was invited to join this newly established Task Force on Africa on a permanent basis.

While I enjoyed participating in the City's international activities and was willing to offer my services as a volunteer and assist with developing African related events, I was reluctant to give up my job in international business. I respectfully turned the job offer down but remained on the Mayor's Task Force as a volunteer.

One of my first assignments on the Task Force was to work with a committee responsible for bringing Nigeria's *"2000 Years of Nigerian Art"* exhibit to Los Angeles. This activity turned out to be another milestone in my life. By now, I had already worked on several community projects and met stars such as Dr. Jester Hairston, of a current sitcom called "Amen." While working on the Los Angeles Sister City to Ghana committee, I would meet many musical icons including Steve Wonder. I even met Huggy Bear, of the TV series, Starky and Hutch, while volunteering on the Kwanza Parade preparations—yeah! This assignment would also present opportunities to work with more established celebrities. Joining me on the art committee, for example, was Sidney Poitier, whom I would never actually meet, but was content to just have my name[8] appear next to his on the art exhibit's brochure, which listed the names of the committee members in alphabetical order. Other members on this committee included Dr. Maya Angelou, with whom I had wonderfully enlightened conversations about her experiences in Africa compared to my own.

Ms. Angelou, an accomplished author, playwright, actress, dancer, singer, director and civil rights activist, confirmed that she knew Professor James Lacy and that they had indeed, both lived and worked in Ghana during the same period of time. When I shared with Ms. Angelou my desire to live and work in Africa someday, reflecting on her experiences, she excitedly told me to go for it! Her enthusiasm was tempered only by what would turn out to be some very wise advice about working and living abroad in general and Africa in particular.

I also had the privilege of meeting Brock Peters (star of the movie *Mississippi Burning*) who was one of the committee's co-chairs. After being dumped (the evening of the exhibit's opening reception) by one of his colleagues who, even after starring in several movies, was still struggling in the industry, Mr. Peters ended up having to escort me home. Apparently thinking I was somebody, since most of the questions at our final planning session (the only one this gentleman attended before the exhibit opening reception), were aimed at me (probably because of my background on Africa in general and Nigeria in particular) he approached me after the meeting. I was very flattered when he flashed a gorgeous smile, but shocked speechless almost when he asked if I had an escort to the reception. Knowing, who he was, I heard myself saying "no," and "yes," when he gallantly asked, "Would you give me the honor?" Although I was nearly floored, I acted as if his request was as natural as the eye on a black-eyed pea.

---

[8] Although my husband was deceased, I decided to keep his name (Philpott) since, not only was it the last name of my children; it was also the name that appeared o most of my legal documents.

Me and Dr. Angelou on the night of the reception, 1981

Before the big night I called everybody, I knew, in this great country of ours, to let them know about my date; and to prove that it was true, I promised to take pictures with him and send them all at least one, (Facebook did not exist at the time). Because he had been a recent box office sex symbol, especially during the Super Fly and Shaft days, everyone knew who he was. The big night finally arrived, and sure enough, my date came to pick me up as planned. I had to pinch myself to make sure I was not dreaming.

Upon arriving at the reception, we ran into Brock Peters at the door, who had come alone. It became obvious the two knew each other after my date introduced me to Mr. Peters. I also noted that my date had proudly winked at Brock after I recommended, we join Ms. Angelou's table, where she sat with several of the City Councilmen with whom I had worked, accompanied by their wives. Moving toward our table I recall feeling like a princess being escorted by both my date and Brock Peters. I felt that our table companions were impressed as well.

As the evening progressed however, I began noticing a little distancing from my knight in shining armor, and later on--what's this, a bit of annoyance in his voice during our small table talk? Having observed earlier that it was hard for him to keep up with the conversation around the table, which made him appear somewhat uncomfortable, I'd made a few attempts at keeping the conversation on something that might interest him--*Shaft in Africa*, perhaps? Finally, my date leaned over discretely, but asked bluntly, "*who are you?*"

A bit annoyed with him by then, especially after knowing what he meant, I jokingly said, "Nobody, just a worker bee." "Why," I asked. I was almost floored when he said, "Well, who do you know--do you have any connections here?" I intentionally

Sharing a smile with Brock Peters and friend (name unknown), 1981

responded with a "no, not-a-one." I did not have to wait long for a response before he leaned over to Brock, who was involved in a stimulating conversation with Ms. Angelou and others. I heard Brock respond, "Sure," after which my date leaned back in my direction and informed me that he was sorry he had to leave, but that Brock Peters would escort me home. Pleased with myself, I remember thinking that at least he waited for me to say okay before he got up to leave. Relieved he was gone; I could now focus on the more interesting table conversations.

On our way to my place later that evening, Mr. Peters, knowing more about what had happened than I, apologized and explained that like many aspiring actors in Los Angeles, my date was very superficial. He went on to explain that people like him try to be seen with as many "important people" as possible, and that it is their belief that strategies such as this are helpful to their careers. Stressing the behavior displayed by my date had nothing to do with me, he insisted I not take what happened personally. I merely replied that it was too bad he wasted a whole evening on me. After we both had a good laugh, I also acknowledged Brock for being such a gentleman, and told him how pleased I was that my evening ended with him escorting me home.

After volunteering for some time for the City of Los Angeles, I presented Mayor Bradley with my proposal on establishing the African/African American Cultural Center. Exclaiming that such a Center was an excellent idea, the Mayor promised to pass it on to several branches within his administration for advice on how the City could pursue on such a project.

Upon finally getting an audience with those officials in charge of making decisions on projects such as mine however, many of them invited me to do everything from requesting that I speak at various events in which they were involved, to inviting me to chair the Los Angeles Sister City project to various countries in Africa. Several even offered me a job in their departments. No one, however, knew how the city could incorporate or even sponsor an

African/African American Cultural Center. I concluded then that the Center would happen in its own time.

Mayor Bradley and I, 1981

TREASURES OF ANCIENT NIGERIA

OPENING NIGHT COMMITTEE

Rita Lawrence • Brock Peters
Co-Chairmen

Carolyn Ahmanson
Jackie Avant
Anna Bing Arnold
Johnnie L. Cochran, Jr.
Lynne Deutch
Elaine P. Feldman
Valerie Franklin
M. J. Frankovich
Darcy Gelber
Harold A. Haytin
Lois Haytin
Mary Jane Hewitt
Edward W. Hieronymus
Marcia Wilson Hobbs
James Hodgson
Maria Hodgson
Phillipa Houston
William G. Hunnefeld, Jr.
Ray Johnson
Jon Lappen

William B. Lee
Hazel Livingston
Sherrill D. Luke
William J. McCann
DiDi Daniels Peters
Vandean Philpott
Sidney Poitier
Earl A. Powell, III
Reilly P. Rhodes
Hans A. Ries
Margot Ries
Rodney W. Rood
Herman M. Salk
Josine Ianco Starrles
Paula Tobak
Milton Williams
Kitty Winn Winston
Jerry Wulk
Edith R. Wyle

HOST COMMITTEE

Hakim Ali
Clarence Avant
Jackie Avant
Richard Bailey
Danny Bakewell
Terry Bell
Devra Breslow
Louise Brinsley
Aurelia Brooks
James Burke
LeVar Burton
Kathryn Carr
Jack Carter
Nancy Carter

Nettie Charlotte
Johnnie L. Cochran, Jr.
Herbert R. Cole
James Coleman
Diane Cornwell
Comer Cottrell
Dave Cunningham
Alonzo Davis
Irwin Deutch
Lynne Deutch
Julian Dixon
Judith Drinkwater
J. Howard Edgerton
George Ellis

212

Welcome
Dr. Yakubu Saaka
Deputy Foreign Minister
of the Republic of Ghana
(West Afrika)

213

REPUBLIC OF GHANA

MINISTRY OF FOREIGN AFFAIRS
GHANA

No. MISC/PF/YS   JAN. 27 REC'D '80   Accra.
                                     17th December, 1979.

Dear President,

       Having eventually returned home, I hasten to
write to express my deep sense of gratitude and appreciation to you and through you and the Executive to all
Ghanaians in Southern California for the warm welcome
and kind courtesies accorded me during my brief visit with
you.

       I was heartened to find that even though separated
by long physical distances your concern for your country's
welfare was an ever-present preoccupation. I was equally
pleased to see that you were desirous to contribute in your
own modest way to efforts aimed at resolving some of our
problems. I cannot over-emphasise the importance of such a
spirit in nation-building and especially in Ghana's present
situation.

       But to recall my advice to you, your collective
efforts would wield much greater influence if all of you
were effectively mobilised into a union working with a
common purpose towards a common aspiration. I have
instructed Washington to consider seriously your request for
assistance and I shall press them to expedite action.

       In conclusion, I would request you most kindly to
express my deep appreciation to Vandean and Eleanor for their
invaluable contribution to the success of our get-together.

       I wish you all the joys of the season and the promise
of peace and goodwill that Christmas brings.

       A very Merry Christmas to you all and a Happy and
Prosperous New Year.

                        Yours sincerely,

                       (DR. YAKUBU SAAKA)
                       DEPUTY FOREIGN MINISTER.

MR. ANTHONY KYEREH,
PRESIDENT OF GHANA UNION,
LOS ANGELES,
c/o MR. ERNEST TETTEH,
WASHINGTON.

OFFICE OF THE MAYOR

December 2, 1980

TOM BRADLEY
MAYOR

Ms. Vandean Philpott
12042 Lamanda Street, #5
Los Angeles, California 90066

Dear Ms. Philpott:

During my 1979 trip to Africa with some members of my Task Force for Africa and Los Angeles Relations, I visited the Nigerian National Museum in Lagos and witnessed the major ancient treasures of this collection being assembled for a travelling exhibition. As you may know, Nigeria is unique in sub-Saharan Africa for its extensive body of sculpture which sustains an ancient history well beyond the usual 100-year life expectancy of most African art produced in wood.

The final selection consists of 100 items of terra-cotta and bronze, spanning more than 2,000 years. For the very first time, these national treasures were permitted to leave Nigeria to travel to the United States—an event every bit as important as the display of the Mona Lisa arranged by the French government. This exhibition opened at the Detroit Institute of Arts in January of this year and was scheduled to remain in the United States only through October to be displayed at the California Palace of the Legion of Honor and the Metropolitan Museum of Art in New York. It was then to return directly to Nigeria.

Since any future opportunity to view these masterpieces in this country was unlikely, the African Task Force worked for more than 18 months to extend the tour, with the cooperation of the Nigerian Ambassador to the U.S., His Excellency Olujimi Jolaoso; the U.S. Ambassador to Nigeria, Stephen Low; the Director of the Nigerian National Museum, Dr. Ekpo Eyo; and the Minister of Nigerian Culture. I am extremely pleased to report that an extension has been granted, and these important Nigerian treasures will now travel to Washington, D.C.; Calgary, Canada; Atlanta, Georgia; and finally to Los Angeles in September, 1981, at the Loker Gallery of the Museum of Science and Industry.

215

-2-

In order to insure that this historic art exhibition achieves the maximum community impact, I am forming a Committee of educators, museum officials, community leaders, and art lovers to assist in our planning efforts. I would be very pleased if you would agree to become a Committ member, which would involve the planning of programs designed to gain the support and involvement of citizen groups in this significant commun event.

As a first step, I have scheduled a breakfast meeting at 8:00 a.m. on Thursday, December 18, in the Executive Dining Room of City Hall (11th floor). Michael Kan of the Detroit Institute of Arts, where the exhibition was first displayed in the United States, will join us for a detailed discussion of our specific charge and possible approaches for achieving it. Please return the enclosed postcard indicating your availability as soon as possible. Parking will be available at the north end of the City Hall Garage off of Main Street.

I hope that your busy schedule will permit your attendance at our meeting. The African Task Force and I look forward to working with you.

Very truly yours,

Tom Bradley

TOM BRADLEY
MAYOR

Enclosure

OFFICE OF THE MAYOR

July 1, 1981

TOM BRADLEY
MAYOR

Ms. Vandean Philpott
12042 Lamanda Street, #5
Los Angeles, California   90066

Dear Ms. Philpott:

This will acknowledge receipt of the proposal to establish an "Authentic African Multiservice Cultural Center" transmitted to my office for review.

Please be advised that I have referred your proposal to Ms. Juanita St. John, who is directing a program funded under the auspices of the "Mayor's African Task Force", with a request that your proposal be reviewed and that the Task Force offer any assistance within its capability to do so.

Very truly yours,

TOM BRADLEY
M A Y O R

TB:lh

cc: Juanita St. John

Back to The Future: San Francisco Bay

Somewhat fed up with the Los Angeles scene, especially since the career path on which I found myself did not seem to be pointing toward my returning to Africa any time soon, I began to long for the Bay Area. There, I reasoned, at least people are not so blatantly superficial, nor did they allow cameras to dictate where their commitments should be. The opportunity to return to the Bay presented itself sooner than I anticipated. During that very time, my company decided to open a branch office in San Francisco.

A short time after we learned about the new office, rumors began to abound regarding an in-house search for someone to develop the market and manage operations at the new branch. In addition to having lived in the Bay Area throughout my adult life and therefore, familiar with its turf, I had also earned my MBA and worked in San Francisco State University's School of Business there. Heck, I had connections! Considering all of this and the fact that I had three years of market development and underwriter experience with our company, I had no doubt that I was at least near the very top as a candidate to open and manage that operation. It soon became too clear, however, that I would not get the position when Tina, an underwriter trainee, who had just been hired, was sent from headquarters in New York for more training from our office manager (in operations management), and me (in market development).

While I initially had no idea, she had been selected for the position, given her background (BA in history), I did find Tina to be a nice person, and we became friends instantly. After learning that she had lived in West Africa, as a Peace Corp volunteer, once we'd complete our many training sessions each day, we'd always find a lot to talk about regarding both our experiences in Africa.

She'd also felt comfortable enough to share the difficulty her Italian family had adjusting when they first arrived in America. I would eventually learn that Tina had married an African, whom she brought back to America with her.

Then one day, our Los Angeles branch manager, Mr. Toliver, summoned me to his office to break the news. He congratulated me for being selected to be transferred back to San Francisco, to assist with establishing the new office and to develop the market for the company's international insurance products. When he had not mentioned who was going to head the operations, I asked who the manager would be. Hesitating, to collect himself before answering, he started by telling me how well I had performed in the Los Angeles market, and how highly qualified he thought I was. "However," he continued, "Home office decided that the San Francisco market was not yet ready for an African American female head of operations; therefore, they chose Tina." He went on to explain that while he knew this may be disappointing, I must know that I was "dam good at your [my] job, especially the way you have with people, which is why you were chosen to accompany Tina." As he talked, my mind raced back to a similar situation I'd experienced years earlier.

***

After several years on the job at a major retail store, I had worked my way up to Assistant Manager in the catalog department. Aiming for a position in top management someday, although it was natural for me to do so, I worked hard and was often praised by my boss. Then one day he brought his young nephew, who had just finished High School, and introduced him to the staff as an intern, working with us for the summer. The young man was assigned to me for training, and because of the rapport my manager and I had, I was not alarmed when he requested that I "teach him everything you know about operations." After a curious six months later, the young man was still there.

Then, one day during one of our planning meetings, and after praising me for a job well done, our manager announced that he was moving on, and that this young man would be taking over his position--as our new manager! I was floored. Just as I was about to voice my opinion on the matter and sensing that he already knew I would be disappointed, I stopped and considered that it may not be worth it. I was a full-time student at that time and, besides this being only one of my two part-time jobs, I decided that a protest would possibly end in having to give up one of my much-needed incomes. So, I chose not to fight, and pushed on.

Like the store manager, Toliver went on to share that he'd observed how well Tina and I worked together and believed the two of us would make a good team. "This is why," he said with pride, "I recommended you, highly." While I knew that this comment about getting along with people was meant to make me feel good about my job performance, I also knew that he was referring to several incidents that occurred when I first arrived (during my initial training) in our office, and the manner in which I handled them.

***

Shortly after arriving on my new job (in Los Angeles), I observed that one particular officemate had an interesting sense of humor, and as the office clown, could often bring laughter to what had the makings for a boring office setting. Considering that I was the only African American in the office at that time, and after a few tests to determine if I could take a joke, made me the butt of most of them. While I could have been offended by some, I was determined to not allow his foolishness to upset me. And, I have to admit, some jokes were rather funny. Additionally, at times, to help maintain my alertness after working on a long project, I would find strategies to make his foolishness backfire on him. For example, knowing that I had been to Africa, one afternoon when everyone in the office was practically snoring, he jumped up, came to my desk, and wondered out loud. "Van, you claimed that you've been to Africa. Did you go by airplane?" Appreciating the moment, I looked up and drowsily replied, "Yes." Well, I find that almost impossible. How on earth could a plane land and take off in a jungle," he managed to ask without breaking into laughter. Half-awake by now, and pretending to be alarmed, I responded with another questioned. "So, you don't know?" "No," he said cautiously, knowing I was up to something "Then allow me to explain," I said loudly, knowing that by now besides the attention of the entire office, I had Mr. Toliver's, in the adjoining office, as well.

"You see," I began, "airplanes do not land in Africa--in the jungle. What happens is, there are certain designated spots over which the air pilot hovers. Having been already briefed on where these spots are located, the pilot notifies the stewardesses to ready all those that will depart at that particular destination." Making the story up as I went, I continued. "A passenger will then be fitted with a parachute and guided to the door. Just as the pilot arrives at the designated spot, the plane's door is opened--the door is controlled by the pilot ya know. At about that same time, the pilot calls out to the stewardess, instructing her to push the passenger out, after which he or she would land on the ground--at that very spot, called, the designated point of arrival." Annoyed by now, our officemate asked, "What if the person misses the spot?" "Oh no!" I exclaimed in alarm, "Nine times out of ten, they will land right on the spot, if not, c'est la vie (That's life)!"

On the floor by now, and knowing that her question too would be appropriately addressed, another officemate continues the backfire and asks, "But Van, how do passengers board for his/her return flight?" My peripheral vision caught view of Toliver standing in his doorway. I could tell that he wanted to stop a joke gone bad, but too curious to hear what my reply would be; he just stood there. Knowing that this had to be good, as the entire office waited in anticipation, I paused briefly to think.

More serious than ever now, probably because even I was not sure how the story would unfold, I began. "Oh, this is the easiest part--take off, that is. Considering that rubber is one of West Africa's largest resources, some of it is used quite creatively. What happens in this case is, a big rubber band is placed around two large trees--in the jungle. When a plane, intending to pick up passengers, hovers over the jungle, each passenger is positioned (on the ground) in the middle of this big rubber band. Two men, one behind the other, are poised to pull the passenger back as soon as they get a signal from the pilot." Buying more time to think, I rose from my desk to demonstrate a pulling motion and continued. "When the signal is given, quickly judging the distance between the ground and the airplane door (having very good calculating skills—ya know), the two men pull as far back as necessary, and with a sling shot kind of motion, let go of the passenger, who flies right up to the door of the airplane and is escorted inside by the stewardess." Barely able to contain himself from laughter, hoping that he had not been noticed, Toliver eased back into his office. By now, the entire office was in an uproar. Our office mate mumbled a few curses and rushed back to his desk, not to be heard from the rest of the day.

Shortly before quitting time that day, Toliver telephoned my desk and asked that I remain after work for a meeting. During our meeting he asked how I was able to take so much joking without getting upset. I explained that I did not take my office-mate's joking personally and, like most in the office, it sometimes kept me awake, especially after I'd had a big lunch with a client. After we both had another big laugh about the jungle story, which I admitted to making up as I went, Toliver became serious. He assured me that I did not have to take this or any other nonsense in our workplace and made me promise that I'd let him know if jokes aimed at me from anyone became too much. I assured him that while I could take care of myself, indeed I would.

The jungle story apparently created so much animosity in this my office mate, who was also one of my initial trainers, his jokes slowly became more hostile and inappropriate; they also were beginning to aim more at me. In an attempt to understand his behavior, my mind began to race back to what I'd learned in one of my history classes about the Dutch war with the British and their involvement in the slave trade. This office mate of mine was a Dutchman and had let everyone in our office (most of whom were of British heritage), know how proud he was of his heritage. As fiercely independent and aggressive traders, the Dutch had a long involvement with slavery. Perhaps, considering I was a descent of those enslaved and was now one of his peers, this may explain his animosity toward me, I thought.

***

The Netherlands revolted against Spanish rule in 1572. In retaliation, Spain closed its Iberian ports to Dutch ships. As a countermeasure, the Dutch began to challenge Iberia's monopoly on world trade, and by 1610 they had established several trading posts on Africa's West Coast as well as the Caribbean. In 1621 they proudly established a Fort at the tip of Manhattan and built a wall (where Wall Street is currently situated) to keep out the Native Americans. By 1630, a significant part of South America too had fallen into Dutch hands, and slave trading started almost immediately thereafter.

The first cargo of Africans to be sold as slaves in North America arrived on the East Coast, at a place called New Amsterdam, a name given it by the Dutch. The enslaved were brought from Brazil in 1646 by the Dutch, who, by the 1660's, controlled most all the West African slave posts. Although the English seized New Amsterdam in 1664 and renamed it New York (one of several incidents that led to the Dutch-English War of 1665-67), the Dutch later appeased the English by allowing them access to the British outpost in Suriname, South America, a place they acquired from Britain during the war.

***

One afternoon, I was busy working on a file and chose to ignore the office fun. Toliver had apparently overheard a conversation in which my officemate/trainer declared that there was no way he was going to comply with a request and train me on all the important aspects of his job. Waiting for his usual punch line, someone asked why. Strutting to the middle of the office floor to make sure he had everyone's attention, including mine, he proclaimed, "Once you train one of them, others will follow and eventually they'll have all the jobs." Apparently taking this as *the last straw that broke the camel's back*, Toliver stormed out of his office, red face and all. Although he was clearly upset, he tried to contain himself while summoning my officemate/trainer into his office.

Not caring that everyone could hear him now, Toliver not only warned our officemate against telling anymore jokes, but he also told him that from then on, he would be monitoring all of my trainings and progress personally, and that if he found any lack, appropriate disciplinary actions would be taken. In addition, Toliver arranged for me to attend more outside classes and seminars "to enhance my skills on new product lines." These seminars were held in both Los Angeles and New York, and much of what I learned, I had to introduce to my fellow underwriters upon my return, including our now meek and humble office joker.

In regard to the potential assignment in San Francisco, Toliver went on to assure me that if 1 took the position to help set-up operations in San Francisco, and to establish a market for our products there, if for no other reason but to help him out, he would make sure that even better opportunities came my way in the future. While I was disappointed (even a bit pissed off), once I realized that this was also my ticket back to the Bay Area, I accepted. When I initially accepted the job in Los Angeles, due to my naivety, I did not know that my potential employer was supposed to finance my move from the Bay Area to Los Angeles. Since I had not negotiated it in my initial contract, they didn't. Accepting this position meant they would, at least, send me back to the Bay--in style. Once there, I projected, I would retain this job while planning my future.

Los Angeles Kwanzaa Parade Participants, 1979

It's Time to Move On

Working with Tina at our newly established office in San Francisco was very pleasant, especially considering how gratefully she depended on my knowledge and willingness to help in the areas of management and operations in which she was deficient, which were many. Additionally, I had no one to answer to considering I had mastered my own area of expertise. And, since our salaries were virtually the same (as females, neither of us were making what we were worth), we did, indeed, make a good team. Against this backdrop, I had few complaints.

As he promised earlier, after nearly three years of successes in the Bay Area, Toliver approached me with a new proposition. He had been offered a position in Japan to begin operations there and invited me to go with him as his market developer. While I thought very seriously about accepting his offer, especially considering the additional international experience it would provide, I could not help but acknowledge that yet again, although I would be given all the perks for accompanying and assisting others to excel in their management careers, I was still not being given the opportunity to wear the title myself.

What if, I wondered, the Japanese market was also not ready for an African American woman running things there? In any case, it did not matter; at that juncture my daughters had both graduated from high school, and my desire to return to Africa had re-emerged, and this time, with a force. In fact, having re-involved myself in much of the same cultural activities in Bay Area's African and African American communities, as I had in Los Angeles, my desire to go back to Africa had grown even stronger. Consequently, although I tried my best to be upset about my superior's refusal to offer me a position (in management) I deserved, I could not help but reflect on both the training and other opportunities I'd received during the five plus years spent with this

229

company, which I felt good about. Not only had I traveled to several major cities to assist with training and/or to receive training myself, when an opportunity for me to participate in a Model Organization for African Unity (OAU) conference, being held in Washington, D.C. (although it had little to do with my job), Toliver allowed me the time off to attend.

And I still smile when I'd recall my stepmother's excitement during her visit with us in Los Angeles, another opportunity resulting from my working for this company. Save for her visits with us to the Bay Area during my graduations, she had never ventured beyond Mississippi and Chicago. She was beside herself with excitement when she discovered what was in store for her in Los Angeles.

My mother arrived in Los Angeles during the time my girls and I were involved (as volunteers), with organizing the City's Annual Kwanzaa Parade. On the day of the parade, the organizing committee members were each assigned a limousine in which to accompany one or more of the many participating celebrities. Having already arranged that my girls ride on the floats, I volunteered my mother to ride with one of the television stars. That star turned out to be Ms. Marla Gibbs (one of her favorites) from the Jefferson's show. My dear mother talked about that experience

Actress Marla Gibbs and my mother, Arris Harris, at Kwanzaa Parade, 1979

until the day she died--three years later.

Posing with other model OAU participants on the steps of our nation's Capital, 1981.

So, while I could have viewed my current situation as a disappointment, it was impossible to do so. I was not only pleased to have given my mother the opportunity to visit two of California's most popular localities San Francisco's Bay area and Los Angeles, my father would also visit these places. Besides, I had already resolved that I was not interested in going any further West in pursuit of developing my career. My oldest daughter had already finished high school by the time we were to return to the Bay Area and decided that she wanted to remain in the Los Angeles area and attend Santa Monica Junior College. My youngest had returned with me and completed high school, after which she headed off to Howard University, in Washington, D.C. It was, indeed, time for me to move on.

I'd become restless with my job sooner than I expected, and after nearly three years, began searching for anything that offered opportunities that would allow me to work in Africa. I was eventually encouraged by a friend, who convinced me that my chances were better if I lived on the East Coast. Having taught at Johns Hopkins School of Advance International Studies (SAIS) in Washington, D.C. he suggested that I apply for the PhD program there. I did so, and shortly after turning down Toliver's offer. I was accepted at SAIS.

Me, shortly After arriving a John Hopkins University, in Washington, DC, 1983

Late Summer

Van Goes [Back] to Washington

By now I had traveled to D.C. on several occasions and was pretty familiar with its politically laced culture. Therefore, I was already prepared to change gears from the laid-back lifestyle that the San Francisco's Bay Area offered. Additionally, having participated in at least two seminars on diplomacy, held in D.C. in the past, I was also ready for any challenge life would offer within the Beltway, at least I thought I was.

Although my purpose for going to D.C. this time was to attend Johns Hopkins School of Advanced International Studies (SAIS), in pursuit of a PhD in International Trade and Economics, while living in the D.C. area I would be exposed to, and learn much more, especially about how our country's decision-makers and other power brokers operate. Besides school, I landed part-time jobs (at different times), at both the Brookings Institute and the Overseas Development Council. And, while there, besides them, I learned about the many other "Think Tanks" that researched everything from why people buy certain pets to how different ethnic groups react to poverty. I recall feeling it a bit unnerving that peoples' way of life was studied to such a degree.

Upon registering at SAIS, I discovered that since my past studies focused on the business aspect of international, it was necessary to do a prep course, in the Department of International Studies, in order to prepare for my new area in Trade and Economics. After qualifying for this one-year program, one would have earned an additional master's degree. It was shortly after this first year at SAIS that it became necessary for me to return to the Bay Area to attend to some important personal business that had not turned out as expected. It was also during this time I would meet the man that was to father my long-awaited son.

***

As I stood in line, along with the other proud new students on that first day of registration at SAIS, several of the students started complaining about how long, and how slow the lines were moving. Some began boasting that were it up to them, they would conduct the registration process in a different manner. When a young man standing directly behind me asked how, and no one had a reply, he jokingly pointed out that since we all knew that we were thrilled to be there, what we were doing amounted to whining. While the group stood silently waiting for someone to defend us, Souman (the young man who posed the question) and I, simultaneously, started laughing. Within seconds the others caught on and joined us.

Having formally introduced himself to me earlier, I already knew that Souman was from the Republic of Benin. He'd also informed me that he was at SAIS pursuing an additional Master's in International Relations. As my mind wandered back to the incident that happened during my first visit to Benin, I thought (out loud), "How interesting!' Forcing me back into the present, Souman asked why Americans always used that [phrase] when they can't think of anything else to say. Finding some truth in his inquiry, I paused to think before answering. "Ya know," I said bewilderingly, "I don't know," after which we both began laughing again, only this time almost uncontrollably, which made everyone else start again also, although I'm not sure they knew what they were laughing about at this time.

Taking an even closer look at him, that day, I concluded that Souman had a delightful sense of humor. I also observed how strikingly he resembled the men on my mother's side of our family, which immediately put me at ease with him. Like most of my family members, one would think he was Asian, were it not for his beautiful dark chocolate complexion. From that point on, Souman and I were on our way to becoming inseparable friends.

I would learn later that while my new friend and I were in different areas of study, we both were in the same African Studies Department. Although he was more interested in the political aspect of Africa's development, as opposed to my area of economic development, I would soon discover also, that we shared many of the same classes. As a result, along with several other students, we eventually became study partners.

As I examined Souman more closely, I'd noted that he had a striking resemblance to my brother and cousins, and that he was extremely handsome. Yet, I was not attracted to him in that manner. After pondering why, I concluded that since he reminded me of so many members of my family, being intimately involved with him would almost be like dating one of my cousins; or even worst, my own brother.

Later on, after we got to know each other better, I would often tease Souman about his never-ending flirtations with the female students at SAIS, many of whom seemed to not help being attracted to him. As a matter of fact, I respected him for not seriously pursuing their overt advances, although he admitted to having "fun with some of them." Not quite sure why these women were so enthralled with him, Souman would often confide in me when some became too bold. Eventually, however, our relationship somehow evolved, and the next thing I knew, only one year after my arrival at SAIS, I was pregnant.

Once I discovered my pregnancy, I was extremely perplexed on how it could have happened. After all, my youngest child had just turned twenty and was attending Howard University a few blocks away. Hadn't I advised both my daughters, just before they each set out for college, not to come home pregnant. Having laced my warning with what I'd referred to as the three B's, I jokingly recited the lyrics of a song that conveyed the same message: "Be young, Be foolish, and Be happy," but added, just don't come home pregnant. Upon their departures, I had finally begun to live a life of freedom and independence (semi, at least) and here I was, nearly thirty-eight years of age, and it was I who had gone away to college and gotten pregnant. Was this my fate in this life, I wondered, to get pregnant just as I was about to embark upon something significant, or life changing. Indeed, this was a mystery.

Sitting in the doctor's office on the day I was told of my condition, I could not help but scold myself for having let my guard down. Reflecting on the possible cooperate, I recalled having chosen the revolutionary infra-uterus device (IUD) as a birth control method. Trusting that it would not cause harm, since my doctor, at the time, recommended it after my body had rejected "The Pill", the device was inserted but eventually traveled out of its proper position and had to be removed surgically. After the surgery I was told that the likelihood of my conceiving again was very slim. Still in shock that day, my reflections turned to the evening my new "best friend" and I set out on a trip to New York.

Attending Johns Hopkins with students from some of America's most affluent families, when these students would take off to places anywhere in the entire world they chose, those of us with fewer resources found other activities with which to busy ourselves during semester breaks. After convincing ourselves that we too deserved a break sometime, while we clearly could not afford a trip abroad. Souman and I reasoned that we could at least take a drive up the coast one holiday weekend.

In preparation for our trip, I arranged with my friend Rachael, who was attending the Columbia School of Law in New York at the time, to put us up for the two nights of our planned get-a-way. Rachael and I became friends during my early years in California. We had not seen each other since my last visit several years earlier, when my company sent me to New York to attend a training seminar on a new insurance product line. She was as excited as we about our visit and promised to spend the entire weekend showing us around New York. I was equally excited to be able to share this experience with Souman, since I was not sure if he had ever traveled beyond the D.C. area at that time.

It was about three o'clock that Friday afternoon before we left the D.C. area, and neither Souman nor I knew what we were in for. With great expectations, we headed toward the Beltway with carefully mapped out plans to reach the Bay in Baltimore by 4:00 pm, at which time we'd take our first break (at the Board Walk), before continuing up highway 95, no later than 5:30 pm. This way, we reasoned, we would be on highway 83, which was a straight shot to New York, by 7:00 pm. We'd surely be in New York by 10:00, no later than 10:30 pm, we reasoned.

I realized that our plans were a bit naive the moment we turned on to the Beltway. The roads were so crowded heading out of D.C. that holiday weekend, I thought (out loud), that everyone within the area must have the made same exact plans as we. Having agreed not to stop at the Board Walk, since it was nearly 8:30 pm when we turned off the Beltway and headed toward Baltimore, I was already showing signs of fatigue. Souman did not have a driver's license and could not assist with the driving.

Having passed through Baltimore, where traffic seemed even worst, it was well on the way to 10:00 pm when we approached the small town of Towson. It was at that point I realized that we had not even departed the State of Maryland. Souman and I agreed that there was no way we would reach New York that night and decided to stop for an overnight rest at the hotel we were approaching. We agreed that we should call Rachael to let her know what happened, and of our new plan to start afresh early the next morning. Since our modest budget did not allow us the luxury of getting two rooms, reasoning that we were both mature enough to do so, we agreed to share a room. After all, we agreed laughingly, "we valued our friendship much too much to ruin it by committing an intimate act without us being an item."

Acknowledging that since it was I who must have been the most exhausted, from the stop-and-go traffic during our short (in terms of mileage) but tedious drive, Souman insisted I take the bed, while he'd retire on the small sofa in our room. I didn't argue. When I finished my shower, however, Souman had fallen asleep on the other side of the bed, where he'd been watching television, which was apparently easier than watching it from the sofa. Not having the heart to wake him up, I eased onto the other side and fell asleep also. Early the next morning, we both woke up at the same time. Souman apologized for sleeping on the bed with me and decided to give me a kiss as appreciation for not awaking him. The rest is history.

***

It had been over a year since I arrived in Washington, D.C. and my household effect had still not arrived from California. I had been talking with the moving company that picked up my belongings before I left California over the past ten months or so, trying to understand why they had not transported them, when I discovered that their telephone had been disconnected! It was then that I decided it was imperative that I go back immediately and investigate.

After making my case for not attending school during the upcoming semester to both the school officials and my closest friends, including Souman, who had difficulty understanding why "these material things meant more than remaining at SAIS until I'd finished my program." I did not quite know how to convey that having grown up with not one picture of my mother or grandparents, and only one of me and my sister from our childhood, I needed to make sure my children would not have the same experience. Although Souman tried hard to convince me to stay, I explained that while I was not so concerned about the furniture, the thought of losing a lifetime of my children', photos, school and other family documents, including those of their deceased father, was simply too much for me to bear. I was not sure he understood, but eventually he finally gave up trying, and I made preparations to leave.

Exactly one week before my planned departure date back to California, I began having a perpetual upset stomach. Initially thinking that it must be something I had eaten during another trip I had taken to Florida. to visit my father's sisters the previous weekend, I tried to ignore this apparent stomach virus. After the "bug" persisted for several days, I decided to see a doctor before my impending 3,500-mile trip across country. The result of my examination was given after the doctor called and insisted on seeing me the day before I was to leave for California.

I had thought long and hard that evening about telling Souman of my situation. Ultimately, I decided not to. After all, he had come to America to pursue his education, not to get caught up in something that negated his efforts. Deciding to handle the matter alone, I went ahead preparing myself for the long trip back to California.

Reflecting on the two other significant relationships I'd had since Jimmy passed away, I was not able to get much sleep the night before my departure. I had actually refused the marriage proposal of one of them because I knew he wanted children, and I was not sure if I could have any more. I cared about this person so much I had secretly tried to conceive. So, by now I was sure I could not, which is why I had long stopped using any form of birth control. In fact, I was among the group of women suing for damages, as a result of the implanted IUD gone wrong.

Against this backdrop, I wondered how this could have happened, and why had fate chosen Souman to father a child with me; someone who lived on the other side of the world--in Africa. Besides, by now I was well aware that there was someone else waiting for Souman to make a decision about her future. More importantly, now that I had raised my children, I had my own future aspirations, and finally the freedom to pursue them. At this juncture, marriage was not in my plans.

Extremely concerned about how my daughters would feel about my pregnancy, by the time I reached California, I had convinced myself that there was no way I could bring this child into the world, and, in effect, become a single parent again, especially after having already raised two children to adulthood. And, while I had successfully done so, I wasn't about to trust fate any further. Gee, I thought, it seemed that each time I embarked on something life changing...

During the next several days of traveling back across the country, it crossed my mind that maybe I should have shared my condition with Souman. Considering my background with Africans, maybe it was my destiny to marry one, I thought. I quickly rejected that idea, however. Having studied African history extensively, as well as having lived among and worked with Africans in the past, I understood too well the vast differences in our cultures. I also knew of the many differences in the past and current value and social systems that could cause a myriad of problems that would act adversely on the best of relationships. And, although I sometimes wished I'd grown up in Africa, I had not. Besides, I was not about to leave my two girls to go off and live that far away from them, possibly forever, in Africa or anywhere else. Having considered all this, it had become very clear what I had to do.

***

Several areas of my previous graduate studies had focused on the breakdown of traditional life in Africa during and after the colonial period. During these studies, I learned about young people, especially young men, who left the traditional life of their village to become city-dwellers or to live abroad. After becoming accustomed to city ways and/or receiving western education, many began seeking a more sophisticated mate. If they could not find one in their own village or was unlucky enough to fall in love with someone while living abroad, many would take the chance and marry the "outsider."

Additionally, I reflected on the sad endings to such situations while working at the Nigerian Consulate in San Francisco, where I witnessed first-hand the many American women that came through seeking help from the Consul General, attempting to get their children back. After living in Africa for years with their African spouses, some of them had returned to America completely broken. They were products of the differences in the value systems mentioned earlier--those that even love could not conquer.

Believing that love would prevail however, young Africans, who left their homes, often broke customs when they married an outsider without their family's approval, which is still a custom throughout much of Africa. After acting on their own, some honestly tried to integrate their foreign spouse into their family upon returning home, only to find that he or she, was rejected. Still infatuated with having a foreign spouse and, in an effort to keep them happy or to encourage them to stay, the African spouse often made extreme concessions and sacrifices, thus creating more resentment in the community.

As for the foreign spouse, after the initial impact of living in a completely different culture wears off, they still had little to no idea how traditional norms would affect their everyday lives; especially that of a female, whose behavior, and expectations to both her in-laws and to people outside her home is under constant scrutiny. Even if she had been somewhat prepped before following her husband to his country, little did she know that she would still be confronted with issues never dreamed of during her western up bringing.

A close friend, who'd gone through this situation explained that "in the beginning, her spouse (as did others in their community with foreign spouses) had initially made every effort and/or concession possible to accommodate them. After the novelty of having someone different from the rest began wearing off, however, or perhaps after maturity, their African spouses seemed to begin appreciating the need to be more aligned with their traditional way of life and wanting to participate more with their peers, he/she soon began understanding that to continue going against cultural norms was not in their best interest. As a result, the concessions become fewer or stop altogether." Although by now, the foreign spouse may have grown in understanding and tries harder to adapt to his/her new-found situation, without his/her spouse's sympathy and support "life became a living hell," especially in a village setting. Because of these new circumstances, and without the support of their far away family and friends, finding it harder to cope, the "pampered" outsider, now faced the inevitable choice to leave; often without their children. In many parts of Africa, the children produced in a union belong to the male's family. Jomo, Kenyatta agrees. In his book, *Facing Mount Kenya*, Kenya's former president confirms that this is the traditional attitude throughout Africa:

A few detribalized Gikuyu, while they are away from home for some years, have thought it fit to denounce the custom and to marry uncircumcised girls, especially from coastal tribes, thinking that they could bring them back to their fathers' home without offending their parents. But to their surprise they found that their fathers, mothers, brothers, and sisters, following the tribal custom, are not prepared to welcome, as a relative in-law, anyone who has not fulfilled the ritual qualification for matrimony. Therefore, a problem has faced these semi-detribalized Gikuyu when they wanted to return to their homeland."

Kenyatta goes on to explain that if their sons wish to receive the blessings of their parents, and be accepted back into their family and clan, "They must divorce the wife married outside the rigid tribal custom and then marry a girl with the approved tribal qualification. Failing this, they have been turned out and disinherited." This attitude, explained and defended in chapter six (*The Initiation of Boys and Girls*), also defends the circumcision process among the Gikuyu. I must admit that until I read his entire book, I was totally against circumcision (female and male) which Kenyatta compares to the Jewish practice, in relation to the whole teaching of tribal law, religion, and morality. After getting a better understanding of the African perspective on family in general, and women in particular, who are viewed as "the salt of the earth [as] they have the most sacred duty of creating and rearing future generations...and therefore are looked upon as the connecting link between one generation and another."

Kenyatta defends that "women must be protected and cared for, not mutilated as suggested by people who do not understand their customs." Given this new perspective, in which the conversation on circumcision is so embedded, I began to wonder that if indeed our society were held to such high moral standards as he describes, perhaps we would have fewer single parent families. And, maybe, young women and their children may not have such a tough time surviving under our current social value system. For the readers who desire a better understanding of how Africans sees life, especially their views on the female and her importance in maintaining the African family, I highly recommend this book. For those who may not have access to it, I have decided to include a portion dealing with the subject of circumcision, especially in relation to the rites of passage of young boys and girls, in an addendum at the end of this chapter.

***

Back in California, when I finally worked up enough nerve to discuss my options with a doctor, he insisted a test be taken to make sure I still had options. After the test results returned, for some reason the doctor asked if I was interested in knowing the baby's gender. When he informed me that the child I was carrying was a boy, I was floored. My thoughts immediately raced back to what my mother had predicted during her spiritual visits with me during my childhood--that I would have three children, two girls and a boy. I quickly jumped off the examination table, got dressed, excused myself, and literally ran out of the doctor's office.

Embracing my mother's words, it was then that I realized I was living a life that had been divinely orchestrated. Although I did wonder why he was appearing so late, after the revelation that I was finally getting this long-awaited son, I had no concern about how I was going to manage raising him at this stage in my life. And, while this too would later reveal itself, at that point I decided to let the situation unfold the way I knew it was going to anyway. Concluding that my girls would just have to understand, I was pleased, though not surprised, to learn that they were delighted at having a little brother. They both returned home for his birth.

Jonathan daydreaming about mom at 3 months, 1985

Addendum
The Initiation of Boys and Girls

The initiation of both sexes is the most important custom among the Gikuyu. It is looked upon as a deciding factor in giving a boy or girl the status of manhood or womanhood in the Gikuyu community. This custom is adhered to by the vast majority of African peoples and is found in almost every part of the continent. It is therefore necessary to examine the facts attached to this widespread custom in order to have some idea why the African people cling to this custom which, in the eyes of a good many Europeans, is nothing but a "horrible" and "painful" practice, suitable only to barbarians. The Gikuyu name for this custom of rite de passage from childhood to adulthood is irua, (circumcision), or trimming genital organs, of both sexes. The dances and songs connected with the initiation ceremony are called mambura, (rituals or divine services). It is important to note that the moral code of the tribe is bound up with this custom and that it symbolizes the unification of the whole tribal organization. This is the principal reason why irua plays such an important part in the life of the Gikuyu people.

The irua marks the commencement of participation in various governing groups in the tribal administration, because the real age-groups begin from the day of the physical operation. The history and legends of people are explained and remembered according to the names given to various age-groups at the time of the initiation ceremony. For example, if a devastating famine occurred at the time of the initiation, that particular group would be known as ngauagu {famine}. In the same way, the Gikuyu have been able to record the time when the European introduced a number of maladies such as syphilis into Gikuyu country, for those initiated at the time when this disease first showed itself are called gate go.

Historical events are recorded and remembered in the same manner. Without this custom a tribe which had no written records would not have been able to keep a record of important events and happenings in the life of the Gikuyu nation. Any child who is not corrupted by detribalization is able to record in his mind the whole history and origin of the Gikuyu people through the medium of such names as Agu, Ndemi and Mathathi, etc. who were initiated hundreds of years ago. For years there has been much criticism and agitation against irua of girls by certain misinformed missionary societies in East Africa, who see only the surgical side of the irua and, without investigating the psychological importance attached to this custom by the Gikuyu, these missionaries draw their conclusion that the irua of girls is nothing but a barbarous practice and, as such, should be abolished by law.

On the other hand, the Gikuyu look upon these religious fanatics with great suspicion. The overwhelming majority of them believe that it is the secret aim of those who attack this centuries-old custom to disintegrate their social order and thereby hasten their detribalization. The abolition of irua will destroy the tribal symbol which identifies the age-groups and prevent the Gikuyu from perpetuating that spirit of collectivism and national solidarity which they have been able to maintain since their beginnings.[9]

---

[9] *Excepted from Facing M. Kenya, by Jomo Kenyatta. PP 129-130, Random House October 1965.

A Missed Opportunity?

Shortly after my son's first birthday, I returned with him to D.C., and not long thereafter, obtained a job in the corporate community again. After about two years, and due to my continual participation in African oriented cultural events, I received a job offer from Africare, an African American Development organization that performs development projects throughout the African continent. It was at this organization that I met and befriended Gladys, from Ghana. During some of our many conversations, I shared with Gladys that my great-grandfather may have come from Ghana. When I mentioned that his last name was Ware, she exclaimed jokingly that I could be the descendant of royalty. More serious now, Gladys went on to inform me about the two Asantehenes (kings), that she knew of with that same last name.

As I mentioned earlier, Katakyi Opoku Ware I, was an Okoyo king that ruled the Ashanti people from 1720 to 1750. Gladys explained further that he was credited with being an "empire builder" of the now disbanded Ashanti Confederacy and had fought successful battles which initiated the Ashanti takeover of the Gold Coast and the Ivory Coast between 1741 and 1744. King Opoku Ware I had two children whose names were Adusei Atwenewa and Adusei Kra.

The second king from the Ware line was Opoku Ware II. Born in 1919, Gladys explained that because he was contemporary, she was more familiar with him. Upon completing college at Kwame Nkrumah University in Ghana, Kwaku Adusei (his Ashanti name) attended school in the United Kingdom where he earned a degree in law. He worked as a lawyer in Accra after returning to Ghana and later, established a practice in Kumasi where he eventually became involved in Ashanti politics. He was nominated king in 1970 after the death of his uncle, King Prempeh II, but before becoming the Asanethene he was appointed Ambassador to Italy. According to Gladys, because of his commitment to the country as a whole, King Opoku II was well respected throughout Ghana.

During some of my earlier readings, I speculated that since my great-grandfather's first name was Ephraim, considering his African background, he may have been associated with the Black Hebrews of Ghana. In his book entitled *From Babylon to Timbuktu*, Rudolph Windsor describes the customs of the Black Jews who had lived in Ghana among the Ashanti. In fact, Windsor points out that having migrated there from the Mediterranean, Black Hebrews inhabited the entire Niger River bend as far back as the 13th century. These countries included the Ivory Coast, Togo, Dahomey (the now Republic of Benin), Upper Volta and Nigeria.

Windsor goes on to discuss how the Black Jews, called the Emo Yo Quaim, of Southern Nigerians, are viewed by others in their area. He says that other Nigerians see them as "Strange People," and explains that these Black Jews refer to themselves by the Hebrew name "B'nai Ephraim" or "Sons of Ephraim." Wait a minute--there's my great grand-father's name again! In the Bible, Ephraim was the name given to one of Joseph's two sons he'd had with his Egyptian wife, who had been given to him by Pharaoh Ahmose I (1580 B.C.) after making Joseph, Prime Minister over Egypt "because of his good work" (Gen. 41:17-44). Could my distant ancestors have come *out of Egypt*, as well?

Windsor expounds that these Nigerians claim that their Jewish ancestors migrated from Morocco, and that this claim is supported by their current language, which is a mixture of Maghribi Arabic and that of the local Nigerians, the Yorubas (see p.131). Pointing out that while they [the Jews] still use the Torah as their spiritual guides, "Their social life is not Torah-controlled, but mimic those of the Ashanti (Ghana) Jews."

***

I had worked at Africare's D.C. Headquarters nearly three years when I was asked to go to Nigeria and manage the operations at its headquarters in Lagos. So, with my little son Jonathan in tow, I was finally off. I would spend the next several years realizing my dream of living, working and traveling on the African continent.

During my tenure in Nigeria, I got the opportunity to attend the First African/African American Summit which King Opokee, also attended. The brainchild of Dr. Leon Sullivan, this first summit was held in the Ivory Coast in 1991. As an employee of Africare I attended the summit as a "worker bee" and did not have much time to mingle with the royalty. I did, however, get to see the King--from a distance. Unfortunately, he and his wife and their entourage were surrounded by so many guards and dignitaries it was impossible to get anywhere near them. Even if I had gotten near, I am not sure I would have been brave enough to ask any questions. And although I worked with some of his staff, it never occurred to me to try and secure a future audience with the King through them.

King Opoku II died in 1995. Although he and his wife, Victoria, had three children, I only know the name of one (Prince Akyeme-Hene). Interestingly enough, while working in Nigeria I would discover that people with Souman's surname also lived in Ghana. Almost overwhelmed by what I felt may have been a missed opportunity (by not exploring both names further), I decided to leave this research to Jonathan, or to future generations of our family that may be interested. It appears that my descendants have their research work cut out for them.

Thank God Almighty, I'm Free at Last

Living in Nigeria was exciting but challenging. Nonetheless, I felt like my spirit had returned home. By now (1990) I knew that I was destined to travel the world just as my maternal great-grand father had done over a hundred years earlier. Finally, I was actually living in the motherland! My only regret was that I did not get to send for my dad as I'd planned.

After losing a second mother (Arris), I had vowed to make sure my father would visit every place in Africa in which I got the privilege of living; especially after, while visiting us in the D.C. area, he surprised me with the revelation that because of his

MARCH 1991   THE CONTINENT

Africare appoints Ex-John Hopkins University (SAIS) Students , Administrative Officer for Nigeria

Ms. Vandean Philpott and Jonathan her son.

The new administrative officer of AFRICARE in Nigeria is Ms. Vandean Philpott graduate of the Johns Hopkins School of Advanced International Studies (SAIS), 1982-84. Ms. Philpott until her recent appointment served AFRICARE in various capacities for about four years at AFRICARE's headquarters in Washington, D.C. An Africanist and mother of three children, Ms. Philpott also an MBA holder confided to one of our staff reporter at Dulles Airport, "I'm happy to be going home to Africa and hopefully contribute effectively to the development process in Nigeria."

AFRICARE is one of the few African-American founded non-profit organization that is promoting grassroots development in many African countries, including Nigeria. Ms. Philpott is based at Ikoye where AFRICARE office is located.

Jonathan and I just before leaving for Nigeria, 1990.

mechanical skills, he had received a job offer to work in Africa when he was younger. He shared that he turned down the opportunity because he felt it more important to bring me and my siblings to live with him in Chicago at the time.

Unfortunately, my father made his transition while my son and I were in the air flying back from Nigeria to visit him after I received notice of his illness. The next year, however, my youngest daughter spent her school summer break with us, during which time we traveled four countries along Africa's West Coast. My oldest daughter would spend time with us later in Southern Africa.

While living in Nigeria was, indeed, a challenge at times, admittedly, I enjoyed every minute of it—well, most of the time. The friendliness, the smells, the social life, the ease of living with people who all looked like me, the real taste of the African foods I'd become familiar with back in the San Francisco Bay Area, all played a role in making the challenges worth it. And, while I was supposed to be living in a poor "third world" country, it was in Nigeria that I first had the experience of flying on a private jet, sailing on a luxury private yacht, and belonging to an elite country club.

Although I was serious about my work and extremely dedicated to doing the best job possible, I was afforded, and enjoyed (as shown below) many the amenities of working for an African American development organization in Africa as well. Further, it was while we were in Nigeria that a string of events happened that let me know why my son had made his appearance at this point in my life. The following are only a few of many occasions that my son, whom I'd begun calling my guardian angel, changed what could have been negative experiences into something good and positive.

After about one year in Nigeria, however, things were getting pretty tough "again" for the locals. Prices began rising so rapidly that it had become difficult for the average family to afford staples such as baked goods (loaves of bread), sugar, gari (a local staple), fresh milk, butter, etc. The situation had not yet impacted the wealthier families or foreign workers like me, who could easily benefit from the ever-increasing exchange rates. So, knowing that I could get more Naira (Nigeria's currency) for my dollars, to make life a bit easier for my domestic staff (which consisted of a housekeeper, a driver, a gardener, and a security guard), I decided to increase their salaries to offset the increase in food prices and other basics they needed.

Jonathan and Janie, with some friends she made while visiting us in Nigeria, 1991.

Additionally, having control over my organization's operating budget, I also increased the salaries of our local staff and/or augmented those difficult to obtain staples they needed by purchasing these items in bulk and distributing them among those that wanted them. Nevertheless, it was still a bit disconcerting when we continued to get warnings that "they" were coming, especially after hearing that the neighborhood in which my son and I lived had been targeted. "They" were the notorious robbers I'd heard about since the early days of my experience with Nigerians. These robbers conducted extravagant home invasions in upscale neighborhoods.

According to the stories being circulated, when Nigeria's economy began to "squeeze the life out of its people," gangs of armed robbers would take from the rich to feed the poor--and themselves. Their colorful mode of operation was to let targeted families, whom they thought benefited from the crisis, know in advance that they were coming after them. Neighborhoods in which foreigners lived were key targets. These gangs were so strong and well organized "even the police could not stop them from going after their targeted victims, once a promise had been made to do so." In fact, rumor had it that some of these gangs were led by the police!

My son and I resided in what one would consider a ritzy suburb just outside of Lagos called Ikoyi, and our block had finally received notice that we were next on the list--two weeks from the date of our notice, in fact. According to those who had past experience, the robbers would probably start from the first house on the block, assaulting one house each night until they reached the end, at which time they would give a one-day notice to their next victim.

Upon the first notice, many on our block had begun their home leaves until the troubles had passed, taking with them as many of the valuables as they could carry. Those remaining were advised to have money in the house, and not resist the robbers if they wished to stay alive.

When the robberies began, I was simply amazed that it was happening just as I had been told. In fact, it was happening exactly how I'd seen it enacted on a weekly Nigerian television soap opera earlier that year.

***

My residence was situated on the ground level in a four-plex apartment structure owned by a rich Nigerian, whom I was told (after I had already moved in), that very few people liked. His family resided in one unit while the other three were rented to three other foreign tenants that included my friend Veronique, who lived on the second level across from the owner's flat. Veronique was from Cameroon and worked as a secretary for her embassy. I was also told, later, that to maximize his money, our landlord would only rent to foreigners because he knew he could charge a higher rental fee. My little son and I lived in the first unit closest to the entry gate, making ours likely to be the first hit.

As our time grew nearer, I noticed that our building's owner, who lived in the flat above us, had increased the guards securing the entrance to our complex. In addition, he installed steel bars blocking the entry to the second floor where he and his family resided. He had also acquired two big German shepherds and kept them just inside, behind the barred upstairs entrance. Although I wasn't afraid initially, by now I was beginning to feel a bit anxious, especially after the local staff jokingly teased that "the security guards were useless in times like these, because on that night, to save their own lives, they would only run away." I recall asking myself why on earth had I brought my little child into this mess.

As the robbers progressed down our block and closer to our home, I'd hear stories about the "brave ones" (mostly foreigners) who were beaten, raped, or even killed, "attempting to hold on to their precious worldly possessions." Trying to remain positive, I resolved that the robbers could have everything they wanted in my house (except me of course) and that if I'd come to Africa only to die by the hands of my African brothers--so be it. I prayed, though, that my little son be spared.

However, when the people two houses down from us where robbed, Dewitt, a fellow American with whom I worked, insisted that Jonathan and I stay at his apartment, in another part of Lagos, for a week or so, or at least until after they finished robbing my house, and our block. I agreed that perhaps this was a good idea. So, I paid my domestic staff a week's salary and left. Two days later, our security guard came to my office to inform me that we could return home now. He also told me that while our compound had indeed been hit, my unit had been passed over. The unit next to me, however, had been stripped clean. This unit belonged to a Lebanese gentleman, who left temporarily for the same reasons we did. The two units upstairs were apparently so well protected the robbers didn't bother to attempt fooling with the dogs.

Perplexed at understanding why the robbers passed over such an easy target as my unit, I asked a group of my Nigerian neighbors, consisting mostly of servants, standing outside buzzing about the latest tragedies, when I arrived that evening, why? While the rest stood buzzing among themselves, one person spoke up and explained that it was because I was "Mama Jonathan (Jonathan's mother), and that everyone knew that!" Although I found his answer puzzling, I said "Okaaay," and returned to my apartment, while they chuckled. I learned later that the entire community knew Jonathan, the barely six-year-old little American boy who played with everyone, including the servant's children. Hearing this, my mind rushed back to a conversation I'd had with our landlord shortly after we moved in. He had come down to my unit to let me know that I "needed to correct" my housekeeper.

***

Once colonization ended, many of Nigeria's elite had adopted and maintained the behavior of their former rulers, that is, allowing their "domestics" to live in quarters constructed for them in the back of the colonizers' homes. Many of these workers would bring their entire family to live in these one-room or two-rooms (in a few cases) spaces. During the daytime hours, while most "Augas" (bosses) were at work, when they were not playing out back, the children of their "domestics" would play games like football (soccer) on the streets with each other. One day, my landlord had stopped at my unit to inform me that during my absence, my housekeeper, Portia, who did not have children of her own, was allowing my son to play with the children of the neighborhood's servants, and that he'd found that unacceptable.

When I told my landlord that I did not mind, as long as the children got along with each other, he looked at me in amazement and warned that if this was allowed to continue, Jonathan was no longer permitted to play with his two boys. When I simply replied, "That's fine," he jumped up, looked at me with a puzzled look on his face, and just before storming out, told me not to expect his family to take Jonathan to the country club with them again either. "Fine," I replied, "We have our own membership passes, anyway." I had not realized that my housekeeper heard the entire conversation. So, I instructed her to allow Jonathan to continue playing with his many neighborhood friends. Here, I feel is a good point at which to discuss colonialism and its effects on the colonized in Africa. I'll get back to our experiences, in Nigeria, shortly thereafter.

***

There is an old African saying that states, "When the whites came to our country, we had the land, and they had the Bible; now we have the Bible, and they have the land..." Colonialism had arrived in Africa on the heels of slavery. Around the mid 1800's

Me, at a wedding while living in Africa.

when traders in slavery decided it to be less profitable, given the world's attitude about the inhumanity of the institution, it had drawn to an end. More importantly, the need for free labor was declining since the new industrial period, while the need for more and more raw materials was rising. Thus, European countries that wanted to be in the forefront of this period, needed to find other ways to develop this newly profitable state that had ignited a new world order. The cheapest way to get these materials, they decided, was to control the land that produced them, and the people who could work this land, thus colonization was instituted.

Before colonization began taking root in Africa, European powers had already established posts along the coasts of the continent, which had been used to successfully store the human resources they exported throughout the world. Since these resources were being brought to them (at these posts), the white traders saw no need to penetrate Africa's unknown interior. It was decided that this same strategy could be used to transport and store the many natural resources contained throughout the continent; thus, Europeans set out on the "Scramble for Africa."

History records several events within Europe that finally led to this scramble. First, an American explorer named Henry Stanley was sent to the Congo by King Leopold of Belgium, to make treaty arrangements with various African chiefs. Having successfully attained this goal in a number of places, his prestige escalated so much that in 1884 Leopold expressed the desire to increase his wealth. By the end of the century then, he could claim an area in the center of Africa equal to the size of all Western Europe.

The second event would show up when Otto von Bismarck, Chancellor of the German Empire, who's goal was to create competition between his enemies, (England and France), and thus improve his position on the European continent at the same time, achieved a similar goal. Around 1885, the Chancellor succeeded after sending his agents to the territories of Cameroon, Togoland, Tanganyika (today's Tanzania), and Southwest Africa. Fearing that

Belgium and Germany would use their African territories as pawns in the on-going power struggle in Europe, other European powers, desiring some of Africa's wealth, followed suit. and the third rush for African colonies began.

By the end of the 19th century, the competition was over when, without the input of Africans, Europeans convened a conference in Berlin and "laid out the rules of the game"--that is, how to split up the Continent among themselves. During this conference they all agreed that while there would be no slave trading, and no interference in the territories of other European powers, in order to achieve their goal, it was necessary to control the hearts and minds of the Africans.

For centuries thereafter, Christian missionaries from Europe began building European styled churches, schools, and hospitals which became important colonial apparatuses. When the scramble was over, only Ethiopia and Liberia were left uncolonized. The educated African elite, like my Nigerian landlord, benefited most while the common man was left feeling bitter resentment. Thus, home invasions by the have-not became a form of coping when the situation became unbearable for them.

Getting back to my experiences, the following is another drama that took place while we were living in Nigeria, during which my little son proved, once again, to be my rock because of his ability to take charge in those rare occasions when I'd just lose it. On this occasion Jonathan got us put up (for the night), in a luxury hotel after we found ourselves stranded overnight at a local airport, in Southern Nigeria, free of charge. During this ordeal, and after having failed at getting any sympathy from airport officials when I explained my situation, I became so upset I actually had an out-of-body experience and could no longer function on this earthly plain.

Stranded at the airport now for nearly ten hours, with tears in my eyes, I finally managed to convince the fifth person to call still another official for assistance. When this one reinforced what others had explained previously: that "absolutely" nothing could be done, I went berserk. I now watched (from what seemed like above) as my little son (now about seven years of age) as he took hold of his mother's hand, calmed her down, and guided her from underneath an airplane, where she had dragged him and perched there--refusing to move. He explained the situation to the authorities, who'd suddenly appeared after hearing about a crazy American woman shutting down airport operations. It was only after this that things began to happen to our advantage.

Basically, after being consistently ignored when I tried to explain that because I was allergic to mosquito bites and could not spend the night in the airport waiting room with screenless windows, it was imperative that I find a way to leave. We had been dropped at the airport by friends at 1:00 that afternoon, about an hour before our plane was scheduled to arrive. After several announcements promising that the plane was expected within the next hour, finally, at 9:00 P.M., an announcer explained that the next plane to Lagos would not arrive until 10:00 A.M.--the next morning! and that we should try and make ourselves comfortable where we were.

I had waited patiently until several other panicked travelers were done making their case for needing to get to Lagos sooner (with no success). Finally getting my chance to speak with an attendant, thinking they would surely understand my situation, I began my sad story. Having already accepted that no planes were arriving until the next morning, each person I tried talking to about getting transportation to a hotel had begun ignoring me after they'd explained that all the taxis had left for the night. When I was also told that none of the airport telephones were working either, therefore I could not contact the people who'd dropped us off (cell phones had not yet hit the market in Nigeria), my sanity disappeared.

Having noted that the only plane that had landed that day was still sitting on the tarmac, although I knew it was bound for

Cameroon, I decided that it wasn't going anywhere without me and my son. In a state of panic now, I really believed that if I could just get out of this small airport into a larger one like Douala, in Cameroon, we'd be okay. With my son in tow, I ran out to the tarmac and attempted to board the plane. Of course, we were not allowed to enter since I did not have tickets. As hysteria set in, I grabbed my little son and quickly positioned ourselves under the plane so that it could not take off.

In shock, in response to my bizarre behavior, the pilots could only stare in disbelief. Pulling away from me, Jonathan ran back to the airport and managed to get audience with several of the authorities I'd spoken to earlier. I am sure that after they saw that I was serious about not giving up my position (under the wheels of the airplane) they had to do something. Apparently, the pilots had already radioed them, and by the time Jonathan arrived, these officials were ready to follow him back to the plane. After discovering they could not coax this hysterical woman out from under the plane, not knowing what else to do, they sent my son.

In the meantime, a military vehicle had been summoned and after witnessing my son perform the task, an important looking officer instructed several lesser looking ones, to escort us to a hotel nearby, where we were to be given a very nice room and, later. a hot meal. After apologizing for the entire incident, the head officer begged us to please try and get some rest and promised that the military would come to escort us back to the airport at 9:30 the next morning. It was not completely clear to me that Jonathan was my guardian angel however, until another incident presented itself a short while later.

***

I was in my office, searching through documents that would prepare me for an insurance renewal meeting with one of our local insurance agents, Shiagu. Shiagu had been scheduled to come by in two days, and needing to have all my questions answered, I wanted everything ready so that he would not waste my time talking about his church again, an indigenous African sect, which admittedly, I was intrigued with, but on this day, did not have the time listen. Suddenly, a pain shot through my head, so intense it felt like fire. My goodness, I thought, what is this?

A short time later, I began feeling very weak. When I finally mustered up enough energy to call my Secretary, Rena, I requested that she get a driver to take me home. Noting that something was terribly wrong, Rena went with me and after helping me into bed, she instructed Portia, my housekeeper, to stay with me and Jonathan throughout that night. Knowing something was indeed wrong, Jonathan slept at the foot of my bed that night.

When Portia entered my room to check on us the next morning, she startled both me and Jonathan when she inadvertently screamed upon looking at me. I still am not sure what I looked like, but after my seven-year-old looked at me, he quickly instructed Portia to go to my office and bring back Dewitt, our American Health Coordinator. A short while later, Rena appeared and began getting me dressed. Explaining that Dewitt had not returned from a field trip, and that she felt it necessary for me to see a doctor. When I asked Rena where she was taking me, she explained that we were going to the clinic located near our office.

After examining me, the doctor concluded that I had malaria and assured my little son, who would not leave my side, that I was going to be fine. He then instructed the nurse to give me a shot. I watched as the nurse removed a needle from a jar of liquid. At that same moment, the warning Dewitt had given me quickly flashed through my mind. He explained that due to a perpetual scarcity of supplies, doctors in Nigeria often instructed their staff to clean and reuse needles. While aware that I should take caution, I was so sick I really didn't care what they used at that moment. Submitting to whatever they were doing for me that day, I convinced myself that, after all, the needles were being disinfected in that solution over there. When the nurses were done, the doctor gave Rena a prescription, for me, along with a list of instructions for my care, and sent us home.

The following morning, I felt ten times worst. I stayed in bed all that day, but by noon the next day, I could clearly feel my life-force slowly leaving my body. During that time, I distinctly remember asking my mother why it appeared I was determined to die and leave this little boy, whom I'd had at such a late stage in my life, in Nigeria. While I do not recall receiving an answer, I do remember reasoning that he should not have to grow up without a mother like I had. If this were going to be the case, I wondered, why had he come to me so late in my life? Forcing myself out of bed, I made it to the living room and crashed on the sofa. Portia was feeding Jonathan. Hearing my stirrings, she came in and questioned why I had gotten out of bed. I instructed her to get me a pen, some paper, and an envelope.

When she returned, with Jonathan now kneeling at my side, I began writing a note to Dewitt. The note instructed him where my daughters were and how to get Jonathan to them. I also wrote notes to my daughters, apologizing for dying so far away from home. After instructing Portia to take Jonathan and the notes to my office, I ordered her to wait there until Dewitt returned from his trip later that day. I was sure I would be dead before they'd return and did not want my son to be there alone with me.

Although I was nearly lifeless now, I was still lying on the sofa (waiting for my mother to come for me) when someone burst through the door. It was Shaigu, my insurance agent. Thinking to myself that that insurance policy renewal must really be important to him, I tried to speak but couldn't. Then I heard him say, "Wake up Madame, it's not time for you to go." As much of a reaction my feeble body would allow, I looked up at him; I made a comment about the policy and laughed. Joining me, he explained that he was there to renew me, not the policy. He then asked if it was okay if he touched my body. Cynically thinking, why not, it won't be mine much longer anyway, Shaigu began laughing again. My goodness, I wondered, had he heard me? Starting from my temples, he pressed, paused, and then moved down to the sides of my neck; then he pressed, and paused again.

Shaigu continued down to my heart, my pelvic, my knees, and my ankles performing the same ritual until ending at the ball of my feet. As his fingers moved methodically down my body, I could feel life flowing back into each part he touched. Wow, I thought as I looked at him in amazement. I started to sit up when he asked me to wait, then pushed the middle of my chest as if to pump my heart. "How do you feel now?" he asked. "Great!" I replied. While I showed amazement, I was clearly puzzled by what had just happened. "You'll be fine then," he said smiling. "Your ancestors have seen to that, by sending Jonathan to you."

Explaining, as he rose from my side, that he needed to rush to his church service, he was gone before I could utter the words, "Thank you." When Portia and Jonathan came in I was sitting up on the sofa. Seeming to not even notice that I was now well, Portia explained that Dewitt still had not returned that evening and that she was instructed to stay with us again. Her behavior left me wondering if she'd even gone to the office this time.

The next morning, I got up and stirred around, waiting for a relapse of sort. When it didn't happen, later that morning, I decided to go to the office and work. Feeling no pain whatsoever, I tried to explain to my staff, who were trying to figure out how I'd gotten over malaria so quickly, what had happened the night before. Strangely enough, everyone seemed to understand. I found it interesting that no one questioned my explanation. Determined to find out more, later that day I tried to get Rena to give me her views on what had happened to me during the past couple of days. She merely smiled and said, "Madame, just accept that you are special."

Janie and Jonathan on a Sunday afternoon at the beach in Lagos, Nigeria 1991

Me, Jonathan and friends on afternoon on the Lagos River in Nigeria, 1991

Janie in a Village in Loko, Benin 1991

Visiting Elima Castle with Janie and Jonathan in Ghana 1991

The balcony of Elima castle where the slave ships could have been seen when they left Ghana

***

When Shaigu had not come for our insurance policy renewal after a week passed, I called his office. I was told that he was not available and that a Mr. Agbola would be handling my account from then on. Although I wrote several letters to thank him, including the ones I wrote after returning to the States, I never heard from Shaigu again.

Me and a Nigerian staff member, at my office in Nigeria, 1992.

As the end of my assignment in Nigeria neared, an official of the U.S. Agency for International Development (USAID), who "had observed my work and noted my ability to get along with people," approached me with a job offer with the Agency. When he revealed that by accepting and completing the required training, I would become a U.S. Diplomat, I almost blurted out loud, Nooo way, especially considering my most recent ordeal.

***

I had been reluctant to accept the job offer from Mr. Chiviroli, the USAID diplomat, until the little voice that had always pushed me forward spoke again, and I stopped myself from speaking just before the words "no way" escaped my mouth. While I was no longer that eager to remain in Africa, given my experience with the mosquitoes at this point, my inner voice pointed out that maybe it would be of value to experience other places in Africa, and that this might be an opportunity to do so, and/or to even work in other parts of the world. So, I cautiously accepted the offer, and committed myself to the 5-year contract trial period, which qualified people seeking permanent careers in the U.S. Foreign Service. I then reasoned that, after all, while I had not solicited it, I was being presented still another rare opportunity; why not accept it? It may even be interesting to serve as a U.S. Diplomat.

My daughter, Janie, graduated during my training stay in Washington. This time, Jimmy's mother came to celebrate with us. While we tried to impress her with all that Washington had to offer, I think that the graduation and the festivities that followed was the highlight of her visit. After all, her son's daughter had graduated from Howard University. At the completion of my training for the Foreign Service, my little son and I were off to Zimbabwe, Southern Africa.

Vandean Harris-Philpott

United States Agency for International Development

Letter of Reference

Vandean Philpott

I am pleased to provide this Letter of Reference for Ms. Vandean Philpott. I have had occasion to work closely with Ms. Philpott in her capacity as Deputy Country Representative/Administrative Officer, for the Africare Office in Lagos, Nigeria. The Africare program in Nigeria is a quickly growing program. Over the past year, Africare has diversified its project portfolio to encompass work in several new sectors, and in several new administrative regions (States) in the country. I believe that Ms. Philpott has been instrumental in assuring that this growing program is on an administratively and financially sound basis. Logistics are not easy in a country the size of Nigeria. The rapidity and ease with which the Africare offices were set up in the new States is, undoubtedly, due to the expertise and industriousness which Ms. Philpott brings to her work.

We travelled together for three days recently. Her interactions with her Africare staff were excellent. She gave clear and precise instructions, in a way that was not at all threatening but encouraging and rewarding. I also noted that she interacted with Nigerian officials in a manner which was thoroughly professional and extremely productive. I do not hesitate to recommend Ms. Philpott for a position with A.I.D. or any other organization which has need of someone with administrative and managerial experience and someone who can produce under very difficult and trying conditions.

Eugene R. Chiavaroli
AID Affairs Officer
USAID/Lagos, Nigeria

276

Me at a going away luncheon in San Francisco just before going to Zimbabwe 1994.

INAUGURATION OF THE
NATIONAL FOREIGN AFFAIRS
TRAINING CENTER
U.S. DEPARTMENT OF STATE
OCTOBER 13, 1993

**Chatting with Secretary of State, Warren Christopher after my graduation from
the Foreign Service Academy in D.C. 1993.**

Part Three

Early Autumn

And Still, We Rise

In order to qualify as a career Executive Officer (EXO), the position for which I was hired in the U.S. Diplomatic Corps, one had to be competent in managing a U.S. Mission's overseas operations. Thus, it was necessary to successfully complete a one-year training program in Washington, D.C., and an additional two-year period of on-the-job training (under the supervision of a seasoned EXO), at an overseas post where the trainee would also function as a Deputy EXO.

Upon completing this three-year training period, the new EXO must participate in a bidding process which is used to determine where he/she would spend the next two years (on their own) as a junior officer. These three years of basic training and two-year first country assignment constitute the completion of a five-year contract agreement that one would have signed upon accepting the position, as a promise to remain in the Foreign Service during the entire training period. At the end of the five years of service, the contracted (dubbed an Intern) could decide if he/she wished to continue on as a career diplomat with USAID, transfer to another Government agency, or end his/her service.

This five-year contract was designed to discourage those who may not be serious about keeping their commitment to the government, in this case the Agency of International Development (USAID), which would have incurred the cost of training, travel and other costs necessary to prepare them for working overseas and/or representing the U.S. as a diplomat. It was only after my initial training that I understood why such a contract was necessary. Long before my five-year contract was to end, I was nearly ready to return home. Somehow, I didn't think African Americans would be subjected to the same discriminatory behavior inside government we experienced outside, especially overseas.

I had discovered years earlier that African Americans are

respected and admired throughout much of the world, including Africa, mainly for having survived the ordeal of slavery and yet become necessary components in both the building and survival of a nation that would turn out to be one of the mightiest of its time. Often, during my overseas travels, people with whom I'd taken time to hold a conversation, would become very excited after hearing my accent and discovering that I was an African American.

Additionally, having had the rare opportunity to live outside the States and looking back at it, I could see that, indeed, African Americans are a remarkable people. I was surprised to discover that nearly everywhere I went we are recognized for both our fortitude and our achievements, as well as for what we had contributed to the USA in particular, and the world in general. I found it an interesting dichotomy however, that inside of the States, African Americans are still made to feel inferior. Why then, I wondered, did it seemed everyone else in the world appreciated African Americans except the people who enslaved us? Even more interesting (I'd sometimes reflect), why is it that many African Americans don't seem to be aware that others in the world view us with such high regards? Thus, given this recent experience that I will talk about, and in spite of the good ones that were to come as well, my soul began longing to be back in America; in the presence of my own people; my immediate family in particular, and African Americans in general.

Although I'd always known that we African Americans were unique, not only because of what my Aunt Mariah had taught me earlier in life, but also because of what I would eventually learn about our entire history ("and still we [rose]"), not to mention my own ability to have survived the many challenges I would personally experience in life. How African Americans are treated here at home, especially women, reminds me of a story once told to me, by an elderly woman, of a man that had a beautiful, competent, and faithful wife. Because this man was so afraid of losing his wife, he would constantly put her down and/or abuse her; thinking that by doing so she would not be aware of her worth and therefore remain with him. Against this backdrop, I promised myself that, indeed, I would return home, if for no other reason but to share my experiences and continue my quest to educate. Before discussing my quest to return home however, I must share some of my experiences in both the diplomatic corps and in Southern Africa.

***

Upon completing our training in D.C., near the end of 1993, I, and the three other interns (all White males) hired along with me, were assigned to our individual post, where each of us would serve our two years of on-the-job training, as Deputy EXO, before acquiring our next assignment where we would be on our own. It had been explained that these initial assignments could be anywhere in the world, so I was elated to learn that I was assigned to Burundi in East Africa. I would soon learn however, that the Hutus, and the Tutses of Burundi and Rwanda were at war and were trying to annihilate each other. I tried hard to ignore the murmurings among the civil servants, at the USAID headquarters in Washington, as they questioned why the Agency would send a single woman with a small child into a situation such as that in East Africa. But as the time for our departure grew nearer, and having carefully monitored the evening news each day, I noted that the violence was escalating in that region of Africa and I was forced to voice my concern. Upon doing so, I was bluntly told that this is what I signed up for when I decided to become an Executive Officer. So, silently assuring myself that my mother's spirit would never allow anything bad to happen to us, I pushed on.

Then, exactly two weeks before my son and I were to depart for Burundi, the State Department called for the complete evacuation of all Americans from both Burundi and Rwanda. While I was greatly relieved, this action left me without an assignment, and as a result, we would remain in D.C. (with my working out of USAID headquarters) for nearly a year before another training post would become available. While working at headquarters, I received several other disturbing revelations. Of the four of us hired and trained as new EXO's, I was paid the least! Why, I wondered, considering that the other trainees were all not only younger than me, but they also had less work experience. And they all had less education (something I'd already learned during conversations with each of them during our training). Two of them were single, and one was married with two children.

The young married couple, with two children, had been assigned to Harare, Zimbabwe, in Southern Africa, which was dubbed one of the best foreign service posts in Africa. Enough said about this point. Needing an explanation about the pay however, I forced myself to go to personnel for an explanation. Seemingly shocked that I would be so bold to ask, the Personnel Officer pointed out that while my assertions were true, the Organization's policy was to base the salary of a new employee on a certain percent above his/her last salary, or salary history. Thus, although a person may be hired for the same job, it matters not if his/her qualifications are less, since it is one's salary history that dictates salary levels.

Having heard this blunt explanation, the reality of which quickly disarmed me, my mind immediately raced back to other unfair situations I experienced during my earlier career building years. I couldn't help but focus on my most recent one however, in which I accepted an outrageously low salary (compared to what I was making at the time, after having returned to Corporate America) just to get to work in the African arena again. Currently, I could feel the Personnel Officer waiting for my protest. I decided, rather, to thank her for being so candid, and left. After all, I had my reasons for being there, which was to experience more of Africa. As I walked out, I silently prayed for another assignment on the continent.

Shortly before the year in D.C. was over, I received notice that

I would be assigned to Harare, Zimbabwe where, due to later unforeseen events, we would spend all of the remaining years of my USAID contract. I already knew that Harare was a rather nice place since Jonathan and I had spent some Rest & Recuperation (R&R) there, when I worked in West Africa. Therefore, I was not surprised when my office mates excitedly exclaimed that Zimbabwe was where only those agency diplomats who had paid their dues" could bid on, and win, considering that both the city of Harare and the weather there were reminiscent of living in San Francisco's Bay Area. And, because the city is situated so far above sea-level, it had few, if any, mosquitoes. I smiled and said to myself, "thank you, mom." Nevertheless, I wondered if they were aware that I knew that my fellow trainee (the one with the wife and two children) had been assigned to Zimbabwe as his first assignment.

We arrived in Zimbabwe on September 13th (my fiftieth birthday). Jonathan and I were picked up from the airport by my trainer and taken to our assigned home. Once our baggage had been placed inside, and we were introduced to a gentle looking lady, who turned out to be our housekeeper, my trainer suggested we (she and I) go to check out where I would be working. While I had observed her very nervous demeanor, when we first met at the airport, I began to wonder if she was a bit looney—didn't she realize we had just completed a nearly twenty-four-hour international plane trip that included a six-hour layover in Europe. Could she not see that I was barely conscience from exhaustion!

In an attempt to get her to think, I expressed feeling uncomfortable leaving Jonathan on our first day in our new environment, not considering that upon our arrival he had run out to examine the swimming pool, showing none of the exhaustion he'd expressed earlier. Seeing that my trainer didn't appear to get it, the housekeeper (an African), whom I'd noticed had been clearly taken aback when she discovered we were African Americans, stepped in to assure me that Jonathan would be fine. So, although I was half dead with fatigue, convinced my trainer was a bit wired, I went with her. I would learn what her problem was within a few weeks on the job.

Although we had been warned during training that an EXO's job could be very dangerous, after arriving at post in Zimbabwe, I would soon learn that the job was also all-encompassing. In addition to being responsible for the proper and productive functioning of an entire overseas Mission, including the safety, security, and well-being of its entire staff, when we first arrived, it was unsettling for me to have to leave my young son at our home with people who were strangers for such long periods of time. An average workday would often stretch late into the evening. And, recalling that the EXO's job entailed being the last to depart Post in the event of an evacuation, although I eventually came to trust my household staff, the reality of having to leave my child's safety in the hands of anyone other than a family member, was to be too much to think about. That is until the appearance of a more familiar problem that soon reared its ugly head, which brought my thoughts back to a real reality.

Jonathan in the pool at our house in Harare, Zimbabwe, 1995

***

Somehow, I knew that it was about to happen again when, during a private meeting with me, a colleague, who was also my superior, raised the question. Not aware of my initial assignment to Burundi, she asked, "How did you manage to get a Post like Zimbabwe as a first assignment?" Not quite sure what she meant since I was in training, it became clear as she went on to explain that posts such as Zimbabwe were considered easy living and were "reserved for long-time diplomats who have paid their dues by serving time at more difficult posts."

The "It" referred to earlier was that intuitive uneasy feeling I'd experienced in the past when working as the lone African American, in a majority of others. Once the others soon got over the initial shock of having an African American with equal or better qualifications in their mist, there was always one who could not help displaying some form of unhappiness about him/her being there. I found her explanation very odd, especially since I already knew that the Deputy EXO preceding me, at this Post (who'd just left to continue his duties in South Africa), was hired at the same time as I and had gone through training with me in Washington. Moreover, were it necessary for him to remain at Post in the event of an evacuation, he had a spouse to take care of his children, who were both older than Jonathan? Why did she not have a problem with him being initially assigned to Zimbabwe, while I was assigned Burundi, I wondered. Sensing her disapproving attitude, I shrugged my shoulders indicating that I didn't know why and responding with, "I'm just lucky like that I guess." Although it was clear she was not happy with my reply. We moved on.

Me in mock village in the City of Harare, 1996

A local resort near Victoria Falls in Zimbabwe we visited often, 1997.

In Their Own Interest

Although I had a wonderful experience living and working in Southern Africa overall, at times my tour of duty there would become extremely challenging. Not necessarily because of the stress-laced EXO work tasks, but due to that particular co-worker referred to earlier, who turned out to be the personnel supervisor for both my trainer and I, In that, her office was responsible for all U.S. personnel issues relating to home and sick leaves, temporary tours of duty (outside of the Mission) assignments, and evaluations. While her initial focus had been on my trainer, it would later be aimed at me--with a vengeance; and yes, I took it personally. For reasons known only to herself, she just did not seem like the EXO initially in charge of my internship, nor me either, apparently. In time I would witness numerous occasions when my trainer would run back to our department, literally in tears, after an encounter with this person.

As a result, at the end of her tour in Zimbabwe, which was also near the end of my official training, my trainer was given a very poor final evaluation by this supervisor. One key point of her evaluation was that she had not provided the proper training for me. While neither of us understood what she meant by this, especially since she'd never mentioned any lack before, nor had she explained what it was, I remained silent and just observed the resulting drama as it unfolded. Although I don't recall being afraid of anyone before, this encounter left me feeling a bit vulnerable, other thing considered. Wow, I thought to myself, can one person actually do that to another?

The resulting fallout from our Mission's Director, who was our supervisor's immediate supervisor, was that since she felt I had not been trained properly, it was necessary that I remain in Zimbabwe another year and continue my training under the next, incoming senior EXO. When this decision came to my attention, my instincts indicated that her superior must have known of her unfair treatment towards my trainer, with whom he appeared to have no problems. Did he also know how she felt about my initial assignment to Zimbabwe and decided to use this as an opportunity to get back at her, as well, I wondered.

While I found it unsettling that no one asked my opinion or feelings on this matter, I immediately recognized that remaining at this Post another year meant even more stability for my son. Additionally, I felt comforted by the fact that by staying put, I would be closer to the end of my five-year contract. I therefore said nothing and accepted the consequences. However, it concerned me that I could be so far away from home and still experience discrimination. Indeed, staying put would allow me the opportunity to make some serious decisions about whether or not I wanted to remain in the Foreign Service (FS). Nonetheless, feeling that whatever was going on with these people, all of whom were already in Zimbabwe when I arrived, I clearly did not enjoy being caught up in their crossfire.

Until Larry Foley, the senior EXO who was also supposed to be my new trainer, arrived nearly five months later, I ran the Mission's EXO operations alone--with no complaints! I'd often wonder if anyone noticed that. I was pleased, however, when Larry turned out to be a very nice person and very easy to work with. I'm sure it helped that I required little training which made his job very easy. Although he never said anything about what happened with my first Senior EXO, he made it clear to me that he knew. I'd learned early on that even when Whites did not like each other, they seldom discussed such feelings with Blacks. So, I pressed on.

After I learned that Blacks in other FS agencies (including those from throughout the diaspora and those from other African countries) were experiencing similar problems, I began organizing events to help us all cope with living away from home a bit easier.

United States
Agency for International Development
USAID / Zimbabwe

Vandean Philpott
Deputy Executive Officer

Tel (0) 720630/720757
Fax 263-4- 722418

Me working in my office on my own as deputy EXO, 1996

Then, a Program Officer, who had worked with our supervisor in the past, was eventually assigned to Zimbabwe and gave us the entire scoop on why, he believed, she behaved the way she did. According to him, rumor had it that during her climb to upper management, she had a run-in with an EXO who assigned her a house she felt did not reflect her status. After endless complaints about the house, instead of getting a new one, she was ousted to another country. Having worked for years in this organization, once she reached a point near the top of the chain of command, she let every EXO know that she had power over them, via the almighty evaluation tool if nothing else.

Having heard about our past drama, this officer concluded that our supervisor's problem was not necessarily with any particular EXO, but rather, all EXOs! He went on to suggest that her behavior towards us probably stems from the fact that although her position is near the top of her category, she realizes that her position is basically on the same level as an EXO, given our ability to make such decisions as housing assignments and purchasing vehicles for all American staff (including hers). Thus, she feels that EXOs still have more power than she does." Additionally, while she did not want to be one, she "envied those who were." Looking at me, he exclaimed that she tended to be even harder on female EXOs. Upon hearing this, I thought, how personal is that! To me, this made it clear of what the phrase "In one's own interest" meant.

It became clear to me also that when it finally occurred to our supervisor that her actions toward my trainer had presented positive results for me, her venom had, in fact, shifted my way. Is this, I wondered, the reason that during the period I managed the EXO operations alone, I remained under such great scrutiny and was constantly harassed about the smallest things—mainly involving the remodeling of her house, which she had convinced upper management was not suitable for her entertaining duties. My natural charm had been severely tested during this period. In fact, it failed me so many times I finally had to tell the woman to get off my back and go to hell. It seemed we got along better after that--at least, I thought so.

The following year, the third African African American Summit was scheduled to be held in Zimbabwe. Since this was basically an economic event, USAID played the main role in organizing it. Having discovered that I had worked closely with Mr. Sullivan's international group before, namely while working for Africare, in West Africa, and already familiar with their setup and other needs, I was asked by our Ambassador to play a major role in assisting with organizing the Zimbabwe Summit, which I did. When the four-day summit actually took place however, our supervisor, whose office was responsible for the logistical scheduling of USAID's personnel to host the Summit's on-site activities, made sure that I did not step foot on the conference grounds. Considering the role, I had played, coupled with the fact that I was the only African American at USAID/Zimbabwe at the time, my absence was felt by everyone, including her supervisor, who was clearly embarrassed, as were our country's Ambassador, who had requested my role, in the first place. While the fallout was sweet, I would still feel the consequences of her silent rage.

In the meantime, when Mr. Sullivan's organizing crew, with which I had worked during the past year, noticed my absence, they threatened to file an official complaint with the Ambassador. I begged them not to, however. After all, I felt that my role at the command center, although miles away, was just as important. Having attended the very first Summit, which was held in Cote'd'Ivore, I felt that I was not missing anything I had not already experienced. At the Cote'd'Ivore Summit, I had met many of the key participants including Mrs. Coretta Scott King, Ozzie & Ruby Dee, and Benjamin Hooks to name a few. Besides, I knew that this person would be writing my evaluation! But, since I already knew Sullivan's entire staff, and being one of the few African Americans at Post, y'all know the after-party was at my house. Enough said.

The first African/African American Summit held in Abidjan, Cote d'Ivoire 1991.

"If a race has no history, if it has no worthwhile tradition, it becomes a negligible factor in the thought of the world and it stands in danger of being exterminated. The achievements of the [African] properly set forth will crown him as a factor in early human progress and a of maker modern civilization "

By Dr. Carter G. Woodson, African-American historian and founder of Negro History Week, now observed as African American History Month

.

Vandean, Carl and Violet, request the Pleasure of the compagny of...
in celebration of Black History Month at a Luncheon to be held at the Residence No 10 Woodlane, Borrowdale.

Starts at 14 :00 Hrs on Saturday 22 February 1997.

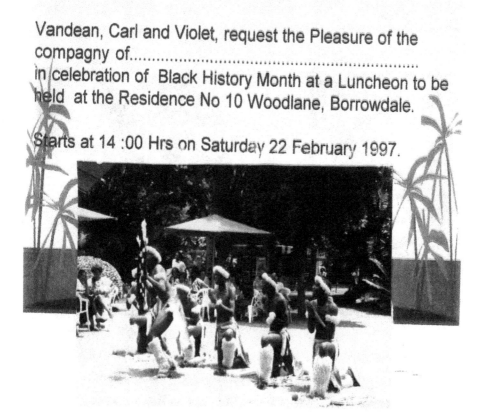

At the first African/African American Summit with Mrs. King, and Benjamin Hooks. 1992

At any rate, the thing I found most disturbing about working for a great organization like USAID, was how one American can be so hard on another while working in a foreign country, especially considering the delicate and sometimes dangerous situations in which one might sometimes find oneself. After all, the entire Mission depended on each of us, for our general safety. However, besides being responsible for the smooth and safe operation of our daily work environment, the EXO is also depended on for after-hours protection, including home safety, and the security of all American employees working in the field.

Considering that EXOs are on the job twenty-hours a day then, I wondered how one individual could be allowed to, not only jeopardize the many outstanding services offered by USAID, but such actions also had the potential of putting the entire Mission at risk by causing unnecessary stress on those with a more noble cause, or like myself (crazy enough to accept such a position), to want to leave the service altogether. This experience also confirmed to me, that like organizations, individuals, too, act in their own interest. Other than this "on the job craziness" living in parts of South African was pretty much like living in the U. S.

Johnnie Carson
Ambassador of the United States of America
and Mrs. Anne Carson
request the pleasure of the company of
Ms. Vandean Philpot
On the Occasion of Dr. Leon H. Sullivan's Visit to
Discuss the 1997 African African-American Summit
on Monday, June 24, 1996
at 6:00 - 7:30 p.m.

Me at the reception held for Dr. Sullivan in Zimbabwe, 1997

During my tour in Zimbabwe, I had the opportunity to do temporary tours of duty in several countries including El Salvador in Central America. Until this assignment, I thought that beside Tupelo, Southern Africa in general, and Zimbabwe in particular, were the most beautiful places on earth. After traveling in Central and South America, I realized that the Creator had made many such places throughout our planet. How then, I wondered, could the human race be so hard on one another? Considering all the beauty that surrounds us, and all the bounty the earth offers, I'd often found myself wondering also, how can we, as conscious beings, even think about hate and war?

While I enjoyed living and working in Southern Africa, and although West African presented more of a challenge, i.e., the hot climate and the abundance of mosquitoes, I noted that there was something about West Africa that was more familiar to me. Thus, I felt more comfortable there. My experiences throughout Africa were many. It was during these travels that I realized that the continent was so vast I would never manage to visit all of it in one lifetime.

And now, after the more than twenty-five years in which I had the privilege of studying, visiting, working with and/or residing in it and, having managed to experience only thirteen of Africa's fifty-three countries, I knew that these were nowhere near representative of the entire continent. Neither were the many books, films, maps, fabrics, paintings, sculptures, furniture, carvings, and artifacts I'd managed to collect and bring back to America to share and/or use as teaching tools. This fact made me even more determined to someday establish that cultural center I'd dreamed about years earlier. In the meantime, I still had one more year before my five-year commitment with USAID was complete. This meant I had to participate in the bidding process for my next post.

As discussed earlier, once the intern completes his/her initial training and performs in his or her chosen position, in my case, as an EXO, in order to move on to an independent assignment, it is necessary to participate in a bidding process, which listed job openings throughout the world. However, since USAID diplomats had been ordered to stay in place, although I didn't mind, this put my progression behind for still another year. By the end of this extended time, I would have nearly reached the end of my five-year contract. So, with a little more than a year to go, the time had finally come for me to participate in the bidding process.

The bidding process required that the bidder select three posts, in the order of preference, among those available at the time. The most desired post was to be requested first, followed by one's second preference, and the third. Toying with the idea that if I got one of my three, all of which were in Africa, in places I had not visited, lived nor worked, I just might continue in the service a while longer. Thus, I chose Egypt in Northern Africa, and two countries in East Africa (Kenya and Uganda). I'd heard rumors, however, that while it rarely happened, if a junior officer chose all posts that may be desired by a more senior officer and missed out on all his/her three choices, the junior would have to accept and go to what was left.

Thinking also that I might not have enough seniority to compete in this very competitive process, especially since I had been at a so called "easy post" for my training and beyond, I reasoned that if I did not get one of my desired choices, and chose to remain in the foreign service, perhaps I should choose a fourth-- which one could do--rather than having it randomly selected for her. So, at the last minute, I decided to throw in a fourth choice. And, considering that I preferred to remain in Africa if possible, Conakry, Guinea was my fourth choice.

I chose Conakry, Guinea because in addition to being a French-speaking country, it was situated in West Africa. And, although I knew that this country was not as developed as Zimbabwe, it was near The Republic of Benin. Not only could we visit Benin during some of our R&Rs, I reasoned, living in a

French-speaking country would prepare us for those visits since Benin is French-speaking as well. I did not realize, however, that a war was brewing in that region of Africa at the time, and that Guinea was very much involved. Nor had I realized that by making this choice, I had played right into the hands of my supervisor.

By the time the bidding process was completed, and the tours were posted, I learned that I had been assigned to Conakry Guinea! Having been well informed about the war by then, which was now in full force, I was puzzled by such a fate. Labeling the situation as bizarre, considering our first assignment was in war-troubled Burundi, one of my colleagues, familiar with my experience in Zimbabwe, suggested that since the person responsible for sending our bids in was my supervisor, she might have had something to do with my getting the assignment; and that my having bid on Conakry, though it was the least of my choices, made it easy for her to get away with it. Whether my supervisor had anything to do with my new post or not, I felt it more disturbing that again I was presented with the reality that being a single parent (accompanied by a small child) had no effect on being assigned to a war zone. And while I did not expect preferential treatment, I did expect a bit of compassion, especially given the stress an EXO faces even during peaceful times. After all, this kind of assignment was given to me before I even met my current supervisor. Indeed, this was my cue to end my Foreign Service career.

Then, just one year before my year in Zimbabwe was to end, in an effort to curtail overseas operating expenses, USAID officials announced that all overseas personnel were to remain at their current post another year. Upon hearing this news, I wondered why I was not surprised that what seemed like divine intervention had taken over again--at just the right time. Interestingly enough, this extended year would be the end of my five-year contract--YEAH! More importantly, it meant still another year of stability for my son.

In spite of my initial concerns and ongoing encounters, I

would get the opportunity to visit and or work in several Southern African countries, including Botswana, Malawi, Namibia, South Africa, Swaziland, and Zambia during my stay in Zimbabwe, something I found very rewarding. In cases when I either could not take Jonathan along, or needed someone to care for him while I attended my temporary tours, I would send for my daughter, (Denise). Therefore, she got the opportunity to travel throughout Southern Africa.

***

Other highlights on this tour of duty, included taking an airplane full of Congress people around Zimbabwe, and escorting Mrs. Hillary Clinton to Victoria Falls which is situated between

Mrs. Clinton expressing her appreciation for accompanying her to Victoria Falls, 1996

Zambia and Zimbabwe--although I would learn later that most of these assignments were given me because I "was the only African

American at post at the time, and that the organizing officials of these trips stated that they did not want the U.S. dignitaries to be surrounded by an all-white staff in a black country." Apparently, the camera shots taken during these visits were going to be shown on the primetime news back in America.

THE WHITE HOUSE
WASHINGTON

June 3, 1997

Ms. Vandean Philpott
USAID
C/o American Embassy-Harare
Department of State
Washington, D.C. 20521-2180

Dear Ms. Philpott:

    I want to extend my gratitude to you for assisting with the details of my trip. Your support was integral to the success of my visit to Zimbabwe. Your help made this occasion a memorable one.

        Sincerely yours,

        Hillary Rodham Clinton

When my supervisor learned that her continued vengeance towards me had not produced the unfavorable results, she expected for me, it was all out war. Having annoyed him too often however and knowing that this was something she was looking forward to doing, our Head of Mission (her supervisor) announced that I would be the person to escort the First Lady of the United States during her visit to Zimbabwe. My goose was cooked--at least she thought it was. Fortunately for me, by then I had convinced myself that I was not interested in becoming a career diplomat. Moreover, I didn't like the feeling that I may have been chosen because I was one of the few Blacks at post. Therefore, I was not that impressed.

So, when Mrs. Clinton came to visit Zimbabwe, indeed I was asked to accompany her to Victoria Falls. During that trip, I recall standing in the distance watching her absorb the awesome beauty of the Falls, just as I had done on my first visit there. I understood when I observed her shooing off the Secret Service people. I smiled. She wanted some alone-time. It was then that I also realized that like most, who had the privilege of visiting this majestic place, she wanted to pray in silence. The scene was very moving. I could not help but appreciate that while she was a very well educated, sophisticated and privileged woman, she was also a humble and gentle human being. Perhaps this is where her strength comes from, I silently guessed.

***

I would also make several life-long friendships while in Zimbabwe, with both other foreign service workers and diplomats representing their own countries, as well as with many Zimbabweans. These friendships included that of Joe and Emma Cunningham, with whom I was totally taken aback when I first met the couple. I could not speak for a moment after being introduced to Joe, during which time he said they were from Jamaica; I am sure the look on my face frightened them.

Jonathan and Chelsie Clinton during her visit to Zimbabwe, 1996

Mrs. Clinton's (far left) vist at Victoria Falls, 1996

Me at Victoria Falls, 1996

My daughter Denise, during her visit to Zimbabwe, 1997

During our initial introduction, my thoughts took off again as I began thinking, my goodness, is this why I came here! Joe's last name was the same as that of my great-grandmother, who was also from Jamaica. Having observed my strange demeanor, Joe asked if I was okay. Feeling I would sound silly, I timidly decided not to express my thoughts on how much he resembled some of my family members, whose last name he also carried.

The Cunningham's and I would share a close friendship throughout my stay in Zimbabwe. I remained too timid however, to bring up the subject of them sharing my great-grandmother's maiden name. Besides, everywhere I'd traveled in Africa, I met people who either looked like, or reminded me of family members and/or friends at home in America. Considering how enchanting my life had been thus far, though, it would not have surprised me to learn that my family was connected to the Cunningham's. Since they had given me their address in Jamaica, I decided to leave this too, for my descendants to pursue, should they choose to. In the meanwhile, I'd just enjoy their friendship while I was with them.

During that extended year I learned that I was due another rest and recuperation (R&R) leave. Having already decided that I was not interested in becoming a career diplomat, or continuing in the foreign service, instead of traveling to other countries, as I often did during my R&R, my son and I went back home to California's San Francisco Bay Area. While there, I purchased a home, in preparation for my imminent departure. Although being in an African country may have offered some comfort for me, I was often presented with the fact that I was still a foreigner on foreign soil. A key component of foreign service training was to instill the idea that relying on and looking out for one's fellow Americans and vice-versa, is very important when away from home. My experience, at this, my first post, indicated that egos were so inflated I could not find any consideration of this rule. As a result, I cannot find words to convey the uneasiness I felt knowing that I could not rely on all of my fellow country-people, were it to become necessary.

Despite my experience in Zimbabwe, I had to recognize that throughout my time in Africa, I had experienced a life very rare for the majority of Americans in general and for African Americans in particular. And by now, I had also figured out why my son arrived so late in my life--to be my travel companion. I also recognized that all I had accomplished so far, was the result of what the Creator had allowed me to and that out of my storehouse experiences, I must find a way to give back; not just to my family, friends, and loved one, but also to my community.

Therefore, I was even more determined to establish that African/African American Cultural Center I'd dreamed about some twenty-five years earlier. Having decided early on during my odyssey in Africa, to collect as many resource materials and any other items representative of the continent as I could afford and/or could manage to bring back home for this purpose, I was pleased that I had done just that.

Having left the Zimbabwe operations in the well qualified hands of EXO Larry Foley, my experience there (referred to earlier) had pretty much convinced me that since I was not interested in becoming a career diplomat, though I appreciated the opportunity. It was now time for me to go home. What happened just after we left Zimbabwe, however, sealed the deal. Several months after my departure from Africa, in 1998 our U.S. Embassy in Kenya, my second re-assignment choice, was bombed and many people died, including several Americans. Two years later, after I returned to the States, Mr. Larry Foley, my second trainer and replacement in Zimbabwe went on to his new post in Jordan. There, he was gunned down by Al Qaida. It was this incident that paved the way for our involvement in Iraq.

Laurence Foley

American diplomat was killed outside his home in Jordan on Oct. 28.

Diplomat's death tied to al-Qaida

■ Jordan says that Abu Musaab Zarqawi guided slaying of Laurence Foley

By Christine Spolar
CHICAGO TRIBUNE

AMMAN, Jordan — Jordanian officials linked the slaying of an American diplomat to a top al-Qaida lieutenant Saturday as they announced the arrest of two men — a Libyan and a Jordanian — who they say confessed to the killing and to working with the terror group.

Abu Musaab Zarqawi, one of the most sought-after fugitives tied to al-Qaida, guided the men in slaying diplomat Laurence Foley and in planning what was supposed to be a killing spree against Americans and Jordanians, including "diplomats, embassies and local police" in Amman, Jordanian officials said.

Foley, a 60-year-old administrator for the U.S. Agency for In-

See DIPLOMAT, Page 15

Diplomat

FROM PAGE 1

ternational Development, was gunned down outside his home Oct. 28.

"Unfortunately, (Foley was) the first and easiest target," Jordanian Information Minister Mohammed Affash Adwan said Saturday night.

Details about the arrests of Salem Saad bin Suweid, a Libyan, and Yasser Fatih Ibrahim, a Jordanian, were sketchy Saturday, and it was unclear how the men were captured.

But Adwan emphasized that the men took orders from Zarqawi, who European and American intelligence officials have identified as a key planner and one of the top 25 people in the

terror web led by Osama bin Laden.

"He directed (Suweid and Ibrahim) in Jordan. He gave them their tasks and the information. He facilitated their stay in Jordan. He helped provide weapons," Adwan said.

U.S. Embassy officials in Amman praised the Jordanian police efforts.

In Washington, the U.S. government welcomed the news of the arrests.

Asked about possible extradition of the suspects, State Department spokesman Louis Fintor said he had no information about U.S. interest in prosecuting the men.

Foley's death, the first killing of an American diplomat in Jordan in decades, stunned Jordan and much of the diplomatic

Suweid   **Ibrahim**

corps, which had viewed Amman as a safe posting.

Since Foley's death, the State Department has offered embassy dependents and non-emergency staff the option to leave Jordan.

Information minister Adwan would not say whether U.S. law enforcement had been involved in the arrest of the suspects.

Adwan said Suweid and Ibrahim were charged Saturday

and turned over to the Jordanian state security court for prosecution.

U.S. intelligence agents indicated Saturday that the capture and interrogation of Suweid and Ibrahim was a "Jordanian operation."

Both men were captured earlier this month and subjected to interrogation by Jordanian intelligence agents, according to news reports on state-run media.

Adwan said the men, during questioning, identified themselves as members of al-Qaida and said they had trained in Afghanistan.

However, state news reports Saturday night said that only Suweid trained in Afghanistan.

Both men said that they had been supplied money and

weapons by al-Qaida, Adwan said, and that they took directions from Zarqawi.

According to a statement on state-run television Saturday night, the men had used $18,000 of an estimated $50,000 allotted for the attacks in Jordan.

"We got the information we wanted," Adwan said. "They confessed to their plans and confessed to killing." He added that the men would face multiple charges, including murder, weapons smuggling and planning terror attacks.

The arrests underscored the increasing importance of Zarqawi, also known as Ahmed Kalaylah, in the global schemes of al-Qaida, which carried off the Sept. 11, 2001, attacks.

Zarqawi, a Jordanian, has been linked to al-Qaida for some

time. In Jordan, he played a key role in plotting to bomb a luxury hotel in Amman in January 2000 — which became known as the "Millennium Plot" in Jordan — and was later convicted in absentia.

In the past year, Zarqawi, who is said to be trained in the use of poisons and toxins, has reportedly traveled to Iran, Iraq, Syria and Lebanon.

In the past two months, European intelligence agencies have described him as one of six regional commanders in al-Qaida.

Germany intelligence has identified him as a leader of a militant group known as Al Tawid. His name has also surfaced in connection with al-Qaida efforts in refugee camps in Lebanon.

Me and Senior EXO Larry Foley, 1997

Me with my staff in Zimbabwe and Larry Foley at my going away party, 1997

Goodbye Zimbabwe! Photo taken of Jonathan and my departure from Zimbabwe with my staff August 1997.

One Last Stop in Africa

Souman kept his promise and came to visit his son the year before we left Zimbabwe. Jonathan had turned twelve and went through his initial Rites-to-Passage ceremony without his father's presence. Although it was a joyous occasion for him since he had many mentors, including several members of the U.S. Marines stationed in Zimbabwe at the time, the child was very disappointed. He was even more disappointed when Souman could not attend his final Rites-of-Passage celebration, as promised. This final event takes place on a boy's birthday the following year, after he has completed a task-intensive year directed by his mentors and community elders. These tasks are designed to prepare the now-young man for becoming a productive member in his community and a good citizen of society at large. This final celebration, which officially declares a young boy's passage into young manhood ends his Rites-of-Passage year, in a ceremony that is witnessed by his family, friends, and community.

Joining me are members of the Foreign Service community in Zimbabwe, welcoming guests to Jonathan's final Rites of Passage Ceremony. From left to right is Carl from Panama, Violet from Bermuda, and US Ambassador Johnnie Carson.

Souman did come for a visit later that year, however. And, knowing that he missed both these very special occasions, he planned something that would not only make Jonathan forget about his father's absence at the events, it would also erase any doubt in his mind that his father was "the greatest man that ever lived."

Jonathan with his father at the Mall, during his visit with us in Zimbabwe, 1997

Before we returned to the States, Souman made sure we understood how important it was that we stop in his country, the Republic of Benin, where he was temporarily living with his oldest son. Soon after arriving in Cotonou, we learned that he had organized several gatherings that would introduce Jonathan and welcome him into his side of his family. Besides my own in Mississippi, I had never witnessed so many people constituting one family in my entire life.

Jonathan was surprised to see so many boys around his age. They all surrounded him, introducing themselves according to family, and welcoming him into the whole. After discovering that they could not get much out of him about America, considering he had not spent much time there, during his life, the boys (and girls) decided to tell him all about Benin. This included showing him all the latest dances.

Before this particular main event was over my son behaved as if he had always been a part of this group. I, on the other hand, had to discipline myself in order to dismiss the fact that I just may have chosen a distant relative to father my male child. It was very unsettling how much Souman's entire family resembled my mother's people, the Wares.

Above Jonathan (middle) surrounded by brother and cousins; (below) Young male cousins showing Jonathan some Benin dance moves.

Jonathan with older brother, grandmother, and two young cousins, 1997.

Jonathan (far right) with some of his father's, brothers, sisters, and their children.

Jonathan ending Rites of Passage Celebration on his 13th birthday, 1997

Me singing to Jonathan his growing up song as he plays the piano.

Souman took great pride in taking us to visit his birthplace, and to where he went to school and grew up. As he told his son about some of his adventures as a young man, I noticed the trouble he was having trying to contain his emotions. He ended by sharing how sorry he was that his children (now numbering five) would not have the opportunity to grow up (all together), in his country, as he and his siblings had. After insisting on taking us on tours throughout Benin, including the beach on which a monument is now situated, constructed in memory of those captured to be sold into slavery, I did not have the heart to tell Souman that I had already been to many of these places before; nor about the deja vu (already seen) moment I'd experienced in 1977. While working in Nigeria (six years earlier), not only had Sean, the young navigator I met during that initial trip to Africa, taken us on several sight-seeing trips, he also escorted me on my first visit to see my friend Mrs. Rosine Soglo, the First Lady of the Republic.

Benin borders Nigeria on the right, and from where I lived (near Lagos, Nigeria), the trip was less than a three-hour drive. Mrs. Soglo and I had become friends when we both resided in Washington, D.C. during the late 1980's. Her husband, Mr. Nicephore Soglo, was employed at the World Bank at the time. She was a lawyer. After retiring from the World Bank, the Soglo's returned to Benin where Mr. Soglo was chosen to serve as the country's Prime Minister in 1990. A year later he ran and won the presidency. After Mrs. Soglo discovered I was working in Nigeria, she sent an entourage to escort my son and me to visit her on several occasions.

Madame Soglo (seated) and members of her staff in the Republic of Benin, 1991.

A visit to Ganvie, a city on the waters in Benin, 1997

More pictures of visit to Ganvie, a city on the waters in Benin, 1997

***

At this juncture in my life, however, I could sincerely say that "there is no place like home," or better still, no place like America. While I shall emphatically maintain that I enjoyed my odyssey, especially having had the opportunity to personally witness the natural beauty of so many places on this earth, including Africa, and would always treasure the good fortune given me to do so, by now my idealism had turned into a more mature and realistic understanding of life in general, and what it was like to be a foreigner in another country in particular. I truly began missing home.

Reflecting back on some of my travel experiences, I recall constantly comparing life in many of the places I stayed for a length of time with life in America, particularly the lives of women. In doing so, I'd often find myself wondering if Americans really understand how blessed we are to be in a nation that, at the very least, honors basic rights. Based on my experiences, I had to acknowledge that from the East to West Coasts, as well as North to South, no matter what one's condition maybe in the United States, at least, one was free to exercise his/her own choices.

As we departed Africa, although I felt a sadness about leaving, I also felt a sense of accomplishment, not because of the jobs I had done, nor the people I had met; rather, it was a feeling I had finally achieved an unspoken task (a destiny of sort), in which I had little to say about participating. I also felt that while this would probably be my last time in Africa, the years we spent living there may just be an introduction for my son and/or later descendants. I felt satisfied.

Visiting the mausoleum erected in memorial of the mass grave of captured men and women who died prior to being loaded on slave vessels at the port of Quidah, Benin.

Autumn

Vandean Harris-Philpott

A Family Reunion in Egypt

Upon returning to the States and settling into our new home in California, my first new job was with the Center for International Trade Development in Oakland, where I began as a Consultant for entrepreneurs interested in doing business in Africa. Concurrently, I taught Marketing and Business Law in the School of Business at Merritt College, also in Oakland.

About a year and a half after my return to California, I was approached by the President of the San Francisco African American Historical Society (AAHCS), who asked if I would assist with their efforts to re-invent the Society's business operations. Although it had existed for nearly a half century, the Society was suffering from an off-and-on existence at that time. I had frequented the facility on many occasions during my university years, seeking assistance with my many research projects. I had also participated in many of the cultural events and other activities the Society provided. Thus, I was pleased to be offered such an opportunity to help.

San Francisco Mayor Willie Brown, myself, Jessie Byrd, President (right) and other AAHCS Board members on left, 1999

I accepted the challenge and thoroughly enjoyed participating in rejuvenating the Society. I also felt honored to do so when I was later asked to remain as the Society's Executive Director. An extra bonus of this position would give me the opportunity to begin sharing the materials I had collected during my stay in Africa. Besides helping to enhance the Society's existing programs, my collection presented me the chance to show Africa in the true glory it deserved.

San Francisco African American Historical and Cultural Society
762 Fulton Street   San Francisco, CA 94102

Gallery & Gift Shop: (415) 441-0640   Library & Archives: (415) 292-6172

Presents

Fragments of Africa

Fragments of Africa is a collection of paintings, framed art, pictures, sculptures, stone, wood and metal carvings, cloths, tapestries, tableware (including serving dishes), video tapes, books, and magazines, dolls, etc. collected by Ms. Vandean Philpott during the years she lived and traveled in Africa.

Ms. Philpott, who ended her career as a foreign service diplomat last May (1998), has lived in several countries in Africa, and has traveled to many others. The desire to live in Africa started here in the Bay Area, where she attended Contra Costa College and San Francisco State University. Having developed into a very active Africanist, Ms. Philpott became involved with organizing various African and African American cultural events at both schools and in her community.

After completing her course work in 1977, Ms. Philpott traveled to and did an internship at several universities in West Africa, collecting materials to support her masters thesis. It was during this time she realized how little African Americans *really* knew about Africa, and promised herself that she must live in Africa, acquire this understanding and return home armed with practical knowledge, written and material resources, and what other items she could bring back to share with her community.

Her first opportunity to work in Africa came when she acquired a job Africare, an African American Development organization, where she spent several years in West Africa. Later, with the US Agency for International Development, she worked mostly in Southern Africa. Ms. Philpott's life and travels in Africa covered a period of seven years and 13 countries.

Ms. Philpott says that it was only after she'd lived in Africa, that she also understood its vastness and diversity. "To claim that the items I have collected over the years are representative of all o[...]
induced extensive, for [...]
the collection *Fragm[...]

Exhibition open dur[...]

By now both my daughters had completed their education, settled down, and started families of their own. Finally, a grandmother, my attention began focusing on our extended family in Mississippi again. Considering that my daughters had only met my mother's family that one time I dropped them off (on my way to Africa in 1977), now that my immediate family was expanding, I wondered if that one brief visit was adequate. Had this visit been enough to cause my children to even want to maintain relationships or keep a connection with our extended families, I wondered? Living so far from them, I also wondered if my grandchildren would ever get to know these relatives, who were very important to me, and our unique family history. This lack of having maintained a closer connection left me in doubt. With these questions weighing heavily on my mind, I began creating our family tree chart. By doing this, I reasoned, if not by sight at least the future generations of my immediate family will know who they are on paper.

It was also at this point I decided to begin a book, documenting what I knew about my mother's family and the story of how my great-grandfather came to North America. Ironically enough, it was also at this point (while researching who's who in my mother's family) I was contacted by my cousins in Egypt, Mississippi. Having heard that I had returned to the States after years of working overseas, one relative from Egypt, Mississippi sent me an invitation to their annual family reunion.

Feeling that this presented the opportunity to introduce my now sixteen-year-old, son to my mother's side of our family, I could also obtain more information to include on the family tree chart I was constructing. So, off I headed for Mississippi, with my son in tow, the summer of the year 2001. Since I was approaching retirement age, I also considered this trip to be an opportunity for me to explore that wild idea I'd entertained about returning to Mississippi someday.

During the 1977 visit to Mississippi, I had observed that our farm in Egypt had not changed much since I left as a child. In addition to several trailer homes, occupied by some of her adult children and/or grandchildren, my Auntie's youngest daughter was the only one that had built a new home at that time. I wondered if I would still recognize it now that more than another twenty years had passed. With this thought, my mind raced back to when I first learned that my brother, sister, and I had inherited my mother's share of our ancestor's land.

***

I was in my early thirties, and after receiving this information, I recalled being a bit annoyed and questioned why I had not heard about this before. Thinking about some of the hard times I'd had in the past, I wondered if knowing I actually had property would have caused me to make different decisions. Justifying my annoyance, I reasoned that had I known I would have, or at the least, felt a sense of security knowing that I had some place to go should I need to--a place that belonged to me.

My initial annoyance had arisen after wondering why we (or at least I, since I could only speak for myself) were being told about this inheritance so late in life. Could the reason be that in order to construct on the land, my Mississippi family needed signatures from me and my siblings for approval because we were part owners? I would eventually learn that this was indeed the case, since the land had not been officially divided between the families as intended, thus a second request to build had arrived. Now, I wondered, would we have ever been told about our inheritance were our approval to build not needed? Recalling that not long after that one cousin secured our approval to build her house, my aunt requested another approval to build a new house for herself. I had casually mentioned to my brother and sister at the time that if this keeps up, all the choice spots would be taken by the time we were ready or able to return to Mississippi and build. At any rate, I decided to dismiss such negative thoughts.

It turned out, though, that my aunt had built her new house on the line that separated my mother's portion of land from hers. My aunt had proudly shown me our share of this property during my 1977 visit, after stating that she hoped that at least one of her sister's children would return and build a home there as well. Having already secured a copy of the deed to our share, I promised her that I would do that someday. The location of her new house, however, made the boundary of each family's land more obscure.

***

Another major change that had taken place on this current visit was that my Aunt Mariah had passed away (at age 113), and Auntie Evelyn, now close to ninety years old, was bedridden and suffered from Alzheimer's. I nearly went into panic mode when I learned that she could not talk and possibly would not recognize me. Realizing that Auntie, being my mother's only sister, represented the only remaining connection I had to my mother, a very sad feeling came over me. I was somewhat relieved when, while sitting at her bedside having what I thought was pointless conversation with her, she tried to respond. Unable to make sounds come from her opened lips, having failed to do so, she tried hard to force them to at least move. When that failed, to ensure that I knew that she was aware of my presence, she squeezed my hand. I also thought I saw a smile on her still and helpless face. During our silent encounter, I looked up at my young son in time to see the tears form in his eyes, just before his sixteen-year-old "men don't cry" demeanor kicked in. Although he tried to avoid my glance, I knew he shared my feelings.

Obsequies

of the late

Mrs. Mariah Lou Ware Cozart

NOVEMBER 10, 1867 – JULY 15, 1980

Zion Spring M. B. Church

EGYPT, MISSISSIPPI

Sunday, July 20, 1980

4:00 P. M.

THE LORD GAVE, AND THE LORD HATH TAKEN AWAY;
BLESSED BE THE NAME OF THE LORD.
JOB 1:21

The Obituary of my Aunt Mariah who made her transition at age 113.

Additionally, unlike my 1977 visit, all eleven of Auntie's children were at the reunion. I'd observed that several of her daughters had some resemblance of how she looked in younger days. This somehow made me feel better. Along with this line of first cousins (whom I'd considered my brothers and sisters since I had spent most of my early childhood years with them), were their spouses, children and grandchildren, and my aunt's great-grandchildren. The group totaled well over 200 people. This, I thought, was remarkable, considering that they all came from this one woman.

Second, third, and fourth cousins from nearby were also present on the day of the big gathering. The group of relatives was so massive Jonathan could not believe his eyes. Besides having a nice time, my return to Mississippi had me so excited, the radical change in the landscape of our farm soon did not matter as much; nor did it stop me from dreaming about the five-year plan I had already developed, before coming, to build a house on our share of our ancestral land.

My cousins seemed as happy to see us as we were them, especially the greatly anticipated viewing of my "little half African son." They were intrigued, however, to see that he "didn't look like an African, but just like [them] us!" Not quite sure how to handle this one, I fought the urge to conduct a history lesson. By not doing so, we ended up having a wonderful time with our family in spite of their innocent naivety about Africa.

What happened later that evening, however, after some of the other lines of cousins and guests departed did cause me to pause. After the candles were blown out and the surprise birthday cake, meant for one of Auntie's sons, had been half eaten, one of her other children announced that it was time for a family meeting and requested the "family" all move into an adjacent room. As I was about to enter the room, this cousin stopped me at the door and explained that the meeting was for family members only.

Upon turning back to join the few spouses and other friends

that remained in the great room, I found it necessary to call on some huge restraint to fight back the tears threatening to burst out of my eyes at any second. Once I had conquered my need to cry, I sat quietly during their entire meeting trying to figure out why I was so hurt by this. Admittedly, I only felt better when after the meeting ended, one of my favorite first cousins, who was in my age group and with whom I'd therefore had more contact when I lived with the family, sat beside me and apologized for his sister's abrasive behavior.

Before leaving that evening, thinking that everyone would be pleased with my decision, I mentioned the possibility of returning home and building a house on my mother's share of our land. I was almost deafened by the loud silence that suddenly fell upon the final leg of our welcoming visit. Puzzled by their reaction, and after a bit of digging for answers, the same cousin that turned me away from the meeting finally blurted out that, "[I was] coming to destroy the many years [they'd] worked to hold on to the land." Speechless, I made a weak attempt at trying to explain that I had no such intentions. All I wanted to do, I said in defense, was come back home to my roots.

While some of my cousins seemed okay with the idea, others were not and saw an intended conspiracy on my part. Although I was surprised at their reactions, I was also somewhat annoyed having to explain my motives. After all, the land in question belonged to my mother and had been passed to my sister, brother, and me after her death. I found it interesting that those against my idea either did not live on the property or no longer lived in Mississippi. Had my childhood fantasy about returning to my roots been too idealistic, I wondered, or was this still another moment of enlightenment?

Perhaps after being in America for over five generations now, our family too, had lost the need to be close to anyone other than their immediate family members. The concept of living in a harmonious village surrounded by extended family appeared to have surely lost its meaning here! I was to learn later that the same thing had happened in other families along Egypt road when their members tried to return home. In any case, I apologized for causing the alarm, after which I suggested that we all forget about my idea and left.

Nonetheless, I felt a bit saddened to discover that my cousins thought my returning to Egypt to build on my mother's share of our land would, in effect, destroy their lives. During the drive back to our hotel in Tupelo, Jonathan inquired about what he described as a sudden atmospheric change among our relatives and asked why. I explained what I believed was the cause and added that it was probably for the best.

In spite of the nice time, we'd had at the reunion, after spending several days in the back woods of Egypt, I had already begun to question if I would be able to live in such a rural environment, anyway. The attitudes displayed by my cousins helped me make the decision - - NO I COULD NOT! Now I understood why my mother had to get out of Egypt. I could hear my son exhale a sigh of relief after I shared my feelings with him. He did not know that my heart was still on living in Tupelo, though, where I was actually born, and still considered my hometown.

* * *

Upon returning to our hotel, I stopped by the desk to inquire about the real estate market in Tupelo. The hotel clerk informed me that she had a friend in the real estate business who would be happy to take us around town to look at some properties. After finalizing the arrangements, the clerk instructed that her friend would pick me up the next morning at 10:00 A.M. My son asked if I had lost my mind. I jokingly assured him that I only wanted to see what the homes were like. He quickly reminded me that we had already toured the city when we first arrived, and I'd taken him to see where I was born earlier that week. I had not mentioned to him that I was considering retiring in Tupelo once he went off to college, which would happen at the end of the next school year.

The real estate agent came by the next morning as promised, and we spent a good portion of the day being shown parts of Tupelo I'd never seen before. I was amazed at both the size and beauty of this small city. I was also convinced that I would indeed return someday. After my very patient son gave me an "okay mom, I've had enough touring," kind of look, I instructed the agent to take us back to the hotel. She said okay but insisted on showing us one last property. Looking at my son, I reluctantly agreed after she promised that it was on the way back to the hotel.

My son and I looked at each other with a "you must be kidding look" when she pulled into a very unassuming gray painted house. While the house was situated in what was obviously a nice newly developed gated community, complete with freshly manicured lawns, it appeared no more special than many of the other homes we'd seen that day. When she pulled up onto the side driveway, sensing our growing annoyance, the agent began to nervously explain that Tupelo was growing by leaps and bounds, and this was one of its newest sub-divisions. We both relaxed (a bit) when we saw what appeared to be a lake in the back of the house.

Dismissing the lake, the agent escorted us around to the front door, and kind of shoved us in as she opened it. Both Jonathan's and my mouth dropped at the same time. The back of the house consisted of windows that expanded across the entire "great room", kitchen, and breakfast nook; and on into a bedroom whose wall continued along the same backside of the house. The amazing view gave the appearance that the house was sitting on the water. It was gorgeous!

After viewing the entire house, I asked the price. Watching my son's reaction to the deck that also expanded the entire backside of the house, I heard my son quietly exclaim, "Yeah, I could live here." The agent responded to my inquiry regarding the price, and the die was cast.

Photo of our house in Mississippi 2003

Full Circle-Tupelo

Having arranged to purchase the house in Tupelo with the real estate agent, contingent upon selling my home in El Sobrante, CA, I was amazed when the entire process was completed in less than three months. During this time, I was able to sell my California home and purchase outright the house in what I thought was Tupelo. After relocating however, I learned that my home was situated in a suburb approximately two city blocks outside of Tupelo, in a small, but quaint suburb called Saltillo, Mississippi. While initially upset that my agent had not disclosed this to me earlier, I consoled myself that I was close enough. I had returned to Mississippi and for the meantime, my soul seemed to be at peace.

My cousins were shocked to learn that I had actually purchased a house and moved back to Mississippi. Interestingly enough, the half that was against my building a home in Egypt did not take it too well. It appeared as if they were anticipating a fight (over our land) which never came and that infuriated them more. Having traveled, lived and/or worked throughout the United States, as well as in several other parts of the world, I had learned to live by the "if it doesn't fit, don't force it" rule. At this stage of my life, my only goal was to learn how to relax, which turned out to be easier said than done, and complete the book that I had started about my mother's family history.

Others of my family, especially those on my father's side who had not been back to this part of Mississippi since following him "up north" decades earlier, and friends that had only heard negative things about it, could not understand how I could "move back to a place like Mississippi." Believing that my relatives should already know why, it took a great amount of discipline to not go into long explanations with some of my friends regarding my reasons. Therefore, I focused on arguments such as a lower cost of living and Northeast Mississippi being at the top of the list as one of

America's nicest places to live--for retirement or to raise a young family.

It was too bad that Mississippi's past reputation continues to over-shadow the fact that some of America's finest African Americans were born and raised there. The list includes, but is not limited to, Alex Haley, of the book "Roots"; television talk show hostess, Oprah Wimphrey; film star, Morgan Freeman; football star, Jerry Rice, actress, Bea Richards; news anchor woman, Robin Roberts, whose father was also one of the original Tuskegee Airmen; actress, Brandy; author and syndicated columnist for the Washington Post, William Raspberry; model Naomi Campbell; and of course, the famous singer, B.B. King--to name a few.

While I do not advocate that one should forget the past ("...for lest one forgets one's history one is destined to repeat it"), I feel strongly that in order to heal the wounds from the past and progress in their development, a people must forgive and move on. Lost in this outgrown perception of Mississippi is the fact that this southern state has more African American elected officials, at the federal level, than any other state in the country. And, at the risk of bragging. I was pleasantly surprised to learn that Mississippi boasts of having one of the largest diversities of both people and cuisines in America. It is unfortunate, however, that Sunday mornings remain the most segregated day of the week in many parts of the state.

When I realized that I often found myself defending the fact that I was moving back to Mississippi, I would stop immediately. I decided that a better strategy would be to invite those who appeared genuinely concerned for my welfare to take a break from their busy lives in the big city and visit me in my small city. I promised them that I could guarantee peaceful early mornings walks and late evening stroll around the lake in back of my home, or even a walk through the nearby woods of the great Native American Natchez Trace.

I went on to promise that afterward, we would dine at their

choice of some of the finest restaurants in the country, which are barely a ten-minute drive from my home, and later shop at one of the largest shopping areas and/or malls, right here in Northeast Mississippi. It worked. Several of my friends came for visits, and upon returning home, spread the news about the "new Mississippi."

Another reasoned for relocating in Mississippi when I did was because my son, who by now was an accomplished pianist, had been offered a music scholarship to attend Tugaloo College in Southern Mississippi. And, while Tugaloo was nearly a four-hour drive away, it was comforting that at least I was in the same state as he. More importantly, my mother had lived there. Whatever the reason, I had indeed, come full circle.

THOMAS WELLS

Tupelo native Vandean Philpott developed an interest in Africa while earning her master's degree in international business. She has served as a worker for Africare and a diplomat for the United States Agency for International Development.

Circle of life returns to NE Mississippi

■ Area native Vandean Philpott has a wealth of knowledge that she's ready to share.

BY M. SCOTT MORRIS
Daily Journal

Wanderlust comes naturally to Vandean Philpott. After all, her mother was an adventurer.

Jane Ware grew up in the Egypt community, just a few miles south of Tupelo.

"She moved to the big city, Tupelo, way back in the '40s," Philpott said. "You didn't find many young black women who left their parents and moved off by themselves back then, I'm told. They tell me she was adventurous and you'll find out I'm the same way."

Jane Ware eventually married Madison Harris, one of the first African Americans in Tupelo to operate his own business. He ran a car repair shop

Turn to CIRCLE *on back page*

Circle

Continued from Page 1A

on East Main Street, the family had a little house on Spring Street, and Tupelo was home.

"My mother died when I was 4. We hung around here until I was 7 and my dad got a job offer up in Chicago," Philpott, 58, said. "I stayed with my aunt and uncle in Egypt until he got settled. That was seven years."

There and back

Since then, Philpott has traveled the world. As a member of the Chicago-based Gems, she performed on the same stage as Diana Ross and the Supremes and provided background vocals for Etta James, the Dells and other artists for Chess Records.

She reared a family in California while earning a master's degree in international business. She served as a diplomat for the United States Agency for International Development in countries throughout Africa.

And through all that, she nurtured a dream of Tupelo as home, the place of her heart.

"When I was living in Egypt, my auntie would periodically take us to Tupelo. When I thought of Tupelo as a kid, I thought of my mother. I thought of my house," she said, the memory bringing tears to her eyes. "I remember all of my life I was going to go back to Tupelo because my mother went to Tupelo. That's why I came back."

Philpott moved to town in October, and she didn't come back empty handed. She's made numerous trips to African countries since first visiting the continent in 1977 on a Fullbright Scholarship.

"Every time I went, I'd bring something back," she said. "I have enough to fill a museum three times over."

"You have filled a museum three times over," her 18-year-old son, Jonathan, corrected.

"You're right," she agreed.

Contribution

Philpott is considering opening a gallery or a museum to display her array of pottery, baskets, paintings, masks, sculpture and more.

While she decides exactly what to do with her collection, Philpott is making herself useful in other ways. She volunteers two days a week at the Cultural Alliance of Tupelo and Lee County's office in Link Centre (the former Harrisburg Baptist Church).

She's also very interested in sharing what she's learned from her many years in Africa with school groups and community organizations. She may be reached at (662) 842-2309.

"Just like my mother, I've been an adventurer and I've brought it all back to Tupelo," she said. "I hope I can contribute something. I don't know what yet but something."

A Dream of My Own

Shortly after settling in Mississippi, during a drive-in downtown Tupelo one afternoon, I pondered how I could best share what I had brought from Africa. I felt blessed to have been able to bring my extensive art collection to my home state. As ideas raced about, my brain stalled on a vision of an art gallery. I began scolding myself for having that thought; talk about work intensive! Had I not returned home to relax, complete my book and possibly start another one? Besides, I reasoned, I have no access to a venue or the resources necessary to obtain one. Even if I had the resources, my thoughts continued, where would a gallery be located? As I concluded that this idea bordered on ridiculous, I decided to head home.

On my way I turned west then north, down Gloster Street, one of Tupelo's main arteries, and what I thought was the most direct route, when suddenly I decided to go back through downtown and take Main Street. This would take me to the freeway (I-45), which was the quickest route home, I reasoned. Upon reaching Main Street, in another split second, I changed my mind again and made a quick left turn on to Spring Street, and there it was, near the corner, a small store with a front consisting largely of windows, one displaying a For Rent sign.

My goodness, I thought as I parked and without pause began dialing the number on my cell phone. A gentleman answered and after my inquiry, said that if I was interested, he could meet me at the space for an inspection. After telling him I was already parked in front of the store, he explained that he was not far away and insisted I wait for him I was shocked at how quickly he got there.

I explained to the owner my reasons for considering his place, which, although very small, I felt was ideal for a gallery, mainly because of its visibility and closeness to Tupelo's downtown traffic. More importantly, it sat at the foot of the Springhill

Community, and I had already observed that Spring Street sat adjacent to Green Street, which is where the home my father built for my mother is situated--the home in which we lived when she passed away. The property owner agreed and explained that the space had been used as a gallery before. After deciding to rent it, at a price one could not imagine, I discovered that the owner's office was in a building on a property situated in front of the house in which I was born, on Frisco Alley. How enchanting, I thought to myself. After the agreements were made, Jonathan and I patched the crumbing walls, painted and made other preparations such as constructing exhibit stands. In no time, Fragments of Africa, the first art gallery of its kind, was opened in downtown Tupelo.

PAGE 6A ■ SATURDAY, OCTOBER 25, 2003

Art gallery opens in Tupelo

■ The current exhibit features stone carvings from Zimbabwe.

BY M. SCOTT MORRIS
Daily Journal

TUPELO — A few pieces of Africa now reside in Downtown Tupelo.

During her years as a diplomat with the United States Agency for International Development, Vandean Philpott amassed an array of African art. On Friday, she officially opened Fragments of Africa, a gallery located at 111 N. Spring St.

"During my time of travel in Africa, I visited 13 countries," Philpott said. "I realized the continent is so vast there was no way I could do anything that included all of Africa, so I called it Fragments of Africa."

Nothing is for sale at the gallery, and there's no admission charge. A Tupelo native who returned to the area last year, Philpott said she wants to share her collection with her hometown.

"I've let some of my collection be used in different (San Francisco) Bay Area museums," Philpott said, "and I wanted to show it to my neighbors and friends in Tupelo."

The current exhibit, Ro-

The Facts

■ The Fragments of Africa gallery at 111 N. Spring St. in Tupelo is open Tuesday and Thursday 12:30-4 p.m. and Wednesday and Friday from 11 a.m. until 4 p.m. It's open on Saturday by appointment. For more, call (662) 322-3231.

mancing the Stone, features stone carvings by the Shona people of Zimbabwe. The collection includes realistic and abstract works.

PHILPOTT

"Some of the things I bought in the villages from the artists, who would literally be working on the side of the road," Philpott said. "(Stone carving) goes back thousands of years in Zimbabwe. When they found out the Europeans liked abstract art, they started doing that."

Philpott said she will change exhibits every three months. She's also working on plans to include work by local amateur artists and students.

Photo of Fragments of Africa Art Gallery, Tupelo, MS. 2003

Vandean Philpott, Owner
111 North Spring St.
Tupelo, MS 38804

662-322-3231   Fax 662-842-2309
Email: fragments001@msn.com

In addition to installing exhibits depicting the diversity of creativity among the people on the African Continent, we also gave lectures, shared books, and showed films on life in different parts of Africa. A new exhibit was installed every three months to which my son and I also provided guided tours. Admission was free.

Feeling that the negative teachings initially taught about Africa were so deeply embedded in our psyche, and that, as it was for me, I understood the difficulty for most Americans to get past them with an open mind and be willing to accept anything other than what they already knew. My son and I pushed on any way.

Although the items in each exhibit spoke volumes in and of themselves, each piece was appropriately labeled. We offered guided tours, which were generally requested after a visitor's self-

Photos of our art gallery, Fragments of Africa, in Tupelo, Mississippi, 2003

tour, that served to elaborate on the supporting visuals displayed that refuted the misinformation often given about Africa. Time was specifically and patiently taken to provide this service because I was convinced that teachings of the past were not only demeaning to the African continent and its people, but to Americans as well, who displayed a genuinely naive lack of knowledge.

As discussed earlier, my travels around the world had revealed that we Americans were among the few people on this planet that did not have a realistic understanding of the many other places and people with whom we share it. I also found that most people on earth speak at least two languages; in Africa, the average was three.

When I did encounter bitterness, ironically, much of it was from African Americans about slavery. I loved this challenge because it provided the opportunity to share more of what I learned while living in Africa. My goal was to make them understand why they were chosen to be brought to America. Although many would not show signs of being impressed, it was clear that my explanation generated a bit of pride. It also generated many speaking engagements at various institutions around the area requesting that same lecture.

After proving that mankind began in Africa, I would argue that Africans were chosen after the so-called founders of America knew that they were (if not the strongest), thought to be among the strongest people on earth. I went on to point out the Europeans looked toward Africa because they already knew that the invaders of America had first tried using the Native Americans, they had conquered to help them build the empire they'd envisioned, only to discover the work required was too much for these already weakened souls. And this, along with the diseases Europeans brought to America almost wiped the native population out. Their

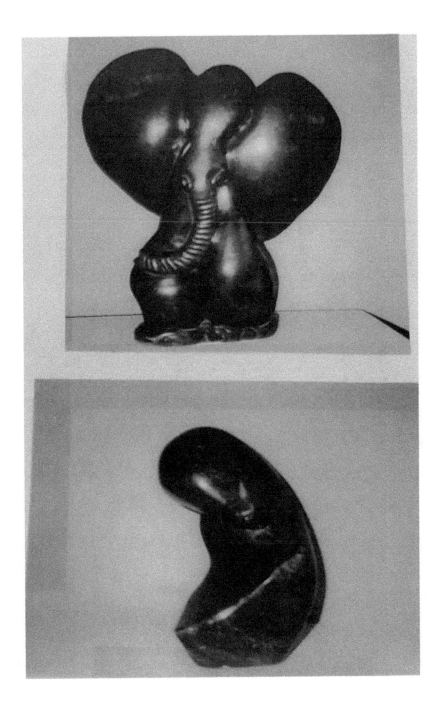

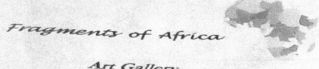

Fragments of Africa

Art Gallery

Presents

Africa's Gift to American

In recognition of African American History Month this exhibit focuses on the many contributions African Americans have made in terms of both human and intellectual resources. In this regards the exhibit features unique carvings of men and women from different parts of Africa, and charts of over 200 patented inventions made by African Americans. The exhibit also features some of Tupelo/Lee County's First in many career areas not opened to African America in the past. Many of these firsts have made their own special mark on Lee County their field.

Additionally, the carvings in this exhibit are of couples from various parts of Africa, including Benin, Cote d' Ivore, French Guinea, Ghana, Nigeria, Kenya, Tanzania, and Zimbabwe, which were selected in recognition of February as sweetheart's month. These carvings are a part of Ms. Vandean Philpott African Art collection.

Africa's Gift to America is the second of many African, African American, and other ethnic art exhibitions that will be shown at the *Fragments of Africa* Art Gallery at 111 N. Spring St., Tupelo. The exhibit will run throughout February.

Gallery Hours:

Monday – Friday   10:30 to 4:30 p.m.
Saturday   Closed during winter months
                                   Also open by appointment
                                   Phone # 322-3231

Admission: **FREE**

111 North Spring, Suite 103

Tupelo, MS 38804

next strategy was to bring over the lower classes of various European nations to do the work. This too failed as did people from other countries when they too could not withstand.

Upon hearing of a people who were not only superior in both strength and endurance, but our visitors also learned that because of the living conditions in Africa (many lived in an environment where they did not have to fight for food and other basic resources to survive), made many hospitable to strangers; even meek, and thus so trusting, it was often joked that "they could easily be fooled." As my Aunt Mariah had often lamented, during my childhood, "why else would a people (in this case, the slave traders) risk their lives and money on long voyages in dangerous seas to capture people 'by any means necessary,' and distribute them throughout their so-called new world?" "For production at the lowest cost possible," I'd exclaim, challenging anyone to refute my claim.

Additionally, realizing that the majority of my fellow Mississippians (Black or White) would probably never get the opportunity to travel the world, my objective for the gallery was to use many of the materials that I had collected to eradicate much of the past misinformation, and by doing so, provide correct information for those (especially in my hometown) that wished to be informed. I felt blessed to finally have the opportunity to share this accumulated knowledge and hands-on experience. Although it was not a capital-producing entity, my efforts at the gallery were both sincere and rewarding.

The gallery also offered seated lectures for school groups and others that encouraged a question-and-answer type conversation. These, too, were conducted only upon requested at which time the group made advanced reservations. Otherwise, the visitor(s) had the freedom to wander through and make his/her own judgments. During my lectures I found it easier to encourage dialogue by revealing that it was only after I'd witnessed the vast differences in each of Africa's many countries that I finally got it.

A lecture being given to a local group of school children, 2004

I shared that this was perhaps because, while I had, indeed, recognized these differences (i.e., in languages, dress, food, customs, structural architecture, etc.), I was so fascinated by this initial impression I had not dealt with changing my narrow-minded attitude—namely, maintaining the idea that all these people were the same and could be treated the same. Consequently, I naively thought that what worked in one place worked everywhere I went. It was not until people began looking at me like I was crazy that I finally figured out that each country (and often, different areas within a country) had its own customs and culture. For example, upon meeting an elder in Cote d' Ivoire, I'd curtsy as I had done in Nigeria only to learn that Ivorians were not quite sure what I was doing. Likewise, it soon became apparent that the protocol I had learned in West African did not work in places like Zambia or Namibia, both in Southern Africa.

During my lectures I made it a point to explain that while I had acquired extensive knowledge through my previous association with Africans, I had to accept that not unlike any subject, it was necessary that in order to achieve a greater understanding on Africa itself, I had to be willing to seek further, especially if I intended to teach. To merely accept only what someone else tells you about anything that you plan to use and/or pursue, can cause great embarrassment.

For example, during my studies I was told that before colonization, many of the countries (especially those concentrated within the same region), were combined lands until they were divided up to fit the needs of the various people who colonized them, i.e., the French, the British, the Germans, the Portuguese, etc. In spite of this dividing, many of the people that already inhabited these areas maintained many of their common values. And although families that lived near or on the dividing lines suddenly found themselves living in two different countries (even though they had not moved), they continued living as they had, before the colonized divide.

By the time I made it to Africa, the information I'd been given about the situation above. while true, was obsolete. Today, (generations later), borders are clearly established, and the inhabitants on both sides have adapted the cultures brought by the colonizer with their own. Currently, one will find that in areas which were once a large, combined region where a great number of related cultures existed are now mixed with that of the colonizer and have created new cultures. These new cultures constitute new countries with very different lifestyles, all of which are not only accepted, but they are also respected by those that ended up remaining on this original area.

My talks would go on to share that it was only after I had traveled to and/or lived-in regions or countries further away, was I able to appreciate the fact that the continent of Africa is a massive body of land, containing more than fifty different countries, and scores of different people, all with different languages, cultures, and traditions. And not unlike other continents on the globe, some which are not nearly as large nor have as many countries, Africa can boast of many different people and many ethnic groups within each country.

Just as Ireland, Britain, France, Spain, Italy, and Germany, for example, are all on the same European continent, they each contain different people that speak different languages, have different customs, laws, and currencies; they all dress differently and eat different foods. The same is true in countries like Nigeria, Senegal, Zimbabwe, Egypt, and Sudan, which are all on the African continent. In fact, the same can also be said about other continents such as Asia, which contain different Asian countries, i.e., Japan, China, Korea, Singapore, Philippines, and India. Therefore, like all the others on the planet, more often than not, the only thing the many people of Africa countries have in common is the various color of their skin tones.

***

Soon the news of both my collection and the activities, offered by the gallery, spread around Northern Mississippi, and eventually caught the attention of some of the movers and shakers in Tupelo and beyond. After several conversations about the lack of education regarding Africa, African Americans, and their history, some of Lee County's (in which Tupelo is located) leaders concluded that the entire community could benefit from having a cultural center such as the potential one I had shared with them; one that could provide opportunities to learn more about African American history, heritage, and contributions both locally and internationally. Very few, however, knew how to make this happen.

Fortunately, having worked with two African American nonprofit organizations by now, and having already gained some insight on this type of entity, I was familiar with both the development and the operational processes. So, on the condition that this core group was willing to put in the work necessary to ensure its success, I volunteered to take the lead. Once these promises and commitments were made, a group of us moved forward establishing and writing by-laws, assembling a board of directors, constructing goals and objectives, and designing a brochure describing same. Next, we acquired our non-profit status, and secured a venue. And, less than a year later, the African

American Historical & Cultural Society of Northeast Mississippi had its opening celebration.

As I looked around our cultural center, museum and library depicting African American history beginning with life in Africa, the voyage to America, slavery, and the contributions and accomplishments made so far by African Americans, I could only smile and appreciate how blessed I am to be able to share what I had discovered, experienced, and learned during my quest to continue my mother's adventurous life, and in the process, achieved a dream of my own. Thank you, mom.

With the blueprint already in place then, the contributions I wanted to make were eagerly welcomed and appreciated. Not only was the African American community intrigued with my offerings, but they were also "proud to know that what I presented was being given by one of their own." They were therefore just as excited and committed as I to the concept of an African American center. Considering how smoothly the creating process had gone, I wondered if my ancestors had something to do with it. The ease at which the ideas I introduced and implemented were accepted was amazing. As I reminisce on my first venture in Mississippi (the art gallery), I am still mystified at how easily and quickly everything fell into place. It seemed that all I had to do was think or speak a need for something and it manifested.

But now, after nearly six years of living in the place of my beginning, I was becoming more and more aware that while I enjoyed nearly everything about living here (except the mosquitoes that dared me to come out on my deck each day after 6 pm), a persistent feeling that something important was still missing from my life, kept imposing on my thoughts. When I would feel this way in the past, I'd often extend my meditations to examine my current situation and evaluate my intentions for doing what I was currently doing and/or being where and why I was at that particular time. I would also examine the results I expected from being at or in that place and time.

After several days of meditating on my current situation, I realized that from an external perspective, everything was fine. Who could complain about having a beautiful home on a lake that's fully paid for, decorated with treasures collected from one's "motherland" and other family heirlooms? When I examined the results of returning to Mississippi, I could find no problems. In fact, as was pointed out earlier, my accomplishments after my return were much greater than expected. I had also been successful in the public realm.

***

AFRICAN-AMERICAN NEWS.........COMMUNITY & CHURCH

A MONTHLY NEWS MAGAZINE   MARCH 2005   Page 18

AFRICAN-AMERICAN HISTORICAL SOCIETY GRAND OPENING

On a bright and sunny Saturday afternoon in Tupelo, Mississippi, the African-American Historical and Cultural Society had its ribbon-cutting ceremony at 104 West Franklin Street in Tupelo. On hand for the festivities were Mayors and city officials from Lee, Chickasaw and Monroe Counties. Also on hand, were the board members of the AA Historical and Cultural Society and many friends and visitors.

Aberdeen Mayor-Cecil Belle, Okolona Mayor-Sherman Carouthers, Judge Rickey Thompson, Vandean

The opening ceremony of the first African American Historical Society of North Mississippi, 2005

In addition to the gallery and cultural center, once the news got out about my lectures and exhibits on life in Africa, I had been invited to schools, churches, festivals, and other events throughout Mississippi to share this knowledge. As a matter of fact, although I considered myself in retirement I can emphatically state that never, in all my life, have I worked so hard--without pay! However, I could also say that never had I enjoyed working hard. So why wasn't I satisfied? The only item left to examine then, were my intentions. What were they?

FRIDAY, DECEMBER 24, 2004

HONORING
Heritage

The detail of
carving on A
shows a feat
about African
"Everything A
make is dec
said Vandean
Philpott. "To
just put a co
gether. They
decorate it."

Vandean Philpott, director of the African American Historical and Cultural Society of Northeast Mississippi said she hopes young people will take advantage
of the group's library to learn about their heritage.

PHOTOS BY C. TODD SHERMAN

ociety seeks to share the African-American experience

BY M. SCOTT MORRIS
Daily Journal

TUPELO – History books don't pour out of thin air. Men and women witness events and record them for future generations.

The African American Historical and Cultural Society of Northeast Mississippi was designed to lect and share the history of cks in the region.

"We want this to be a storehouse of history of African-Americans in Northeast Mississippi," said Vandean Philpott, the society's director. "The truth is American history is the

The facts

■ **What:** African American Historical and Cultural Society of Northeast Mississippi

■ **Where:** 104 Franklin Street, Tupelo

■ **Hours:** 11 a.m. to 5:30 p.m. Tuesday to Friday, Saturday by appointment

■ **Info:** (662) 620-1845

history of all the people here in the area, not just black folks.

The grand opening isn't scheduled until February, but the soci-

ety's library and museum are open for business at 104 Franklin Street in Tupelo. The facilities are for everybody, but there's a particular interest in children.

"It's good for young people to learn their history and to see African-Americans are doctors, lawyers, judges, engineers, teachers, firefighters and everything else," Philpott said. "It's something to aspire to."

Learning

There's an exhibit on display

turn to **HERITAGE** or **back page**

The African American Historical and Cultural ety of Northeast Mississippi's gallery at 104 Franklin Street in Tupelo includes a display compares the way African-Americans and Afri lived in the days following the Emancipation mation.

358

Heritage

Continued from Page 1C

that shows how African-Americans lived at the time of the Emancipation Proclamation. It's contrasted with household items that were used in Africa at the same time.

"There are some similarities, but the thing they really have in common is the cooking pot," Philpott said. "That's the tie that binds."

The walls feature dozens of prominent Northeast Mississippians, including Plantersville Mayor Viola Foster, Aberdeen Mayor Cecille Belle and Okolona Mayor Sherman Carouthers.

The heart of the society's effort is the library, which features books written by and about African-Americans.

There are hopes children will become historians. Philpott said the society wants to encourage students to start their own family trees, even if they can go back only to their parents or grandparents.

"Maybe someone can find it 30 years from now and add to it," she said. "You have to start somewhere."

Help wanted

Vera Dukes of Tupelo has been compiling histories for Carver School and Spring Hill Missionary Baptist Church for years.

"I know other churches keep histories," Dukes said. "That's what we're trying to get people to bring, so we can collect it all in one place."

Philpott served as director of the African American Historical Society of San Francisco for three years, and she knows the new organization won't thrive without community support.

"We want people to contribute because it belongs to them," Philpott said. "All you have to do is fill out an application and come to meetings. The purpose of the meetings is to determine what this place will be like."

The board of directors currently includes Philpott, Brandi Alexander, Nathaniel Stone, Charles Bouldin, James Ford and Kenneth Mayfield, but membership is open to change as more people get involved.

"I certainly don't plan to be the director forever," Philpott said. "This has to be bigger than one person."

Short-term plans include building an exhibit about Carver High School. The society is soliciting graduation pho-

C. TODD SHERMAN

Vera Dukes has been working on histories of Carver High School, as well as her church. She invited other African-American historians to bring copies of their labor to the African American Historical and Cultural Society of Northeast Mississippi in Tupelo.

tographs and other memorabilia.

Long-term plans include partnering with the Oren Dunn City Museum to integrate Tupelo's history.

"This is about telling stories," Philpott said. "I think that's important for African Americans and everyone else."

LEE INDUSTRIAL HEADSTART VISITS THE AA HISTORICAL & CULTURAL SOCIETY IN TUPELO

About 47 headstart students from the Lee Industrial Headstart of Verona attended the AA Historical & Cultral Society on February 23, 2005 in Tupelo, MS. The group was greeted by the AAHCS's President, Vandean Philpott, with a smile and a wealth of knowledge about African cultural, a video and artifacts and painting from Africa. Before leaving, the children got a chance to dress up in African attire. The finale was when two children were chosen to dress as African prince & princess.

Photo of some of the Activities the Society offered, 2005.

Vandean Harris-Philpott

Through My Mother's Eyes

I had returned to Mississippi, and during the seven years that I've been here it seems I have accomplished more than I ever imagined—without (it seems) really trying. I'd struggled for years to achieve results like these in California. One could argue that the reason I was able to accomplish so much in such short a time, is the people of Tupelo.

Shortly after relocating here, I would soon learn that, like other places in the South, Northeast Mississippi in general, and Lee County (where Tupelo is located) in particular, had also encountered its share of resistance to accepting the new order of things--that is, those regarding human and civil rights, and issues of racial equality.

However, African Americans here made it clear they too, were fed up with accepting the old order. Thanks to Tupelo's decision makers, during that time, who were insightful enough to understand that change was inevitable, many of the associated problems that came with resisting change were avoided. Having understood that it would not be in the best interest of their citizens to fight against these long-awaited rights, the region's decision makers took a more prudent approach, and thus adverted many of the conflicts they'd witnessed in other places.

Knowing that African Americans have always been vital to the growth and development here, Tupelo's leaders were wise enough to concede that by continuing to acknowledge their contributions, Tupelo could continue the growth and success it had always experienced. So, when the protest began, instead of resisting, they met with African Americans and explored a more positive approach to giving all of Tupelo's citizens the opportunity to continue contributing to its future, rather than waste time destroying it. Their efforts paid off.

MARCH FOR FREEDOM

Tupelo, Miss. Nov. 25, 1962

Springhill Missionary Baptist Church   Noon

Affirmative Action Now
Stop Klan Terror
Fight Discrimination

During my meditations, it had been revealed to me that while my accomplishments were indeed something, I could be proud of, the one thing--the main reason for my returning to Mississippi (to re-connect with the family I had left behind during my childhood) had not happened. In fact, although some of them would call me from time-to-time (to let me know they had seen me on television or had read about me in the newspaper), considering how many relatives I had here, few had ever visited the gallery, the society nor any of my lectures.

After some serious thoughts on this issue, it eventually became clear to me that having been removed from this family, I subconsciously came to view them as the only link to my birth mother (who had died when I was merely a baby). Since leaving Mississippi, somewhere early in my childhood, I began believing that I had to get back here and be among my larger family in order to feel whole again. And, after realizing what I believed was my mother's adventurous dreams, I'd convinced myself that the final step was to share what I had learned with my family.

Teaching young children about the geography and people of African, 2006

My intentions, then, were to return to my ancestral land (in Mississippi), build a house and live a village lifestyle like the ones Aunt Mariah told stories about and what I had actually experienced while living in Africa and, thus, fulfill my childhood fantasy! The reality, however, is that this was my dream, not theirs. Moreover, this (my larger family), as I had known it to be, no longer existed. This revelation forced me to acknowledge that this too, was an issue in which members of my family were not even aware. Thus, I have to accept that these feelings I'm now having are mine, not theirs. Reflecting on those initial family reunions, to which I was invited and attended as an out-of-state guest, like others in this guest category, I was warmly received because I was an extended family member. When I returned to reside in Mississippi however, the reception appeared laced with suspicion.

Although I had been greeted as a family member during previous visits to Egypt, once I relocated, I began feeling like a distant relative that had to be accepted, if for no other reason than that of being a relative, and one to be treated with caution. However, after acknowledging that these were my feelings and expectations, I found it necessary to forgive them as well as myself. And while my observations from that point on confirmed that although my Mississippi relatives had not behaved as I'd expected, there was little need for me to take their behavior personally. I would eventually learn that although my people did indeed love each other, not unlike other families I had observed in the South, they did so from a distance. So, as it was my nature to try and understand new cultures, my inquiring mind needed to know why. The answer, I was to discover, was simply SIZE!

***

I began focusing on the experiences of my second, third, and other levels of cousins (up and down Egypt road), who like myself, returned after having moved way, as well as those of friends and other acquaintances I'd met with large families in the Tupelo area. They had all revealed the same dynamics. Those in families that had remained (especially on farms), had grown so large, most did not have to go outside of these units to socialize or even find friendships. My goodness, I remember thinking after one of our events, under these circumstances, one could attend a "small party" where nearly one hundred people were in attendance and discover everyone there was related! These self-contained family units often have so much internal drama to deal with, including fighting about land inheritance rights, most do not have the time nor energy to deal with issues from outside, especially traveling to the city to attend a lecture or view an exhibit--from Africa or anywhere else. Therefore, most do not.

Moreover, many have not been socialized to interact with

people other than immediate family members--that is, those of their brothers or sisters (and their many children), and their own children. Except on special occasions many rarely ever socialized with others, until church services on Sunday, or during funerals. Reunions, then, not only give extended family members a chance to come together and be nice to one another every one or two years, it also presents the opportunity maintain a connectedness, or if for no other reason, that to present some with a chance to catch up on the latest gossip or show that one is doing better than the others. Once the reunion is over life goes back to normal--that is, individuals have little time to deal with those with whom they are not immediately attached to, even if they live in the same town.

This new way of living left me feeling more disconnected than ever. Suddenly, I began to understand it all through my mother's eyes. Perhaps because she was born a very outgoing and social person, she found it necessary to leave such an environment. Like her grandfather, she wanted to expand her life and experiences to include other people and cultures. This was a trait I apparently inherited from her. But while I enjoyed an expanded environment, for some reason, I also needed to return to my "roots" so to speak.

At some point during my life, probably after our 1977 visit, which brought back many childhood memories of playing freely on the farm surrounded by scores of cousins, listening to stories told by our elders around the fireplace at night and handmade presents we made for each other as birthday and Christmas gifts, I had begun spending a great deal of time thinking I had been deprived of this "happy environment" from whence I came. Compelled to recapture it; not only for myself but for my small family, whom I believed had somehow also been deprived since we lived so far away from our larger fold, I'd made yet another five-year plan. Now, having achieved this goal, I'm beginning to wonder if perhaps people tend to remember only the good times, and for this reason, childhood memories sometimes get distorted.

Returning to the fold (even from a distance) has taught me

that, as in most situations, it is not the size, but rather the quality of the family that matters. In fact, large families can be hard on individual members as well as the parents of those individuals. Reflecting on my early years with her family, I recall how my auntie dealt with the stress of having so many children to raise and nurture. In retrospect, I now have even more respect for her. Thank you, Auntie, for taking us in.

***

After examining my current feelings (of something missing), I found that while wanting to return to my source, and thus, re-unite with our greater family might have been a good reason for returning to my birthplace in Mississippi, I began to realize that by leaving my family in California I was, in effect, perpetuating this (my) feeling of disconnectedness that I had felt a great portion of my life. More importantly, I began to see that I had left behind what I was searching for all along--a family of my own. Considering all that I was experiencing perhaps I was finally able to see things through my mother's eyes.

The Black Business Association of Mississippi

Presents To

Vandean Philpott

The "People Who Make a Difference Award."

2004

In Recognition of Outstanding Service

And Dedicated Leadership

To the Community

Up Until Now

Looking back on some of the family experiences I've had since my return to Mississippi, I now realize that ultimately, it just maybe one's immediate family that matters most, no matter the size. In my desire to come back and be a part of my greater maternal family, which now consists of over five hundred, it is becoming clear that I was also hoping to find remnants of my mother, and thus, myself.

Up until now, I have enjoyed my life in Mississippi and all I'd experienced there. Once my talents became known, and with my desire to share them, I've been invited and traveled to churches, schools, museums, and other cultural venues throughout the State, lecturing about my travels and sharing my art collection. Jonathan and I had also participated in some current history making activities, such as promoting the election of our country's first African American president.

That connection I was hoping to achieve with my mother's family however, never really happened, at least not as I expected-- that is, the one I left behind in my youth. As mentioned earlier, I have accepted that this is my issue, not theirs. In never being invited to Egypt to share my African experiences, I sometimes felt like Jesus of Nazareth, who was accepted everywhere he went except his own hometown. In pursuit of higher education, Jonathan had joined his father's family on the east coast. The few family interactions I did experience after he left, helped me to realize that in my quest to find and reclaim the family I thought I had lost, I, in effect, had left the one God blessed me with (my children and my grandchildren) back in California!

This revelation became even clearer each time I'd leave a family outing, mostly with second and third level cousins, whose roots also began in Egypt but are now living in towns nearby, or those on my father's side which I'd often visit. During my drives back home after some of these celebrations and events, I'd note that although I enjoyed them, I also felt like something very important was missing. For example, during visits to social gatherings given at the homes of my cousins, I had observed how the mother in a family (who was often in my age group) was treated. Surrounded by her children, grandchildren and in some cases, great-grandchildren, although she'd fuss and complain most of the time, they all treated her with utmost gentleness and respect. As a result, one could actually feel the sense of contentment emanating from her. I'd often leave these occasions feeling sad and lonely. And, after returning to my big, beautiful, lakefront home, I'd began longing for the closeness of my own children--remember, the ones I thought had either come in my life too early or too late. I'd then began wondering, what on earth I would do if I didn't have them. Although I initially enjoyed having a place in the South (if for no other reason now) than to have a place that my children could visit each summer, I began to regret buying the house.

***

Perhaps it was time for me to go. If I do decide to leave Mississippi, before departing this time I decided, I would leave something I treasure as close as possible to where my mother died.

Jonathan branching out on his own.

During the years I've spent here in this Tupelo suburb, I've tried to become the gardener that my grandmother, Ada, was. And, true to my nature of trying to be among the best at anything I take on, after joining the local gardening society, I went all out, including having a greenhouse built in my backyard. It would not be exaggerating to say I went a bit overboard.

The seedling I planted early each spring would produce some of the best plants and flowers in the show that the society I joined conducted each year--just before the upcoming planting season. The winner would get a prize. Although I never won, I had fun trying! At any rate, it occurred to me that the Springhill Community Garden is situated a stone's throw from the home my father built for my mother. That's it! donate my greenhouse; in her name, as a monument to my dear mother. Perhaps this greenhouse will still be standing, as was our house, when and if my descendants decide to conduct further research on our family. This research must surely bring them to Mississippi.

***

It has been said "You can't go back." I say that all depends on the reason one wants to. Sometimes there is a need to go back in order to go forward. I went back to Egypt to find myself, the self I left behind during my childhood, and discovered that the self I was looking for had left with me. More importantly, I learned that in many ways, this self was my mother, my grandmother, and all of my past ancestors whom, as with all humans, the Universal Spirit had allowed to come to earth to represent itself. In the way it chose for my family, I continued on after they did their parts. This included my going to Africa and returning to teach about it. I am convinced that my children and later descendants will continue after I depart.

When asked if I had had the chance to choose differently, would I have still come back to Egypt? I must admit that I believe I would. One major consequence of my time in Mississippi was recognizing that a complete spiritual transformation had taken place, not only in my life, but in America. As proclaimed by many Americans of African descent my age (65) and older, when it happened, I never thought I would live to see and experience such a major shift. President Barrack Obama, dubbed "America's first **Black** President" was sworn into office on January 20, 2009, and for some reason, I was happy to be in Mississippi, the land of my birth, when that happened.

What remains an enigma to me is why this, our first African American president, is labeled the first Black president. Mr. Obama's mother is Anglo American, and his father is an African from Kenya. This, to me, constitutes a true African American. Yet, instead of celebrating the fact that this young, naturally intelligent, well educated, articulate, and seemingly sincere man represents the best of both races in America, the majority continue to label him the first Black President. This begs the question--what constitute a Black person? Frankly, I still am not sure who came up with this idea of people being Black or White and why since, in all my entire life and travels, I have never actually seen a White nor a Black person—and I am not being naive nor am I being facetious.

It appears that because he is tagged Black, as of this writing, he continues to experience an unusual amount of animosity--from both races! The Blacks seem to feel he is not black enough, and the Whites feel he is not white at all. To date (2009), our president has made great accomplishments. Yet, everything he has done so far has been questioned at best, or highly criticized to the worst degree. The poor man is not only blamed for events that happened before his presidency, but even those before his birth! I refer here to the ideas expressed by the Reverend Wright, who is a contemporary product of racism in America, and who often speaks candidly to his congregation about the effect's racism has had on him, and those of African descent.

To Vandean,

Thank you for the significant role you have played in supporting this administration and the Democratic Party.

***

Reverend Wright became a cause for suspicion, only after it was discovered that the President, whose wife is a so-called authentic Black American, was a member of his church. Although the Reverend lectures consisted mostly of historical and current facts regarding the attitudes of European Americans toward and treatment of American Africans, and how one should deal with these attitudes, before this discovery, no one even cared about what he nor others like him thought or were preaching to their congregations. Because our President attended this church, however, he was said to have the same "radical" ideas as the Reverend; never mind the fact that President Obama was raised by an all-white household, and in a white environment throughout his entire childhood. And, while he may have experienced racism as an adult (since many outsiders were not aware of his ancestry and considered him Black), he could never know the extent of the Reverend's pain.

Yet, the President was literally condemned because of Reverend Wright's views, by both the media, and America at large! To chill the ever-rising controversy, the President decided to leave this church. Currently, however, he is being criticized for not belonging to a church. This type of scrutiny and condemnation continues on as of this writing.

***

As I reflect on my odyssey to Africa, I remain in awe of how it was manifested, but more so, how it turned out. It was in 1977 (on my first trip in West Africa) on the beach in Benin that I experienced one of the most powerful spiritual moments in my life; Benin would also be the country in which I would experience my last—some twenty years later. It was also where the father of my long awaited came. When Souman learned that my son and I were finally leaving Africa, he invited us to Benin so that we could meet his family. During this visit he took us to his birthplace, in Quidah, where a large mysterious tree is situated. After telling us the story of this tree, my heart became very heavy.

Souman explained that this, called the Auction Tree, was

372

where Africans were brought soon after being captured from various parts of the interior, and where they were to be sold to the slave traders. He went on to explain that the captured were blindfolded, then made to circle the tree several times. He boasted that many Africans had a very keen sense of direction in those days and this was done so that if one were lucky enough to escape, their captureres knew that they could easily find their way home. Thus, this ritual, around the tree (now dubbed the Tree of no Return by the locals), was done to confuse them. After explaining the tree's purpose, Souman insisted that my son and I walk around it in the opposite direction, three times. "This way" he asserted, "when you die your souls will return to Benin where it belongs." Humbly I complied.

Jonathan and me going around the Auction tree, 1997

Against All the Odds

I am grateful for having the experience of returning to Mississippi, if for no other reason than to give my son this experience. However, he has now gone away (to the D.C. area, where the African side of his family resides) to continue his education. And, finding myself really on my own, after more than forty years of raising children, I have finally had time to get to know me better; not as the "motherless child, the fallen (singer) star, the unwed mother, the single parent, the struggling student, not even the corporate manager, the foreign service diplomat, the professor/lecturer, the executive director, and the worst of them all, the victimized Black American female, facing every kind of discrimination imaginable--but the real me. During the many quiet times I've had alone here, I've intentionally set aside time for reflecting, and putting these reflections in the form of a book. In doing so, I often find myself wishing I had gotten to know myself sooner. But I wonder if that's possible?

I also wonder what my life would have been like had I not "jumped seasons." Taking all of my experiences into consideration however, I must acknowledge that I am pleased the way things turned out--I still kind of like me. I am now convinced that maybe both the so-called good and bad choices we make during our journey through life is all in the Creator's divine plan for us. Perhaps, our true transformations take place only after we have traveled most of this journey in the unconscious state in which we began--during our spring years. Recognizing, then, that I am that little perennial, who, like those that came before me, had to endure all that I did, and against all the odds, I made it. Whatever the case, I can sincerely say that my life has certainly been one of enchantment, and that I am extremely satisfied.

Nevertheless, it appears I now have another decision to make. Will I remain here in Mississippi, and spend my WINTER years where I began SPRING? Or will I rejoin the family the Creator has blessed me with—remember the one I thought either came too early or too late? Whatever my decision, one thing I know for sure is that I am most grateful for both my past and this present moment. And finally understanding how it works, as my next season unfolds, I find comfort in knowing that the choice I make will be right for me. I look forward to the possibilities that are yet to be lived during my winter years.

Late Autumn

To Be Written...

Acknowledgements

I wish to thank my two daughters, Denise, and Janie, who seemed to understand that although I did not know much about parenting, graciously traveled the first part of my life's journey with me with few of the problems I'd witnessed in other families. The awesomeness of having these little humans for whom I was totally responsible, in terms of their future contributions on this planet, not only grounded me, having them also inspired me to learn more about our ancestry and, as quoted by Anthony Browder (at the beginning of this project), "...to preserve our history and culture and then pass it on to the next generation."

Starting a family at such an early age created an almost urgent need for me to understand and preserve information about our family's role on this collective stage I call earth. When my daughters grew up, became young women, and set out on their own journeys, I decided to rekindle my own quest to see and experience as much of this world as I could. This quest often took me to places far from home, and them. And, while they would benefit from my adventurous nature, which often provided opportunities for them to travel as well, I wish them both to know that I appreciated their patience and understanding.

I also thank my son Jonathan, whom I am convinced came here (when he did) to be my guardian angel. Since he arrived just as I'd begun my long-waited adventures, while Jonathan's late arrival in our family first presented as a surprise, it would unfold as a wonderful gift. Although he was a small child, when I literally dragged from continent to continent during my travels, he consistently proved to be my rock.

While I credit my parents (which included several of both my mother and father's siblings) with instilling many of my core values, I must credit my children for many of the lessons I learned from them. In their own unique way, each of my children have taught me many of life's values, most of which, I believe, were responsible for all of my achievements and successes.

Thank you, Cousin Georgia, who at the time of this writing was ninety-five years old, and still able to recall life with her best friend, my mother, thus giving me the foundation for many parts of this book.

Many others have touched my life--far too many to mention here, so I'm going to trust that you know who you are. However, I must acknowledge Professor James (Jim) L. Lacy. As a mentor, adviser, and friend. Jim always seemed to show up whenever I needed guidance and/or just a strong shoulder to lean on. I can only hope that somehow, he knows how much I appreciate him. I also thank Dr. Maya Angelo, who unknowingly gave me the courage to pursue my dreams of living in Africa when she shared with me her own experiences and provided valuable advice on how I should proceed.

A very special acknowledgment goes to Luther Murphree, a young Caucasian man who, after observing my frustration during a day-long unproductive search for my ancestor's records in the archival section of Mississippi's Bureau of Statistics, came to my rescue. Just as I was about to give up, he approached me and asked if he could be of assistance. Although young Luther did not work for this organization, he not only told me where to go and find what I needed, he literally took the time and escorted me to the correct building, which turned out to be several miles from where I was searching in Houston, Mississippi. After showing me how to search for the information I wanted, he also helped in finding several family documents I didn't even know existed. Among them I found my great grandparents marriage certificate, dated 1874. Thank you, Luther.

Finally, I thank Soumanou Salifou, producer and editor of The African Magazine, for spending many hours proof-reading and editing my initial manuscript, as well as those spent couching me on how to best present my experiences in written form.

The Seasons of Life

THE SEASONS OF LIFE

"For every *thing* there is a season, and a time to every purpose under the heaven…"* Ecclesiastes. 3:1-13

Womb/Birth	SPRING PREP Time			SUMMER Time to SOW			FALL HARVEST time			WINTER Time to REST			Death/Grave
	Early	Mid	Late	Early	Mid	Late	Early	Mid	Late	Early	Mid	Late	
Ages:	0 - 10	11 - 17	18 - 25	26 - 35	36 - 50	51 - 60	61 - 64	65 - 75	76 - 79	80 - 85	86 - 89	90 →	
Time to:	Be Nurtured	Develop	Learn	Produce	Provide	Mature	Reap	Retire	Share	Relax	Enjoy	Wait	

The lilies in the field teach us the splendor of Gods *wisdom and love*. Never trying to become a rose, a petunia, or a tulip, they bend and sway, blossom, and fall at God's magnificent plan. They are content to show forth the glory and splendor of his gift during the *seasons* in which they have been blessed to express themselves.

"Enjoy each season you enter into. Try not to *Jump* seasons, especially those of mid and late spring, for these are *the developing and learning seasons*." Grammy Van, 2009.

Remember: Do not EGO trip (*Edit God Out*). As do the lilies in the fields, practice listening for, and obeying, that *small voice within*. *It is* God's guidance.

* …A time to be born…; A time to embrace, a time to refrain from embracing…; A time to love…; A time to plant, and a time to pluck up that which is planted…; A time to do good in life. A time to die… " He hath made every *thing* beautiful in his/[her] time; also he hath set the world in their heart; …no man/[woman] can find out the work that God maketh from the beginning to the end…; Man/[woman] can enjoy the good of all his/[her] labor, **it is the gift of God.**"

Traditional Ghanaian Names

When a child is born in Ghana, until his/her official naming ceremony, which usually takes place one year after birth, he/she is given a name assigned to the day of the week the child was born. Called the Kradin name, this (day) name is carried throughout the child's life, even after the child receives his or her regular name, which will be decided on based on characteristics observed during the first year of life.

Day of Birth & Attributes	Female	Male
Monday: calm, tranquil, and cool; skillful and adept under pressing conditions.	Adwoa, Adozo, Ajoba, Ejo	Bobo, Jojo, Kobie, Kojo, Kwodwo
Tuesday: warm, gentle, eloquent, and compassionate	Abena, Abla, Araba	Ebo, Kobena, Kwabina, Kweku
Wednesday: mischievous, vicarious, vigilant, and daring	Aku, Akuba, Ekua, Ekuwa, Kuukuwa	Kuuku, Kwaku, Kweku
Thursday: Eager for battle, a big rock in one's pocket, and skillful in dealing with people.	Aba, Yaa, Yaaba, Yaayaa	Ekow, Yao, Yaw, Yokow
Friday: wisdom and tenacity, the adventurous wanderer	Afi, Afua, Afie, Efua	Fifi, Kofi, Yoofi
Saturday: possesses the medicine for snake bites, able to reverse bad situations	Ama, Awo	Ato, Atoapem, Kwame, Kwamena
Sunday: unknown	Akosua, Esi, Kisi	Akwasi, Kwesi, Siisi

African Adventure

A View of Victoria Falls which separates the Countries of Zambia and Zimbabwe

Me and White House news reporter returning from Victoria Falls, 1996.

Limited photos of our stay in Botswana, Southern Africa 1966

Jonathan with our friend at the Equator, Denise, at animal park

**Our Visit in Malawi South Africa
1995**

At our friend's village, Belo: The City of Blantyre, 1996

Photo of our visit to Swaziland

A mock village and Our host house in the city.

City scenes in Windhoek, Namibia 1997

Photos of Zambia

Bibliography

Chavis, Grace L, *Reflections on Africa*, Exposition Press, Hicksville, New York, 1975 Davis, Ronald, L.F., *The Black Experience in Natchez:* 1730 —1880, Mississippi, 1999.

De Vore & Sons, Inc. *The Holy Bible*, Family (King James) Version, by, Wichita, Kansas — 1951

Du Bois, William E. B., *The World of Africa*, International Publishers, New York, 1964.

Gimbutas, Marija, *The Language of the Goddess*, Los Angeles, 1989.

Kenyatta, Jomo, *Facing Mt. Kenya, Vintage Books*, New York 1965.

Stone, Merlin, *When God was a Woman,* Harcourt Brache Jovanovich, New York, and London, 1978

Wright, Kai, *The African American Archives*: The History of the Black Experience through Documentation, New York, 2001.

CPSIA information can be obtained
at www.ICGtesting.com
Printed in the USA
BVHW091955190422
634526BV00001B/1